A Taste for Sailing

A Taste for Sailing

John Lewis

Terence Dalton Limited
Lavenham, Suffolk 1989

The photographs and sketches are by the author unless otherwise attributed

Published by
Terence Dalton Limited
ISBN 0 86138 073 8

Designed by John Lewis FSCD
Text set in 10/12pt Baskerville
Printed in Great Britain at
The Lavenham Press Limited, Lavenham, Suffolk

To the memory of Doddy Kahn
and to Rowland,
      Maurice,
      Dod,
      Bill,
      Lun,
      Arthur,
      Monny,
      Freddy,
      Kit,
      Kenneth,
      Jack,
      Frank,
      Philip,
      Keith,
      Guy,
      Bert,
      Fred,
      Taff,
      Bob,
      Charles,
      Paddy and Old Captain Waters
      and all those who helped to give me
      a taste for sailing

Charts and plans

Contents

The "punt" on the beach at Seasalter.

The "punt" in the little dock at Oare Creek.

Model of the "punt". I made this while filling in time on an anti-aircraft gunsite in Berkshire during the winter of 1940.

Part one

1 That first boat

I found her down on Gillingham beach, if beach is the word for
that noisome oil-bespattered Medway foreshore. She lay among the
debris of rusting oil drums, old motor tyres and the rotting hulks of
abandoned tore-outs. Poor thing, she had clearly come down in the
world. She had once been the pride and joy of an old friend. The
very apple of his eye. Since then she had passed through many
hands, some of those not too gentle. I never discovered what her
name was. She was always referred to, not altogether in an
uncomplimentary way, as "the punt". In those days, just before the
second world war, the word punt put me in mind of young men in
boaters and blazers whiling away golden summer afternoons
poling (or should it be punting) dewy eyed maidens along the Cam
or picnicking at Henley to the distant strains of the Eton boating
song or to the tinny sound of a portable gramophone, and the well
loved voices of Messrs Layton and Johnson.

She wasn't that sort of a punt. She was no lady from Shallot or
anywhere else. She had never glided through long fields of barley
and of rye, she came of humbler, rougher stock. All the gliding she
had ever done was when her previous owners had pushed her
down some muddy foreshore into tumbling estuary waters.

She was a fourteen-foot-long flat-bottomed centreboard boat.
She was battered and dirty, the paint was peeling off her and she
had the dingiest suit of sails I had ever seen. They looked as though
they had been made of old flour bags, as indeed they may well have
been. She wasn't a very promising object, but she was a boat and
she did float. The price asked for her was only £5 and after some
haggling I got her for four pound ten. That odious beach under
the lee of Gillingham gas works did not seem the ideal place to fit
her out, so for another pound the man who had sold her to me, a
rheumy-eyed old longshoreman, agreed to tow her round to the
River Swale and to deliver her to the *Shipwright's Arms*, which lies at
the junction of Faversham and Oare Creeks. I still have the receipt
by me. It reads: "Fourteen foot sailing punt with mast, spars,

rigging, jib and mainsail, 1 pair seven foot oars and rowlocks, floorboards etc . . . £4. 10. 0d. To Towing to Swale and delivering to Oare Creek, or Shipwright's Arms if tide not fair . . . £1. 0. 0d. Total £5. 10. 0d. rec-d with thanks, T. Baker."

And so I became a boat owner. At much the same time, I found a wife. She was pretty, she was clever, she was impatient and her name, charming and inappropriate, was Griselda. She is the better half of the we in this modest tale. Her sufferings provide much of the substance.

A week or so later we found the punt lying in Oare Creek. Rowland Hilder, who had once owned the punt, had a beach hut near Whitstable Bay. He suggested that we could fit the boat out there more easily than at Oare Creek. So with his help we sailed her out of the Swale and on to the beach at Seasalter, where we rubbed her down, repaired her as best we could and painted her a chaste grey with an Indian red gunwale. We tarred her bottom, varnished her spars and rove new rigging.

It was a transformation; she looked—at least to my eyes—a thing of beauty. And after all these years, I love the memory of her still. Ill though her sails set, she was a splendid boat in which to learn the first rudiments of sailing and boat handling. In those sunny, blissful, fool's paradise months of July and August in 1939 we had little thought of war as we sailed across Whitstable Bay and up and down the creeks of the Swale.

We made our base in Oare Creek, living in tents at the back of a little cottage, where an old man called Captain Waters lived, looking after a few boats and the sluices that drained the marshes.

The punt was a splendid roomy boat, with her flat floor and lack of side decks. She could even be used for cruising. Rowland, when he had cruised in her, had carried his food and spare clothing in large water-tight tins—kips, I believe he called them—which stowed under the thwarts or up in the bows. She had a heavy iron centre plate, which we soon learned to use as a sounding device. And she was very, very heavy to row. But sailing on a reach she was as stiff as a wooden leg, with never the least tendency to dip her rail.

During her life, the punt had a number of different rigs. The one that suited her best was a balanced lug with a large overlapping foresail. This rig had a low centre of gravity, and under it she never looked like capsizing. In contrast to those racing dinghies which spend most of their time upside-down, this seems to me a commendable quality. Incidentally, we never needed to sit her out—the crew merely shifting their weight to the weather side of the boat, keeping their weight low in the boat. I have said that she had a flat bottom; in fact it had a fair rocker to it, nearly a six-inch rise in fourteen feet. This, with her considerable beam and her flared sides, was the cause of her stiffness.

Chine boats may pound a bit in a seaway but there is some quality about them that no round-sectioned boat can match. This is partly due to their initial stability and the additional weatherliness given by the submerged chine, which seems to get a surprising grip of the water. The punt drew only a few inches, and with her centreboard down only about two feet, so clearly her windward performance was not that of a racing dinghy. But considering her other virtues it was none too bad, and her capacity as a load carrier seemed infinite. Though we never sailed her far she had a reputation for good behaviour in a seaway, for as a young boat she had once crossed the Thames Estuary. It was when Rowland Hilder had her. On a quiet day he left the Medway for Burnham, but as so often happens in those waters, a bit of a blow got up and he got caught out, got thoroughly wet and probably rather frightened. The punt was as buoyant as a seabird but inevitably shipped quite a lot of water, so he went aground on the lee side of the Buxey sands, put on dry pants, bailed the boat out and made himself a pot of tea. After a rest, high and dry on the bank, he relaunched the punt and sailed into the Blackwater river to find gale warnings were out, and not one of the longshoremen would believe he had crossed the estuary—much less that he had had tea on the Buxey. I suppose it was a rather remarkable exploit, particularly as the punt was a completely open boat, with no foredeck or side coamings. Ted Baker, her builder, would never put any decking on these boats; he always kept them completely open. He used to say that they were more buoyant and much safer that way.

Rowland sailing the "punt" on to the beach at Seasalter.

She was without doubt the best five pounds' worth I have ever had, and all the thought in the world and the most careful consideration could not have given me a better boat to learn on.

As for somewhere to keep my boat, I found it at the point of delivery.

The Swale lies between the Isle of Sheppey and the north coast of Kent. At its western end it is crossed by the swing road and railway bridge—the only (frequently interrupted) communication between the island and the mainland. Creeks run southwards to Sittingbourne, and Conyer, Oare and Faversham. In the nineteen-fifties barges still travelled up to Sittingbourne and Faversham, but it must be many a day since any commercial vessels visited Conyer or Oare.

11

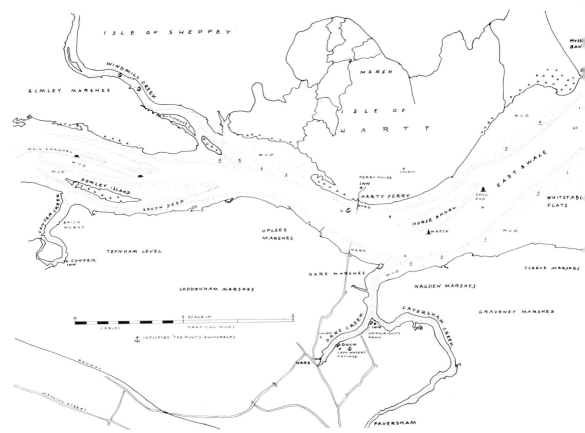

Chart of the River Swale and Oare and Faversham Creeks.

The hilly country behind Oare is rich fruit country, and used to be covered with mile after mile of orchard where they grew the Kentish Napoleon, the most luscious of eating cherries. Oare itself was a village of no distinction, set on the side of a hill. At the foot of the hill, the road crossed the creek and there used to be a track running off to the left, strewn with boulders and full of potholes. This track crossed a dyke by means of a rickety bridge and led, after about a quarter of a mile or so, to a large iron shed which blocked the view. Just beyond this shed was the nicest little dock you could ever wish for, set at right angles to the creek. It had originally been built to serve the barges that came to collect the bricks from the neighbouring brickfield. Now it only served as an outlet for the sluices that control the level of the water in the drains

12

Oare Creek and the *Shipwright's Arms*. Oil on paper sketch by Griselda
Lewis, 1942. Griselda did this sketch after we had grounded on the last of
the ebb. I did a watercolour facing the opposite way.

that crisscross the marshes. Here two or three craft could find a
very comfortable, sheltered berth. At the back of the sluice gates
lived Captain Waters. He not only "kept an eye" on the boats but
looked after our punt as though it was his own. From this little dock
the creek ran on for another half-mile or so to the junction with
Faversham Creek. Here there was a barge repairing yard and the
Shipwright's Arms mentioned on our receipt could be seen crouching
under the sea wall, with the masts of one or two yachts or a barge
showing beyond.

The *Shipwright's Arms* was an interesting old building of white
painted clapboard, like so many Kentish houses. On the first floor
there was a deep balcony that peered over the high sea wall. It was
said, with what authority I don't know, that Turner had painted

there. But the legend that it had been a smuggling centre was more than likely. The whole time that we knew it, it had a curious haunted atmosphere.

Tidal creeks such as these are pleasant places in which to keep a small shallow boat; and if there is a nice little dock, as there was at Oare, it means you can go aboard your boat at any stage of the tide without getting either wet or muddy. Such creeks nearly always dry out at low water, and on those occasions we used to leave the boat at the *Shipwright's Arms*. Another point in favour of this creek was that from the *Shipwright's Arms* to the Swale it ran due north, so that one rarely had a head wind either coming in or going out into the Swale. Once out in the Swale, if the wind was fair and the weather was good and there was an R in the month, we could sail over to Whitstable and eat oysters and drink beer; or if too windy for that, there is a lovely creek running north-westwards into Sheppey, between Eastchurch marshes and Elmley Island. This is Windmill Creek, taking its name from some long-defunct windmill. Here from about half-flood tide we used to bathe, picnic and watch the birds, and drowse away a hot summer afternoon, then drop down on the ebb to the pub at Harty Ferry for a drink before sailing home.

There were times when we had to wait for the tide to turn; it was surprising how much rowing we did trying to stem unfavourable tides on windless evenings. However, the lesson of tides and their importance was only one of the many things we had to learn.

There were a few yachts moored off Harty Ferry, as well as one or two lying at the *Shipwright's Arms*, but when out sailing we more often than not had a Goldfinch barge, an oyster boat or an inshore trawler for company. It was all a very far cry from the Solent or even the Burnham river, but none the less agreeable for that. And there was always Captain Waters. He gently chided us for our mistakes, praised us for our successes and mothered us in a hundred different ways. He was a great comfort.

With the declaration of war we thought that all our sailing would come to an end, but in fact we were able to snatch a few days here and there. Captain Waters continued to look after the little boat, and though the Swale was boomed at Shellness we had plenty of water to sail on. I believe sailing at all was quite illegal, the Admiralty in their dreary perverseness taking a delight in keeping everyone off the water. However, no-one stopped us, though on one occasion we had a bullet through the mainsail. Where it came from or who fired it at us we never discovered. We accepted it as a natural hazard for being able to sail at such a time. The *Shipwright's*

The *Shipwright's Arms*.

Arms, now more isolated than ever, had an uncomfortable atmosphere. We had a feeling of being far from welcome there, and few indeed were the visitors in those days. Later we heard strange and highly improbable rumours of Nazi uniforms having been found in the cellars. Whether there was any truth in this I never found out, but the lonely marshland inn had become a perfect setting for a spy hideout, for gun-running, for smuggling or any other nefarious and melodramatic activity that war-strained imaginations could think of.

Apart from coastal patrol aircraft in the daytime and the throb of German bombers at night, it was as peaceful as ever. We used to stay in nearby Faversham, at the *Ship*, where under the good management of the Widow Wadman we fared surprisingly well. At night, we slept in a bedroom with a bed as large as the great bed of Ware, under a vaulted ceiling, pargetted with Tudor roses.

These brief sailing interludes had come to an end by 1942. I visited Oare Creek next in 1944. I had been abroad for over a year and had had no news from the old captain. It was a sad return—the old man was dead, his cottage gutted with fire and our beloved punt derelict, with sides stove in and with every movable part missing; chopped up for firewood, so we learnt later.

Griselda in the "punt". Summer, 1939.

It was sad, a very minor war tragedy, but the little boat had done its job. I was henceforth a lost soul to all earth-bound recreations. I was "bitten" with boats—and all that that implied.

If this were a book on "how to be a yachtsman" or "how to take up sailing", it would be full of sound advice on "the ideal little ship". Learned remarks would drop from my pen about lines and tonnage, about fibreglass and moulded ply, about whether the sail should be made of terylene or polythene, and so on. Well, it isn't that sort of book.

As for my first boat, as I have related, choice never entered into it; and I truly believe it seldom does, which is probably a good thing. If the beginner were able to pick and choose his ideal craft, it is most unlikely that he would think her ideal for long. Yachtsmen who have been sailing all their lives never seem to be able to choose, build or buy the right boat, so why should a beginner be blessed with any greater perspicacity?

The important thing is to have some sort of boat. There are only two limitations. One is that she will stay afloat, and the other that she can be managed by one person without too much difficulty. The first of these provisos might seem obvious, but I do know one proud owner of an old cutter who has to keep his boat in a mud berth, where the high spring tides will only just reach her, for she never floats, having a bottom like a basket. However, he lavishes much paint on her topsides, and she looks very handsome viewed from a distance.

Presupposing that you can find a boat that will float, you are now faced with what you can manage by yourself. This is important, because if you have to depend on someone else as crew, or captain or mate, you may spend most of your time on shore waiting for them, or afloat arguing with them. Sailing boats that can be managed by one person are either little dinghies or boats with "inherent stability". A ten-foot dinghy can be sailed under most conditions and kept upright by a ten-stone man, boy or girl. This is not to say that a five, six or seven-stone man, boy or girl couldn't sail them under most conditions, but they wouldn't have enough weight to keep them moving and not capsizing in strong winds. Boats with "inherent stability" are ones that don't turn upside down *easily* . This stability is achieved by putting a lot of weight in the keel, or by giving the boat a flat bottom, like a barge. The limiting factors here are the size of the sails and the weight of the anchor. It has been said, I believe by Mr Uffa Fox, that the maximum size of mainsail that *one man* can manage is about 500 square feet. Some man! Most beginners would find themselves being pulled through the fairleads if they tried to manage a sail of half that size. As for anchors and their weight, another authority gives 56 lb as being a reasonable maximum. As far as I am concerned, a 28-lb fisherman can be quite heavy enough, if no capstan, winches, pulley-haulies or other mechanical comforts are available. Let there be moderation in everything—including the size of your first boat, the size of her sails and the size of her anchor.

I suppose people take up sailing for a number of different reasons, and some, perhaps, for no reason at all. There are opportunities in this pastime, for every kind of human attitude and manifestation of folly. The follies rank high and range wide, and tend to be innocent, if "pride of ownership", one of the major sailing follies, is not to be considered too venal a crime.

The curious fact that each season many boat owners spend fewer hours afloat, or at least under way, than they do working on or fitting out or talking about their boats might make many a landsman wonder at the logic of such an activity. Logic clearly does not come into it, and a lot of enjoyable "sailing" is done in armchairs, bars, trains, buses and the office.

Some sail because they like adventure (and they usually get it), some because it is a world set tidily with conventions (these quickly develop into "yachtsmen"), others from a romantic disposition, with stirring thoughts of flying clippers or the Spanish Main (these tend to archaic rigs and often never get their unwieldy craft afloat); others because they have a competitive spirit and like to race (these are usually wet and argumentative) and yet others for a whole number of reasons, among which may be the desire for the peace and quiet which are so hard to find on land today.

Whatever the attitude to it—and with boats and weather an attitude may change—sailing is about the most absorbing, time-wasting recreation invented by man. As a means of locomotion or transport, if anyone can think of a slower way of getting from B to A, I should be interested to hear of it.

And apart from American football, mixed hockey, or all-in wrestling, there can be few sports in which one can get so hurt, bruised, strained or wrenched and generally banged about, in such a variety of ways, and often without realising that one was, at the time, hurt, bruised, strained etc. And the reason for this state of amnesia is plain, crass, unadulterated *fear*. Fear of the sea and fear of the wind, fear of shipwreck and fear of imminent dissolution— and only too often fear of making an ass of oneself.

One's attitude during peaceful, sunny, gentle armchair voyages is quite different from one's attitude when caught in a squall on a lee shore, with too much canvas up. And whether that shore be the rocks of Tierra del Fuego seen from the deck of a sinking Cape Horner or a concrete breakwater seen from the thwarts of a waterlogged dinghy, the feeling is much the same—it's all a matter of scale.

It seems to me that the happiest people are those who know their limitations. And in sailing, limitations loom up from every direction. There are the personal limitations of pocket, and time, and strength and knowledge. There are also the very real limitations of what a boat or yacht can or cannot do. A big deep-draught yacht cannot easily sail in shoal waters, and a very little shallow-draught boat may be quite unsuitable for ocean voyaging. A very old yacht may do quite well for pottering about in a sheltered estuary, but it would probably open up and go straight to the bottom if it had to face the strains of the open sea.

It would seem to be a reasonable idea to decide what sailing you want to do and to limit your boat to that, yet it is remarkable how many yachtsmen don't do this. The number of ocean cruisers and ocean racers that never go outside the limits of the Solent is one manifestation of this folly.

I formed a taste very early in my sailing career for what might be called A to B sailing. That is, very small voyages with definite objectives. The first objective I ever had was a cream tea. We used to sail the punt up to the old town of Faversham for a very filling cream tea for the reasonable sum of one and six (7½p). Our voyages nowadays which, at the most, involve a North Sea crossing, are not much more adventurous and always end in a meal. A self-awarded reward of virtue, or at least achievement, or quite often a consolation prize for having failed to get anywhere in particular. And that has added another philosophical crumb to my attitude. If wind and tide all seem determined to prevent me from going somewhere, I go somewhere else, where they are less obstructive. The elements are bigger than we are, it's better to let them have their own way.

Sailing can certainly humble one. Opportunities of making a fool of oneself in a boat are unlimited, and picking up a mooring in a crowded anchorage with a gallery of spectators is one of the best. A most curious meteorological phenomenon is that on the calmest of days, as soon as I approach a mooring, violent winds blow from the most unexpected quarters, and on windy days, the wind usually increases to hurricane force at this moment.

In sailing, the unexpected always seems to happen, but one constant factor I have found, and that is year after year, when summers have been cold, wet and windy, on whatever day in October or November or even December that I decide to lay up my boat, the sun shines and there is a soldier's wind, and I sail her with apparent skill to the little dock where she spends her winter months. Whether it is like a horse with a clumsy rider making for the stable, or whether it is to persuade me that it is worth fitting her out again next year, I don't enquire too deeply. Whatever it may be, I return to my armchair sailing, full of quite unjustified confidence in my abilities as a helmsman.

2

The desire for a larger boat

Having in a few short months learned, as I fondly imagined, to sail the punt, though I had no wish to sell the punt, I felt I could graduate to a boat with a cabin. I had no idea of being a "yachtsman". In fact I suffered from some kind of inverted snobbery about yachts as such. I wanted a "boat" as like a workboat or smack as could be. How I arrived at this state of mind, I have no idea. It was, I suppose, just about as fatuous as the opposite extreme of thinking that nothing but a Cowes or Clyde-built Class racing yacht would float.

In the Autumn of 1940, on a forty-eight hours' leave, I went over to Gillingham to see old Ted Baker, the builder of the punt, for he had, so I had heard, "a smack" for sale. This turned out to be a most curious craft of immense beam, a sweeping counter and no bilges, and, as I was to discover later, ripe and rotten. She lay afloat in Whitewall Creek, and on that grey misty November afternoon she looked quite impressive. She was a little black cutter with low freeboard and long bowsprit. She was 26 feet overall, and though Ted Baker was a bit vague about her origins, he thought she'd been built "up Barkin' way" somewhere in the second half of the last century. What she began life as it would be hard to say, but when she came into my hands, as she did that day for £20, she was registered as a fishing boat, with the letters S4 painted in white on her black topsides. She was clench built, gaff rigged with wide side decks and a long cabin trunk roof.

We rowed out to her and I scrambled aboard. A piece of the capping rail came away in my hand, the coach roof appeared to be cracked from end to end and the canvas deck was ballooning up in bubbles. "Nice little pump," Ted Baker remarked hopefully, working a handle back and forth with abandoned energy. A trickle

Omega had a massive bowsprit.

of rusty water seeped overboard. "A bit rotten, isn't she," I suggested, poking fitfully about with a pen knife.

"Nah, she's not rotten. Good little old boat. They knew how to build boats when they built 'er. Just you try and poke your little knife into that there cabin side." I tried; it was as hard as iron and the blade of the knife snapped off.

"There, wot did I tell you. Give her a quick clean up and a coat of paint and you won't know her."

Somewhat encouraged, I peered up the mast, which had gaping shakes half an inch wide running up it.

"What's she sail like?" I asked dimly.

"Nice little sailer she is," Ted replied, "scratchy little boat to wind'ard." That comforted me. It would be nice to have a boat that was "scratchy to wind'ard", whatever that meant. Also I had suddenly discovered the pleasure of being able to walk about *on* a boat rather than scramble about *in* a boat.

Omega in Whitewall Creek.

I walked forward. Her bowsprit was set between massive bitts and disappeared over her bow into the far distance. It seemed as long as a telegraph pole. Impressed by much that I saw, I walked aft, my eyes already blinded with visions of her breasting the waves of the estuary. I climbed down into the cabin. It had a damp and fusty smell. Ted Baker followed me in and sat down by my side.

"Ain't too tidy. The chap wot I'm selling it for, he's bin livin' aboard, and weren't too nice in his ways. Bin trying to avoid the army but they caught up with him. That's why this is going so cheap."

I looked around me. The paint was peeling, the mast step crumbled to pieces in my hands, and how she smelt! Even I in my innocence could see she needed a lot doing to her, but she seemed a lot of boat for the money. Ted Baker must have divined my enthusiasm was waning; seeing his sale going for nought, he said with a genius born of despair:

"You hadn't noticed that brass lamp hanging in gimbals. Proper little ship's lamp that is." That did it. In that damp and sleazy cabin, reeking of stale cooking and foul bilges, the little lamp gleamed out. Soft lamplight, a cosy cabin, thoughts of a quiet night swinging to her anchor up some quiet creek. It was the lamp that was my undoing.

The boat was called *Omega*, but everyone pronounced it "Oh Meagre". Poor *Omega*, she never sailed again! I hadn't reckoned on the length of the war. After another five years on the saltings her condition had not improved; but I had her surveyed, and the surveyor, God rest his soul, said: "Yes, considering her age, she's not in too bad condition. Put a six-inch by one-inch oak wale right round her, that should strap her together." I had no idea what a wale was, but I had her towed up to a boatyard above Rochester Bridge to have this mystic operation done. They had more important work to do, and there she slowly fell to bits. I had rescued the lamp as soon as I bought her. I still have it. It must be the most expensive gimballed lamp afloat today. But that was not quite the end of *Omega*.

Our brief halcyon days came to an end in 1942, when I was sent off to Canada to start a Canadian Army Camouflage School in British Columbia. Boats and sailing seemed far away, though I had a few outings in a Star class boat off Vancouver, and on my way back to Britain spent an unforgettable day at Lunenberg in Nova Scotia, where they were still building the Grand Banks schooners. It was there that I met old Carl Zinck, one-time foreman of the gang that built the *Bluenose*, the winner of the International Fisherman's Race against the pride of the United States fishing fleet, schooners from Gloucester such as *Columbia*, *Thebaud* and *Henry Ford*. Mr Zinck was working on a schooner that was about a third planked up when I met him.

"The one hundred and eighteenth I have worked on," he said. "I've been here man and boy for forty years." I asked him about *Bluenose*. He leaned on his adze and thought for a moment:

"She was a fast ship, but she was a big 'un. Bigger than most. Something went wrong with her lines and she came out much fuller in the bows than her owner expected. He made an awful fuss and said he wouldn't take delivery. We didn't know what to do, there wasn't enough thickness of wood to cut it away, so we left it."

Bluenose going to windward off Halifax, Nova Scotia.

Bluenose was built by Smith & Rhuland's yard at Lunenburg with Carl Zinck as foreman in 1921. She ended her career while trading in the West Indies, by striking a reef off Haiti in 1946.   *Photo: MacAskill*

"Did it matter?" I asked.

"Matter! it was that fullness in her bows that kept her head up and instead of diggin' her nose in, she just rose up and planed her way along." He spat on his hands, picked up his adze and with a half-swing shaved off a wafer as thin as a piece of paper. As if satisfied with his skill, he stopped and said:

"We used to think that to make a boat a good sailer she had to have plenty of grip of the water. Not after that we didn't."

On the seventy-mile drive back to Halifax we passed innumerable little anchorages. Tiny little harbours and small winding estuaries that pierced the coast obviously provided the most perfect summer cruising grounds for those that liked ditch crawling and "gunk" holing.

I wondered how long it would be before I was afloat again.

3

To the East Coast

I left the army at the end of 1945 and got a job with a nice old-fashioned firm of printers in Ipswich. On my journeys to London from Ipswich I had noticed, about ten miles short of Ipswich, the estuary of the Stour. The train rumbled across the bridges that spanned the two channels at the head of this wide, shallow, muddy river. At high tide, as I first saw it, it was a great silvery sheet of water, sparkling in the sun from the popple that never seems to be absent here. On the south shore there was a jumble of houses that clung to the side of a hill. This I discovered was Manningtree. It seemed to me that it might be a possible place to keep a boat and incidentally to live. So one September afternoon Griselda and I took a bus there. It was a cold, blustery day and the little town looked rather bedraggled as we wandered round it. We saw one or two nice little Georgian houses that would have suited us splendidly, but they were quite patently not for sale. We had almost completed our circuit, for the town is very small, when we came to a small triangular green, with a half circle—a reverse crescent as it were—of large plain grey-brick eighteenth-century façades. And one of these façades was obviously shielding an empty, almost derelict house.

It looked as though it had been bombed, and it was far too big for the two of us, but anyway we walked round it and found in the garden that lay behind it an old man burning leaves.

"Is this house for sale?" I asked him.

"It might be," he replied with typical Essex loquacity.

"How much?" I asked again.

"Would £300 be too much?"

"Good Lord no," I stupidly answered, thinking of all the odious little villas we had been offered from £5,000 upwards.

"Well," he retaliated with some relish, "I think they'd want £350."

We pushed our way through chest-high nettles to the garden door, which collapsed as I touched it. Inside the hall a little black cat lay dead. She could have died within the last few hours. We

Cumberland House as
we found it.

stepped over her and inspected the house. It was quite derelict; the
wind and the rain had been blowing through it for I don't know
how long. Half the stair treads and most of the bannisters were
missing; all the fireplace surrounds had gone. Wallpaper hung in
streamers down the walls and the roof was full of holes. Yet both of
us saw none of this. We were bewitched by the proportions of the
rooms and the size of the windows and, impossible though this may
sound, by the atmosphere of the house, which seemed to be saying,
"If you save me, I'll repay you."

As far as I was concerned, the house was ours. And in spite of all
the good advice given to us by architect, surveyor, friends and
relations, we bought it.

After we'd signed the contract, our new next door neighbour
popped out and said:

"You know why it was so cheap, don't you? BUGS! Brought by
the evacuees, dirty things; it's been fumigated twice, but you'll
never get rid of them." She was not referring, I presumed, to the
evacuees. This gloomy prophecy was not fulfilled, for we never saw
a bug (or an evacuee), though the first summer we were there we
had a plague of fleas. In subsequent summers they became fewer
and fewer, and more and more emaciated, until they were no
more.

Cumberland House after restoration.

And though ultimately we spent many times that initial £350, we got our house near the water, and we loved it.

When I mentioned to people in the neighbourhood that we were going to live in Manningtree, they raised their eyebrows.

"Manningtree—isn't that where those two funny little towers are? Surely there's no water at Manningtree, you can't sail there and nobody lives in Manningtree, do they?"

The facts were: Manningtree, pop. 619, early closing Wednesday. 69 miles to London; H.W. 1 hour 15 minutes after Dover; 7 foot of water H.W. neaps at the Council Quay. Vessels lie aground at low water. That explained the "no water" remark. Well, mine was going to be a cruising boat—so, like many a coaster of old, I could wait for the tide. Or so I thought.

Manningtree had once been a prosperous little port. Its time of greatness was in the eighteenth century. This was shown by the façades of the houses, most of them having been re-fronted in that expansive time. It still had an occasional barge calling there to unload timber. Its nearby neighbour, Mistley, had (and still has) a considerable traffic of barges and small coasters that load and unload at a quay which was once backed by a magnificent range of nineteenth-century maltings. At the Manningtree end of the Mistley quay there are still the two funny little towers like sugar casters. They are all that remain of Robert Adam's exquisite little church. And if it hadn't been for certain action that we took, they might not be there now.

At Manningtree a shallow-draft boat can usually get away from moorings on the Church mud about two hours before high water. The town is faintly industrial, with timber mills and maltings. There was once a brewery, but that is no more. Every other house used to be a pub—there are still six and an off-licence. And across the water on the Suffolk shore is the plastics factory—I believe the oldest plastics factory in the world. There are days when the little town looks a bit dirty and uncared for. In the summer time a few trippers scatter the streets and the foreshore with fish and chips and ice cream papers. And there is a certain amount of smoke (though clean air bills and the electrification of the railway may put an end to this). It is muddy and there are few yachting amenities. There is not much to recommend it for day sailing but for a really shoal-draft boat, which can lie aground happily for half a day, there is much to be said for it.

For one thing, having laid a mooring there are, at least at the time of writing, no further fees, charges, rents, etc. There are no harbour charges, and no slipping costs—for you just sail up on to

The remains of Mistley Thorn Church, 1947.

Sailing barge unloading timber at Taylor & Butler's yard, Manningtree.

Reminder, one of F. W. Horlock's barges, getting under way on her last voyage under sail in 1947. She was built at Mistley in 1929 and was Thames Champion barge in 1929, 1930 and 1934 and Medway Champion in 1929 and 1934. She traded with the British Xylonite factory – "the oldest plastics factory in the world" – carrying carboys of acid and raw alcohol from Limehouse Cut on the Thames to Brantham.　　*Photo: Roger Finch*

the beach and when the tide goes down you can scrape the boat's bottom or do whatever you want to.

The summer arrived. We had no boat and no plans for a holiday, when Griselda said, "I remember going to Orford once—let's go over there and see if we can hire a boat and perhaps find a pub to stay in. Anyhow, we can do some sketching."

The following week we went over to Orford by bus which dropped us in the village square, almost under the walls of a most imposing Norman keep. We walked down to the quay and the first thing we saw was an encouraging notice which read:

"Oysters supplied daily, apply G. Brinkley."

"Let's see if we can get some," I said, "but I wonder who G. Brinkley is?"

"Better ask that chap over there." Griselda pointed to a thickset, white-jerseyed character who was rubbing down the topsides of a small yacht. I walked across to him.

"Can you tell me where I can find Mr Brinkley?"

"It depends which Mr Brinkley you mean. There's me and there's my cousin."

"It's about the oysters," I said, pointing towards the shed.

"That's my cousin George. He is off down at the layings—down in Butley Creek. But he'll be back teatime. I'm Vic." With which he removed his cap as if to formalise the introduction. He was a handsome, grizzle-haired man, with keen blue eyes. I liked him on sight. We told him we were wondering if we could hire a little sailing boat and if he knew of a comfortable place on shore for us to stay.

"Yes, of course. I've got a little 14-foot boat—that's her over there"—and he pointed to a tubby little clinker-built boat at anchor just above the quay. "As for somewhere to stay, well, there's the *Crown and Castle*, and there's the *Jolly Sailor*, but I reckon you'd be most comfortable at Old Brewery House. Kept by a French lady just up the road there. She's all right, she speaks English."

After some searching we found Old Brewery House—a pretty long low white house with walls covered in climbing roses. It proved to be all and more than Vic Brinkley had indicated. As for Vic's little boat, her name was *Jenny* and she was a somewhat aged Alde one-design rigged with a gunter-lug. The first time we went out in her all went well until it came to picking up our mooring. Wind and tide were together, and it was a four-knot spring ebb tide; and a little cabin sloop had anchored just downstream, blocking our line of approach. At the first attempt I missed the moorings hopelessly. The second time I managed to poke *Jenny's* bowsprit straight through one of the little sloop's open ports. Fortunately the river was deserted and no-one was there to watch my antics. We finally got free and at the third attempt Griselda was

29

Orford Castle. Watercolour sketch.

able to grab the mooring buoy as we hurtled down on to it.

In our first days of sailing our ignorance spared us much worry, and that special saint who watches over fools in small boats allowed us to get properly bitten with the love of such a pastime. By the time we had reached Orford he must have decided it was time to teach us a few salutary lessons. During those two weeks at Orford we learned two, one in each week.

One morning, as the wind was blowing straight up the river and the tide was ebbing, I thought it would be a good opportunity to sail down to have a look at the seas breaking on the shingle banks. We tacked down to the end of the shingle spit past Havergate Island, reaching the mouth in a surprisingly short time. Ahead of us the sea was swirling over the bar in an ominous manner, so we rather hurriedly came about and, with the mainsail boomed right out, we started running back.

Jenny, 14-foot Alde One-design, at the mouth of the Orford River. Watercolour sketch.

"She does well with the wind aft, doesn't she? They run well, these little boats," I blithely remarked.

"We seem to be going through the water quite fast, but why are the river banks going in the same direction as us?"

"What do you mean?" I looked at the shore, and sure enough the banks were going faster than we were. "Good Lord, we are being carried backwards! How extraordinary! That means that the tide is running out faster than we are moving through the water."

"For God's sake, don't start moralising about the logic of the situation. Let's do something."

Some anglers on the shore, seeing our plight, ran hither and thither in their excitement, beckoning and shouting advice to us, of which we could hear nothing. Slowly we edged our way backwards towards them. At length, as we drew nearer to the shore and out of the full force of the stream, we found we were holding our own.

Then little by little making headway. In a while the power of the ebb lessened and we were able to make our slow way back to Orford.

That was the first lesson. Never sail down a tidal river on a spring ebb tide if you want to get back, and particularly if there is a dangerous bar at the end.

Below Orford, that is, between Orford Quay and the mouth of the river, sailing is interesting and varied. The river winds and even divides in two to circle Havergate Island, where since 1951 the avocets had nested. And sailing up the river, on the port hand is Butley Creek, which winds and twists in a north-westerly direction for some three or four miles through pretty country, between wooded hills and reed-lined banks.

From Orford to Aldeburgh the river is straight, featureless, windswept and often rough. It is an unendearing stretch of water. From the river, one's approach to Aldeburgh is from Slaughden Quay. It is rather the back end of the town and looks like it. But I like Aldeburgh with its old flint and colour-washed cottages, its RNLI lifeboat resplendent and toylike in shining blue, white and red, its Victorian villas and Edwardian hotels.

Our introduction to Aldeburgh had been to help in a small way with their Festival of Music and the Arts. Those early Aldeburgh Festivals were fun. They had a refreshing mixture of amateurism and professional expertise. Inevitably the later festivals became more professional, more fashionable and perhaps less fun. But Aldeburgh, at least for a couple of weeks each summer, has a lot to offer anyone who cares both for sailing and for music.

Aldeburgh is two-faced. One side faces the North Sea and a long shingle beach. Here are the hotels and the boarding houses and also, rather incongruously, the Moot Hall, very much restored and standing isolated on the edge of the beach, as if left by the tide; as indeed it has been, for much of Aldeburgh is now beneath the waves. The other face is to the west, where at Slaughden Quay the river no longer runs straight into the sea, as it once did, but turns south, sheltered behind its ever-growing shingle bank. It was to Slaughden that we came a day or so later, for we had a fair wind and a flood tide and we were bound for Snape, where an ancient bridge barred further attempts at navigation, at least for sailing boats with fixed masts.

From Slaughden our course ran due west, leading through wide mudflats with a north bank that had perched on it one or two large houses. We sailed on to Iken, where an old church stood in a romantic tree-grown setting. Once past the point we came to a pool

Iken Church. Watercolour sketch.

below Iken cliff, and there we anchored and had a picnic on the beach. On the last of the flood we followed the river's twisty course through reed-covered banks to the hump back of Snape bridge. We went ashore and were struck by the beauty of a great group of nineteenth-century maltings. Under the shadow of these hand-some brick buildings we found a very nice little pub, appropriately called *The Plough and Sail*. When we had had a couple of pints we found that the brightness of the morning had passed. The sky was now overcast and streaked with low-lying wind-torn clouds.

"Doesn't look too good," Griselda said, buttoning her mackintosh tightly up to her neck. "Hope it doesn't rain before we get back."

"I hope it doesn't blow too hard. We'd better reef her right down."

The wind was on our beam as far as Slaughden, but once we had turned into Sea Reach it was right in our faces. My heart sank at what I saw before me. The river was a livid coffee colour, and advancing towards us were endless ranks of white-capped waves. I comforted myself with the thought: "After all, it's only a river, it's not the sea, it can't really be rough." And then we were into it. I luffed for a squall and *Jenny* pushed her nose right under. Water

33

Orford Quay, Force 8 south-westerly wind. Watercolour sketch.

sluiced along the coamings and we were drenched with spray. By bearing away rather than luffing we survived for a while. Driving gusts of rain and sleet did not improve matters. For what seemed an interminable time we tacked backwards and forwards, sometimes making a little ground, and then on the next tack losing it, and all the time we were getting wetter and wetter and more and more water was coming aboard *Jenny*. With the tide against the wind a vicious steep sea had built up, and to my inexperienced ears the wind had a most ominous sound about it.

"Do you think we'll get there?" Griselda asked, her face streaming with water.

"I hope so—Oh look out!"

We had just cleared the martello tower that lies about a quarter of a mile below Slaughden and were coming about on the port tack when we were hit by another squall. It knocked us flat. The sea came pouring in over the gunwale, but somehow we managed to right her and with water above our knees I made for the bank. Lurching crazily, *Jenny* took on more water at every roll until at last she either sank or she grounded; I never quite knew what had happened. We found ourselves up to our waists in the water. Somehow I got the sails down and Griselda staggered ashore with the anchor.

Wet through, we sheltered miserably under the sea wall waiting for the tide to drop so that we could bail *Jenny* out.

"Fancy being wrecked in a river! Oh, I hate sailing," Griselda sobbed, "it's so—so humiliating!"

"Better than being wrecked at sea, at least we can walk ashore."

"But, I don't want to be wrecked anywhere, and I've broken all my nails!"

As soon as the tide had dropped enough we bailed *Jenny* out, lashed down the sails and spars, made sure the anchor was secure and started to walk back to Orford along the top of the sea wall. And only then did we properly appreciate the power of the wind. We could practically lean on it. We struggled and fought our way into the driving rain and sleet. As we battled our way along I had just sufficient wit to notice that though there was quite a sea running on the other side of the shingle bank, it was not nearly as rough as in the river, where the wind was against the tide. Inside the river the ebb of course runs towards the mouth and almost due south, whereas in the North Sea the ebb runs north. The path on the top of the sea wall was as slippery as a greasy pole and the bank was riddled with rabbit holes. We fell over innumerable times and Griselda on one occasion gave her ankle a nasty twist.

"Oh God, how I hate this!" she wailed, "I expect next time you will really drown us both." I couldn't think of any answer to this, so I said nothing. It took us two hours to reach the RAF ferry opposite Orford Quay, by which time we were not only wet but cold, exhausted and bedaubed with mud. The thirty-six-foot RAF harbour launch that took us across the river was nearly swamped. As we climbed up on to the quay I saw that some curious buoy-like objects were hanging from the flagstaff.

"What are those things?" I asked the RAF boatman.

"Those things! Gale cones, of course. South-westerly gales forecast. They were up there this morning, before you ever started. That's why you had the river to yourself!"

And that, more painfully learned, was our second lesson. To look out for gale warnings.

The rest of our stay at Orford was uneventful. A curious thing happened on the day of our shipwreck. Vic's dinghy, which we had left at *Jenny's* moorings at Orford, had broken adrift and disappeared. After the storm had cleared we went up to Slaughden in Vic Brinkley's motor boat to pick up *Jenny*. There, nestling against her side, carried by wind and tide, was the missing dinghy.

4

Pequod, the little whaler

From my first boat, the punt, I had, if nothing else, become a besotted, unregenerate boatowner; from *Omega* and our experiences with *Jenny*, I had become convinced that nothing but a cabin boat would serve my needs.

With *Omega* disintegrating in the Medway mud and secondhand craft fetching vast sums (for this was the year after the second world war), I turned to the pages of the yachting magazines for consolation and inspiration. And there I saw the prettiest little Viking ship—a little eighteen-foot whaler, half-decked, sloop rigged and with a centreboard, a Colin Archer stern, and planned as a camping cruiser. It was Kenneth Gibbs' Matelot class. How seductive are the plans of boats!

It was a fair-sized folly for anyone with as little experience as I had to go in for building a boat, but to try to improve on the design, as I did, was even more foolish. I wished to put a cabin on her and to change the centreboard for leeboards, thinking that the small cabin would be unbearable if cut in half with a centreboard case. So I wrote to Kenneth Gibbs, the designer-builder of this little craft, asking him if he would be willing to make these changes. He agreed, though I imagine with some reservations. And so on our return from Orford I placed my order, with delivery promised for the following summer.

Then followed a winter of unimaginable bliss—of planning the details of my first cruising boat. What rig—gunter or Bermuda? I plunged for gunter. What kind of anchor? I chose a little ploughshare-shaped contrivance, and it used to cut through our mud like a butter-knife. The colour scheme? We chose black for the topsides and a bright varnished mahogany for the cabin sides; for the deck, after much argument about smooth or non-slip deck paint, we chose the latter, and it attracted dirt like anything. And then we started thinking about the domestic arrangements—the position of the galley and what sort of stove it should have and where the lavatory should be and how we should carry water and where we should store stores—and all this on a waterline of about

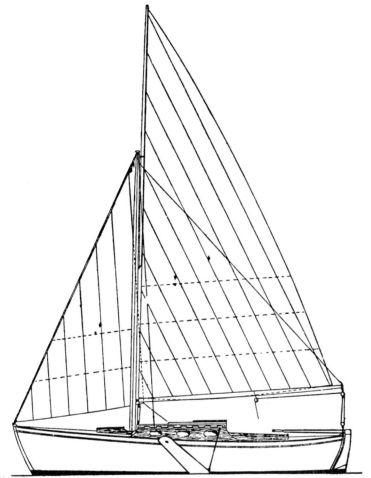

Sail plan of *Pequod*.

sixteen feet, with about three feet of headroom in the cabin.

I wrote endless letters to the designer-builder, which he answered more or less good humouredly. I had to write to him, for he was half way across England—and therein lay another foolishness. I was working in Ipswich, a neighbourhood dotted with first-class boatbuilders, and I had to go and have my boat built on the upper reaches of the Thames. This resulted from picking on this pretty little design—and as the designer was also a builder he naturally enough wished to build it. Hence the letters, about all kinds of matters of which I had only the haziest knowledge—

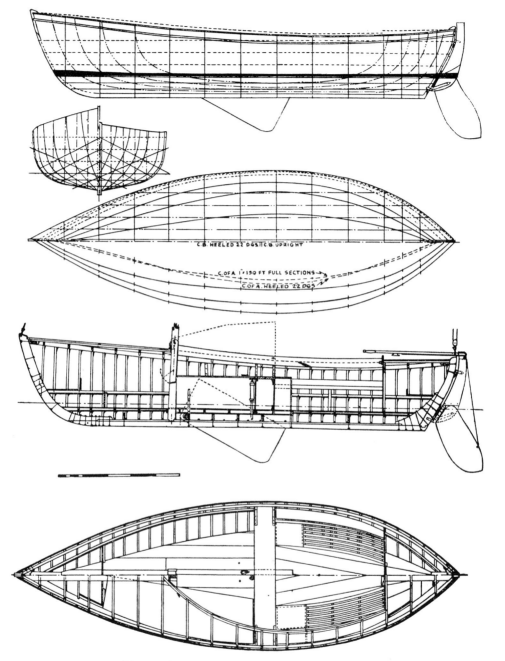

Lines and construction plans of Kenneth Gibbs' Matelot Class, forerunner of *Pequod*.

whether she should be planked in iroko, sapele or makore, none of which I had ever seen. (In fact I chose Canadian Rock Elm, which was as hard as iron, and showed as little propensity for taking up as that material would—which was something of a disadvantage in a clench-built boat.)

The colour and treatment of her sails was a subject for further letters. I was all for treating them with fish oil and red ochre, like a barge's sails. Here the fishing boat complex was coming out—but fortunately the builder managed to persuade me just to accept the colour and not the fish oil. Proceeding on the same fishy tack, and thinking of her whaling shape, I named her *Pequod* after that ill-starred vessel in *Moby Dick* . . . "A ship of the old school, rather small if anything, with an old-fashioned claw footed look about her . . . A noble craft, but somehow most melancholy!" But my *Pequod* was going to be anything but melancholy; she was going to be a trim little whaler, "fit to sail the seven seas", or at any rate a fair share of the North Sea.

"Dad says your boat's come and where is they to put it."

The speaker was a fat square little girl whose speech was impeded by the fact that she was sucking a gaudy iced lolly.

"Thank you June, I'll come right away," I answered.

"Dad says she's a proper pretty little boat, Dad says," she continued, removing the sweet and holding it up, apparently for my admiration, "Dad says, she's spoilt by those old leeboards. What did you put them on for?" Her sing-song voice soared up an octave.

I was loath to pursue the conversation, in case of any other too percipient remarks, and anyhow I wanted to see my boat, so I gave her sixpence to buy another gobstopper.

"Thanks ever so, Mr Lewis. Never you mind what they say about your boat. I think she is a proper pretty little old thing." And she was away to see the fun of the unloading, and probably hoping for some disaster.

When I reached the waterside, I found *Pequod* perched high on a lorry, surrounded by a gaping crowd. I spoke to the lorry driver, asking him how he proposed to unload her. He removed his cap, scratched his head and looked vacantly round him.

"Thought you'd have a crane" was his sole contribution to the problem.

"Ain't no crane nearer than Parkeston Quay and that's British Railways. Can't expect any help out of *them*!" The speaker was a wizened little man with a twitch in his eye.

Monny, the father of the lollypop-sucking maiden, now came to the rescue. Monny had been christened Mons because he was born at the height of that terrible battle. "I reckon we could lift her off. She's only a little old boat, after all."

"Of course we could lift her off. Fancy wanting a crane to lift a little boat like that!" The speaker this time was Monny's brother, known as "young Arthur", a blue-eyed, grey-haired, kindly man.

"Yerrs, we'll soon have the little boat down," chimed in another onlooker. And without more ado, half a dozen of them scrambled on to the lorry and heaved and pushed the boat into the outstretched hands of the crowd, which now included the Doctor, the Town Clerk and the Parson. The latter laid hands on the stern of the boat with such exuberance that he pulled the horse adrift. Even the oldest inhabitant, old Joe Lucas, left his interminable sawing up of driftwood to come and see the fun. *Pequod* landed with a bump right in front of him, for, "little old boat" or not, she was a bit heavier than they bargained for. His beady old eyes darted here and there, then with a look of unutterable contempt he squeaked: "Call that a kebbin, do orl right for keepin' 'ens in," and with a thin cackle he stumped off to his woodpile.

"Don't mind him, Sir, he hasn't got a kind word for anyone since his daughter don't let him go on the water any more, not since he turned his punt upside-down, out collecting driftwood last winter. Anyhow you can't argue with him, he's deaf as a beetle." Old Joe's disapproval of the unfamiliar was a characteristic of the East Anglian. That quite often, as far as my boats were concerned, this attitude of the Manningtree watermen was entirely justified was possibly fortuitous.

"Young Arthur", who had explained away the vagaries of the oldest inhabitant, was now busy organising the stepping of the mast and the setting up of the rigging. In half an hour *Pequod* was ready for the water, albeit minus a horse which some other kind helper had taken off to the blacksmith to be welded.

And all this without so much as by your leave. I and the lorry driver were clearly people not to be reckoned with as far as boats were concerned. We were the kind of people who thought in terms of cranes! So I paid him off and turned to settle my accounts with the hoard of willing helpers, only to find that they had all melted away, except "Young Arthur".

"I just stop to say that I think we ought to get her off to her mooring when she floats. Looks to me as if a storm is blowing up. Anyhow, she will be safer out there. You know, you can't trust everyone round here. High water won't be much before midnight, so let's say I meet you here at eleven o'clock."

"That's most kind of you, but what about my paying for the unloading and everything?"

"You don't want to worry about that, we likes to see a new craft on the river. Easy name to remember too—Peapod."

At 11.30 that night we climbed aboard *Pequod*. To an accompaniment of thunder and lightning, Arthur Woollard towed us off to our mooring, a shiny, gleaming, cherry-like spherical metal float. As I made her fast, the Manningtree sky was torn apart by a great jagged fork of lighting that seemed to plunge straight at us. And with that, it started to pour with rain. We were soaked in a moment. "Better get out of this," Arthur yelled in my ear, "it's fair streaming." We scrambled into the dinghy and were soon ashore. As we sheltered in the old gun shed Arthur said: "This is all because you didn't launch her proper, with champagne and all that. Very jealous, the Almighty is . . ." As he spoke there was another cracking peal of thunder. "He's putting on a nice old show, band and all," Arthur concluded.

At the weekend my brother-in-law joined us for our maiden voyage. We dallied over our lunch and set off in the afternoon on a falling tide.

"She seems to go all right," Griselda remarked encouragingly. Her brother Edwin, assuming their family mantle of pessimism and speaking with the authority of an ex-RNVR commander of a Landing Craft, Infantry mark II, added the comment: "Anything that'll float and has a rag of sail up goes all right with a following wind and the tide under her. Wait till you try to get back," he ended ominously.

They were prophetic words, and my pride of ownership suffered its first rebuff when off Stutton Ness we came about and turned for home. The ebb tide seemed to have increased in velocity and the wind was becoming fitful. After six abortive tacks across the wide expanse of the Stour we found ourselves considerably nearer Harwich.

"Better drop the hook, hadn't you?" Edwin spoke, "otherwise we'll find ourselves out in the North Sea or piled up on one of those mudbanks. Anyhow, I've got a stomach ache, so I'm going below—if you can call it that." And he dodged down into the little cabin. We anchored and furled the sails and sat quite peacefully for a while watching the tide sluicing by. Slowly great whalebacked mounds of mud came into view. In half an hour we were surrounded by acres of mud, though by good fortune we were anchored on the edge of the main channel.

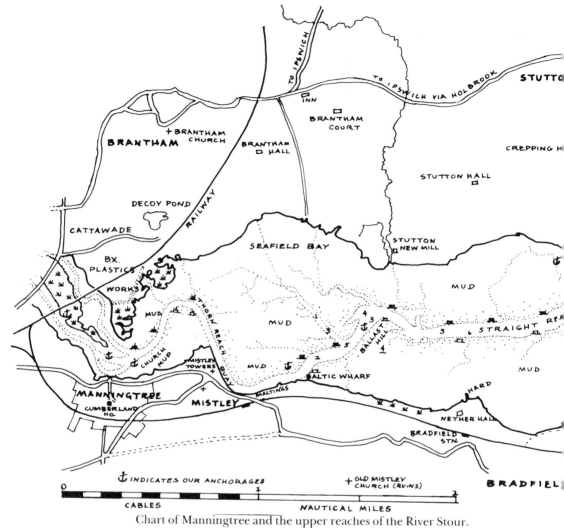

Chart of Manningtree and the upper reaches of the River Stour.

"How long do we have to wait here?" Griselda asked hopefully.

"Only till the flood comes up. We should have felt it ages ago, but something must be wrong with my calculations." This was met with silence.

Night had long fallen before anything of the flood could be felt. A slight breeze had sprung up and soon we were tacking backwards and forwards, as blindly as a beetle in a bucket. The only guidance I had was the lights of Parkeston Quay, and these I resolutely tried

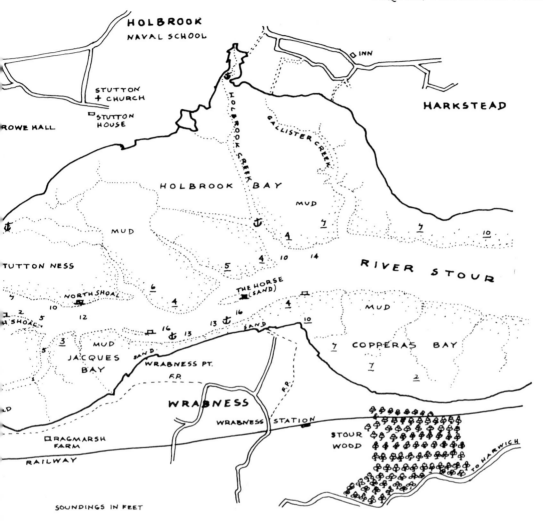

to keep astern of *Pequod*, judging quite rightly that if they were ahead of me, we should clearly be going towards Holland and the wastes of the North Sea instead of to our own dear beds. All went well for a while, though we touched twice before coming about on to a new tack. Somewhere about midnight the wind piped up a bit and we found ourselves careering along. A light suddenly shone in front of us and we spun round almost in our own length, just missing the third Woollard brother, Freddy, out babbing for eels.

Unaware of his peril, he gave us a civil "Goodnight" as we careered off into the darkness. It was a pitch-black night, without a star to be seen. A sudden flurry of rain hid the Parkeston lights, and then with a shuddering bump we hit the only hard shoal in the river, appropriately named Ballast Hill, for there the old coasting brigs and schooners bound for Mistley would drop their ballast before coming up to the quay to pick up cargo.

We seemed not only to have hit this unique obstruction, but to have climbed right on top of it.

"If I'd been you, I'd have called her *Excelsior*—anyway, there's less motion up here," my brother-in-law remarked as he helped me to drop the sails. "Put the anchor over, light the riding light and let's have a nice sleep till morning." I gloomily followed this advice, but sat for a while in the cockpit while the others feigned sleep below. Soon we were afloat again, but the wind had dropped away and all was still and quiet. I heard the distant cry of a redshank and then the putter-putter sound of a motor boat. In a few moments Monny Woollard and his old father were alongside. "Give us a line!" the old man shouted, "time you was home an' abed." Before the others had struggled out of the cabin, our anchor was up and we were away. Thus, ignominiously, we were given safe conduct to our moorings. The Manningtree church clock was striking two as we rowed ashore.

"That will teach us not to go out for an afternoon's sail on a falling tide," Griselda sleepily remarked as we tottered up the hill.

A week later we started on our first cruise. After a busy day finishing up various jobs and getting things ready for our holiday we reached the waterside, some time after the tide had turned. By the time we were aboard and had the sails up there wasn't much water under *Pequod*. Obviously we hadn't learned one lesson yet. We set off and sailed exactly fifty yards over the Church mud before we grounded. A large burly waterman known as Lunn paddled over to our rescue. We heaved and pushed, but to no purpose. In a few minutes even his punt was aground.

"Tide was dropping fast. You didn't ought to have left it so late. I reckon you're there for the night, but you won't come to any harm there, that's certain." He pushed his punt off and paddled away.

I felt a certain tenseness in the atmosphere. This was not lessened by Griselda giving herself a resounding crack on the head on the very low cabin top.

"It's more like being in a coffin than a hen-coop," she muttered tearfully. "Well, I hope you're satisfied now you've got your blessed boat. Come on, we'd better have some supper. Oh God! what's that?" A dismal blaring cacophony of noise had suddenly hit our offended ears. I bobbed up out of the cabin, and there, not forty yards away, were massed bands of the Salvation Army, presumably having their annual jamboree, eisteddfod or whatever they call such hideous occasions in East Anglia. We ate our supper to a mournful dirge, with a chorus of "Wonderful words, wonderful words . . ." We washed up to a pious hymn sung to the rousing pantomime tune of *Maggie's Been and Caught Another Cold!* and climbed into our sleeping bags while they were blaring out their own private version of *The Bluebells of Scotland*.

"What a lullaby!" Griselda remarked, "do you really think a boat is all that important?" I couldn't think of an appropriate answer, and anyhow she probably wouldn't have heard it, for the bands were having a final lung-bursting jam session on what sounded like *The Man that Broke the Bank at Monte Carlo!* They must have shot their bolt with this, for there followed silence. Exhaustion or thirst had driven them away.

Pequod with her nearly flat bottom sat quite upright in the mud. I lay awake for a long time pondering over the incomprehensibility of women and trying to get comfortable in a fleabag which became more and more like a straightjacket as I turned and tossed about. There was a determined draught blowing down my neck, so I pulled the fleabag over my head and comforted myself with the thought that at last I had got my boat in which I could actually sleep. If only I could sleep . . . then, in turning over for the fortieth time, I gave my funnybone a monumental bang on some projection or other. As I lay nursing my agony I thought I heard a small voice say:

"Jolly well serve him right." But I may have been wrong, for when I spoke to Griselda I met no response but her quiet, even breathing.

We awoke next morning to sunshine and the flood tide already trickling up to us. We dressed and breakfasted in the cockpit, for the so-called galley—a primus stove—was placed in a locker under one of the side benches, a relic of *Pequod's* original design, which had been that of a half-deck camping cruiser.

"This is heaven!" I blithely remarked.

"It's all right on a fine day," Griselda replied, "but what happens to these cooking arrangements when it rains? I suppose you expect me to cook under an umbrella!" The effects of last night had apparently not yet worn off.

By the time we had washed up *Pequod* was afloat. A light wind was coming out of the west and was setting up a tiny popple, so that the surface of the water was pricked with over a million points of light. As the 8.0 am Ipswich bus lumbered along the Walls from Mistley we were away and standing off for the Hook buoy. To make amends for our earlier misfortunes we were given a perfect sail, with a gentle soldier's wind taking us down the Stour. Fearful of going aground, we kept devoutly to the channel, with a depth of anything from twelve to twenty feet of water under us. We skirted Mistley Quay, where a timber barge was already being unloaded, then turned out from Baltic Wharf to the north of Ballast Hill, eastwards to Stutton Ness; as Holbrook Bay opened up we crossed to the south shore under the trees and cliffs of Wrabness, and back into the centre of the river through the cocooned reserve fleet of destroyers, corvettes and frigates that lay in Copperas Bay. These were all new waters, for we had never been below Stutton before. The little boat handled pleasantly and pulled the flat-bottomed dinghy without much fuss. We experimented with the leeboards and found that with only a foot of board submerged our leeway was greatly reduced. Her straight keel made her slow coming about, but she showed no desire to miss stays.

We jibed over as we passed Harwich and turned for the open sea, which lay shimmering before us.

"You take the tiller, I want to look at the chart." Griselda obediently took the helm as I unfolded Stanford's chart of the Thames Estuary. It was a battered copy which I had bought second-hand during the war, and on which I had with loving care and very little knowledge of what I was doing made various corrections and additions, based on long outdated Admiralty Notices to Mariners. As our entire (proposed) cruising ground occupied an area of about three inches by six on this large sheet the chart was somewhat out of scale. However, it matched the binnacle—a treasured monstrosity of shining brass that had been looted for us by an N.O. friend.

"South, 20° West," I announced, feeling rather like a Trinity House pilot bringing in his first liner. "With that we should fetch the Pye End buoy. Well, look at the compass, can't you? How can you expect to keep on course by just looking over the bow."

"I'm not looking over the bow, I'm looking at the buoy," my wife replied.

"Heavens, there are a lot of buoys here; unless you follow your course by the compass you might put us aground."

"Well, it's got its name on it, so I suppose it must be the right one. Here, you drive, then you can look at your precious compass as

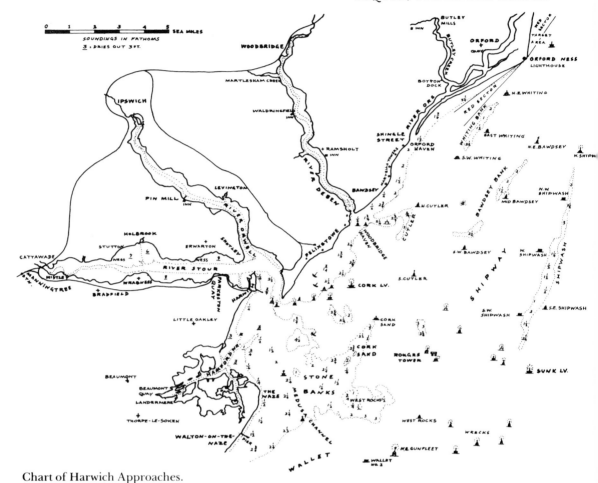

Chart of Harwich Approaches.

much as you like, I'm going to sunbathe." And with that she pulled off her jersey and spread herself out on the side bench, leaving the tiller swinging idly. I grabbed it nervously, then, finding there was little pressure on it, let it go. *Pequod* continued to sail on her course, then bit by bit edged up into the wind.

"Oh, what a clever boat, she sails herself!" I said.

"Which is just as well, considering how much we know about it," Griselda replied.

As we came up to the Pye End we began to feel the ebb running out of Hamford Water and the Walton Backwaters. Our wind was still fair and just strong enough for us to stem the tide. One by one we passed the buoys that mark the channel into the Backwaters. By the time we reached the High Hill the Pye Sands were beginning to uncover. They provide a splendid breakwater against an onshore wind, and a formidable danger to anyone coming through the Medusa Channel.

A row of can buoys on the port side showed the entrance to the Walton Channel. We ignored the wastes of Hamford Water to the west of us, for the ebb tide was now running strongly, and what little wind there was was coming from that quarter. We were only just able to stem the stream up the Walton Channel and crept silently past two creeks opening on our starboard. The second was full of moored craft, and called, so we learned later, the Twizzle.

"I think that's the Walton Yacht Club," I said, pointing to a building that lay about half a mile ahead of us. "We shall be able to go ashore there and get milk."

"Well, you'll have to walk," Griselda replied, "we're aground." As she spoke the dinghy gently bumped into our stern. I prodded about with a boat hook, but we were aground all right and the wind had practically died away.

"I hope you're pleased with your boat," Griselda said as we stowed the sails. I stood for a moment with a tie dangling from my hand, looking at my little boat with some pride. We had completed our first voyage from A to B—or almost to B. It had taken us some five and a half hours and, after the false start, it had all gone according to plan. It was all eminently satisfactory, and I had conveniently forgotten about last night.

"If you want any milk in your coffee, you'd better stop day-dreaming and go and get it before the dinghy dries out." Chastened, I hurriedly finished stowing the sails, climbed into the dinghy, rowed up to the Yacht Club and walked the half mile into Walton.

"It is rather fun," Griselda admitted, as we were finishing our lunch, "but if we are going to eat in the cabin I think I am going to get the most awful indigestion—it's such a cramped position." It was rather cramped, for the cabin was only about the size of a coal scuttle, but I felt at that moment that such things were a negligible price to pay for the pleasure of being afloat in one's very own boat.

In the evening we sailed through the moored yachts in the Twizzle and into a large landlocked lagoon called Horsey Mere, which separates Horsey Island from the mainland—but separates it only at high water and only just then, as I discovered as we touched with our leeboard. Ahead of me was a small cutter, hopelessly aground, so we reluctantly came about and returned through the Twizzle, very nearly fouling a large smack with an immense bowsprit.

Our second night afloat was spent quietly in a little creek, barely more than a ditch, just off the Walton Channel. No itinerant bandsmen disturbed our sleep this time. With great ceremony I lit our little brass lamp, and in its comforting glow we lay stretched out on our bunks, talking and reading. The quiet of the night matched the perfection of the day.

"If it's always like this," said Griselda drowsily, "I think I shall like it after all."

The next morning we left our anchorage on the ebb tide. Out in Dovercourt Bay we found a bit of a lumpy sea and a wind that had moved right round into the east. It was an even brighter morning than yesterday, but the sky had a hard look about it and the surface of the sea was a tumbling greeny grey. *Pequod* seemed to manage all right, though in fact not until we were approaching the Pye End did we come into unprotected water. Here we met the ebb from the Stour and the Orwell, and that with a contrary wind set up what looked to us quite a vicious sea. With our sheets freed and still with no great power in the wind we swooped along. Inside Harwich harbour the sea was, to us, surprisingly rough. Leaving Bloody Point and Shotley on our port we stemmed the ebb into the Orwell. The lower reaches seemed undistinguished, flanked as they are by low-lying marshes, but once we had rounded Collimer Point the thickly-wooded river banks rose steeply on either side. Pin Mill was our destination. It had been our ambition to go there, but it was not until we had passed two long lines of mooring buoys in Butterman's Bay, where not so long ago Captain Erikson's grain ships had tied up, that the wooded cliffs opened up to show a small group of houses on the water's edge and a number of moored yachts, barges and other small craft. It made a pretty picture, seen from the water.

We anchored inshore of the moored craft and then, after a hurried tidy up, rowed up to the hard. We tied the dinghy to a post alongside the hard, which was very muddy, and walked up to a little inn. The rather grimy, paper-and-cigarette-strewn bar was a sad disappointment after the offshore view, and five minutes after our arrival a charabanc disgorged a shouting horde of trippers, so after the briefest of drinks we returned to the dinghy and rowed back to *Pequod*.

"It's fatal to have preconceived ideas about places. Ever since we read somewhere that Pin Mill was the 'Gem of the East Coast' I've had a mental picture that that place does not live up to," I said.

"I wonder if pilgrims find Mecca all it's cracked up to be," Griselda replied. When we got back to *Pequod* we found a motor cruiser anchored almost within spitting distance, with a radio blaring out dance music. We were to discover later that it didn't need a crowded anchorage to make another boat moor alongside. In deserted creeks we have had just the same thing happen. It must be something to do with togetherness.

"Let's get out of this!" We set sail as quickly as we could and were soon threading our way through the anchorage.

We sailed a little way upstream and grounded on the east shore opposite Cat House Point. Our going aground this time was intentional, so that we could have a night undisturbed by the wake of passing steamers. The tide was ebbing fast and we were soon surrounded by mudflats. It was an evening of undisturbed quietness and we quickly dropped off to sleep. We were getting used to sleeping practically in the open air.

"John, wake up! Wake up! Something awful is happening!" I came slowly out of a deep sleep. The air was filled with an appalling clamour.

"What is it? War?" I gasped as I struggled into the cockpit. There, fifty yards away, was a weird contraption, ablaze with lights and setting up a tremendous din.

"What on earth is it, it looks like a Mississippi showboat."

"Oh, it's only a dredger. Fancy you waking me up for that!"

"Fancy waking you up! Only a moron could sleep through that noise. Bloody thing! Oh, isn't it cold?" With these words she dived back into the cabin.

"You wanted a night aground, and this is what you get for it."

"Never mind, let's have a hot drink," Griselda said. She soon had the primus going and in a little while we were happily sitting on our bunks drinking hot coffee and eating some very splendid fruit cake.

"As we can't move, let's hope the dredger can."

"Extraordinary hours people keep on the water. There are those oafs kicking up that awful din and probably fishing up quite unmentionable things from the bottom of the river, and you and I drinking coffee and eating cake all at two o'clock in the morning. Well, it is certainly a change from being on land." As she was speaking the dredger stopped its dredging as suddenly and as inconsequentially as it had started. The quiet after the noise was startling. After a while, the silence was broken with a clanketty clank, clank, clank, clank. Then quiet, then the same noise again. Then another silence. Then the noise again, but more softly each time. We waited for a while until I couldn't contain my curiosity any longer. Looking out of the cabin door, I saw that the lights of the dredger were now some way off. It was shuffling off in a furtive, crab-like manner. My wife peered over my shoulder.

"Damn good riddance, now perhaps we shall have some peace."

We awoke to a cold, windy morning. The wind was still in the east. The primus blew out three times before we could get it to work and cooking breakfast in the cockpit was no pleasure.

It was no day for going outside, so we beat down to Shotley, then turned to run up the Stour. Wrabness offered no shelter, for the moored yachts were rolling their decks under, so we sailed on until we reached Stutton Ness and there in the lee of the tree-covered point we anchored opposite a nice little sandy beach.

We spent the next few days in the Stour, going ashore at Stutton and Wrabness for milk and eggs. The following Sunday the wind had backed to the north-west, so we decided to try for Aldeburgh. With the wind in this quarter this meant a run down to Harwich and out to Landguard Fort and a close reach up the coast past Felixstowe, past the entrance to the Deben and Shingle Street and then a turn to port into the reputedly difficult entrance to the Orford River. The only thing we really knew about this entrance was that it was impossible to enter against the ebb.

Bearing in mind all we thought we had learned about tides, we left Wrabness with about an hour and a half of the ebb tide still to run. The wind was fitful until we had passed Erwarton Quay, when it started to veer round, first to the north, then as we cleared the point at Landguard Fort it began to blow from the north-east. The last of the ebb was still running and for a while we didn't do badly, but as the tide turned the wind freshened and became still more easterly. Foolishly we did not reef. For a while we sailed in company with a gaff-rigged five tonner, which seemed to be making better weather of it than we were. Sailing close hauled, we were able to luff or spill the wind from our mainsail, but now with the wind and tide against us our progress became slower and more uncomfortable. We kept dipping our rail. At what stage I began to feel anxiety, and when that anxiety turned to plain fear, I am not sure. Griselda was crouched in front of me on the cockpit bench and I could see her knuckles gleaming as she clutched the coaming. She turned and said, "You may think this fun—but as for me, I don't like it much."

"All right, let's turn back, it will be easier running." And thus must have spoken the helmsman of the "Ship of Fools". The original, great fool! With head to wind, even with too much canvas

51

up, a novice can keep some control over a small boat. But with too much canvas up before the wind may the Lord help you, for you certainly won't be able to help yourself.

So I put *Pequod* about and very nearly put her under as well, and then we were off. We swooped and careered and yawed about and twice very nearly broached to. Bawdsey Haven was there one minute and gone the next, and so very nearly were we, for through our yawing motion I produced two bad jibes in quick succession. The tiller was nearly pulling my arm out and the yard was bending like a willow. We appeared to be travelling in an undulating trench of water with the waves on either side of us much higher than our heads. I thought "Another broach to and we've had it! We shall be done for, dead and drowned. And our new boat too!" There was no question of anxiety now, I was really frightened. And as always when I am frightened my mouth goes as dry as a sun-baked sandshoe. As for my wife, for once she said nothing.

The second of our jibes happened as I was trying to avoid running down the wreck that lies off Landguard. With the jibe the horse pulled right out from its fastenings and nearly pulled me overboard as well. It was just as well it happened then, for in a moment we were under the shelter of the point and could round the fort in smoother water. Coming towards us was a coastguard cutter. They came up alongside us and the coxswain shouted "We thought you were in a bit of trouble, so we were just coming out to give you a hand." I thanked him effusively.

"Oh, don't mention it," he replied, clearly embarrassed, as he turned his boat away with a wave of the hand.

"How kind of them!" said my pagan wife, her eyes filling with tears as they tend to do if anyone acts towards her in a particularly Christian way.

"It's a bit of a relief to think there is someone watching out every time I make a fool of myself."

"Please, please, don't do that sort of thing *ever* again." I promised that and a great many other things and professed great contrition as we reached across towards Harwich. We came about and stood over to the Shotley Spit buoy, passing under the stern of a fine Smeed barge, which ironed out that nasty short sea as if she had been a steamroller.

We felt too nervous and shaken to run up the Stour, so we crossed over into the shallow bay that lies between Harwich and Parkeston and there we dropped the hook. Dod Porter had said as we left Manningtree that we would never get to Aldeburgh with the wind in the east. "You go out and have a look at it. If you don't like it, you can always come back." We had, we hadn't and, I felt, we jolly nearly didn't!

We fed and drank strong coffee and held a post mortem on our folly. I blamed the boat and her designer and her builder. I blamed the weather and I blamed the sea. The only person or thing I didn't blame was myself. Griselda took care of that in the way that good wives have, when they know husbands have made benighted fools of themselves.

As it grew dark I put up the riding light and we undressed and got into our sleeping bags. Griselda, exhausted, fell asleep immediately, but not a wink of sleep did I have all that night through. First of all I started worrying about my incompetence, then about our boat and if it was the right boat, and finally about whether any boats really were worthwhile. Just when I might have dropped off to sleep the first of the night packet boats departing for the Hook of Holland set us a-rolling and bouncing about. I looked out. The lights on the train ferry jetty seemed to be in a different position. Were we dragging? Next a flotilla of liberty boats from the reserve fleet roared past us. Again I thought our anchor wasn't holding. Then trains either for or from the ferry started shunting backwards and forwards. This went on for an hour or more, and no sooner had that stopped than a couple of fishing boats anchored on either side of us. A lengthy boat-to-boat conversation was carried on over our heads about the misdoings of Edith and Hilda. Whether these were the erring daughters of the righteous fishermen or whether it was the name of a boat I couldn't quite make out. Several times I went out into the cockpit and shivered in my pyjamas as I tried to discover how much we had dragged. The lights on the jetty, the anchor lights, and the winking buoy lights seemed to be dancing the lancers. At one moment we were dragging down on the jetty, at the next a moored lightship was bearing down on us.

When morning came we were in exactly the same place as we had been the night before.

The next day, still feeling chastened after our experience off Landguard, I patched up the horse and then with the flood tide under us and a falling wind we sailed and drifted up to Pin Mill. There was an almost dead calm as we threaded our way through the anchorage. It was a still and lovely evening and flock after flock of curlew flew over, stirring the air with their bubbling cries.

"This does seem to be a life of contrasts," Griselda said, as we sat in the cockpit watching the shore lights reflected in the water. "I must say I prefer it this way."

The next morning, a Sunday, the river was as smooth as polished marble and there wasn't a ghost of a wind. After a lazy breakfast we got under way, using the sweeps to give us steerage. An occasional puff helped us until we reached Shotley, when a steady little wind came up, but it was too late, for we had missed our tide up the Stour. It took us a very long time to pass Shotley pier. Beating through the Reserve Fleet against the ebb, we thought we might do better to pass on the Erwarton (and shallower) side. We clearly thought wrong and went firmly aground. As the afternoon wore on, we finished most of our rations. We didn't float again until after dark, by which time half a gale was blowing. And from the direction of Manningtree, for now that we were going home the wind had gone out of the east. So we stayed where we were and I put out another anchor. We went hungry to bed.

Monday morning, at the time when I should have been clocking in at my job, found us still high and dry, under the shadow of the Royal Navy. We breakfasted on the remains of the coffee, two very small and very dry pieces of bread and two sour green apples. We then waited for the tide to float us off. At nine-thirty the water was beginning to trickle round us when I noticed a boat, a pinnace I think, coming towards us. Just short of the edge of the channel and forty yards from us it stopped and we were hailed by a naval officer. The only word I could catch was "*food*", so in no time I was in the dinghy and pushing myself over the mud.

He was an amiable young N.O., who, after hearing our plight, took me aboard *Tyrrean*, his depot ship, ordered rations for us, and asked me if I wanted to telephone anyone.

"Can you telephone from a ship?" I asked ingenuously.

"You can from this one," he answered, so I took advantage of his offer and in a few moments I was explaining to a somewhat surprised employer that we were marooned and starving and had been rescued by the Royal Navy. He granted me leave of absence; there was little else he could do.

"Will this be enough for you?" the N.O. asked, handing me a loaf of bread as big as a baulk of timber, a large slab of butter and some tins of sardines. I assured him that it would be more than enough.

From *Tyrrean's* deck *Pequod*, now afloat, looked no bigger than a matchbox. "Would you like a tow off?" the N.O. asked me. "You're on a lee shore."

I thanked him and said we would like a tow, thinking that the pinnace would do duty as a tug, but not a bit of it. An enormous vessel that looked to me like an ocean-going tug (I believe it was only an MFV) came churning alongside the depot ship. We

Mistley Quay with barge approaching.

boarded her and I saw that my dinghy was already tied up alongside. Soon we had reached the limits of the channel which the MFV found by going aground, to the ill-concealed annoyance of the N.O. and more shouting than I would have expected from the silent service.

"Can't get any nearer," said the N.O. "You get into your dinghy and we'll throw you a line, and you can pull the cable after you." I climbed into our little flattie and rowed a yard or so when they threw me a light rope, about the weight of a clothes line. This I made fast to the stern thwart and started rowing. I didn't make much headway to begin with because a mutton-headed AB had made the other end fast to the MFV. After more shouting and the realisation that about twenty feet of line wasn't going to bridge a forty-yard gap, they bent another and rather heavier rope on to the first. All the while I was rowing away from the MFV and being drawn back to it for all the world like a yo-yo, those wooden toys that spin backwards and forwards on a piece of string.

"All clear now," the N.O. shouted. "We've bent on plenty enough." So off I went, rowing with all my strength. The light heaving line was followed by a heavier rope and then a cable and a heavier cable and yet a heavier cable. The last one could have supported the bower anchor of the *Victory*. I rowed harder and harder, but instead of getting nearer to *Pequod* I was being swept furtheraway, and even further from the MFV, at the mercy of a vast bight of rope which was being tideborne and carrying me upstream. As I reached the point of exhaustion the N.O. blithely sang out:

"No go, I'm afraid. I will let you have the cable and we'll think out another plan." And with that they cast their end of this great series of ropes into the water. There was nothing I could do but pull it aboard the dinghy. Now that little flattie was a pig to row, a beast to tow, but she could carry a load, and on that Monday morning she proved it. I pulled yard after yard of heaving line, grass rope, manilla sheet, tarred Italian hemp and a great horrid stiff sisal cable into the dinghy. And all of it of course dripping wet. I must have looked like some demented spider hauling in a gigantic web. I was soon submerged under a mountain of wet rope and was drenched to the skin. At last I had it all aboard, and the dinghy's freeboard was reduced to about a quarter of an inch. I gingerly extricated the oars and, sitting right up in the bows, I started to make good the half-mile or so I had drifted upstream. I made poor time of it.

"Hurry up!" came the now familiar voice, "can't wait all day. I'm putting off a boat's crew to lend a hand."

At last I came up with them and handed the line and cable and all the rest of it to the bo'sun of a gangling crew of National Servicemen in a whaler. Their performance was hardly any better than mine, but eventually we got the line aboard *Pequod*. I had warned the N.O. to take the tow gently and not to go too fast, but he had assured me that there was no fear of that. So I was hardly prepared for the sickening lurch with which our tow began. In a moment we were careering madly up the Stour at a speed that *Pequod* had never travelled before and would never equal again. The dinghy was flying through the air behind us like an ill-balanced kite. At any moment I thought she would turn over and fill up, but in less time than it takes to write this we were well clear of the Reserve Fleet. With some difficulty I freed us from that unwelcome cable and cast off. Our change of velocity was so sudden it felt like hitting a wall. I have never taken a tow since.

So we sailed up to Manningtree and handed *Pequod* over to Albert Porter for the fitting of a new horse and also to see if he could locate a mysterious leak. Leaks in boats always appear to be mysterious, whether in the bottom or the top. Where the water actually appears inside is, as far as I can see, never on any occasion at the point where it comes in from the outside.

A week later, it was a Saturday, we were awoken at 4 am by the ringing of an alarm. It was already sunny, though a haze lay over the river. Kenneth Gibbs, the designer of *Pequod*, was staying with us to try out *Pequod* and to answer all my complaints. I was determined at least to go out to sea, and as the wind had settled down in the southwest it did seem likely that we should be able to get out of the river, even if we could not get back. I only hoped it would be a little rough so that the designer could see how his boat handled under such conditions.

We left our moorings at 5.40 am and under a light south-westerly breeze we dropped down the river on a course for the North Beacon. We jibed over at the Hook buoy and held a broad reach up to Mistley Quay, theatrically lit by the low morning sun. The high maltings blanketed our wind but the ebb tide carried us clear of the buildings so that we again picked up the breeze. We sailed through the lines of destroyers and rounded Landguard Fort two hours after leaving Manningtree, some twelve miles away. There was a very slight popple in the Rolling Grounds, but once clear of that the sea was even smoother than the river had been. Gibbs was at the tiller smoking a pipe. Ahead of us was the same five-tonner that we had seen on our abortive trip to Aldeburgh.

Pequod. The leeboards did not improve her looks.

"Let's have a little race with him," he said, "just ease that jib slightly, now a bit in on the main, not too much—yes, that's about it." It was as if someone had opened up the throttle. *Pequod*, leaning over slightly, began to clip through the water. The chaps in the five-tonner watched us, with surprise and then with dismay, come up on them and sail right through their lee. I was dumbfounded. There was clearly more to sailing a boat than just sitting there holding a tiller. It struck me then that there was more than one way that this sport could cut one down to size.

For the rest of that summer we sailed *Pequod* about the Stour and the Orwell. She was a nice little boat, and she was a very pretty little boat, but she was *little*. So at the end of the season I put her up for sale and made a pound on the deal. Any shortcomings she may have revealed were almost entirely due to my ignorance of what small boats could and couldn't do. At the same time I was quite unaware of this fact!

5

About conversions and boatbuilding

Pequod, my little whaler, had been sold and the only boat I had was *Omega* and she was disintegrating down on the Medway. However, she did provide the slender basis for my next boat, for I had her sails and the small brass lamp. One evening late in November, down on the foreshore at Manningtree, Dod Porter introduced me to his nephew Bill, who had just retired as a Chief Petty Officer after thirty-two years in the Navy. Bill was a stocky little man, barrel chested and somewhat pigeon toed. He walked with a rolling gait that would have done credit to any film extra taking part in a deep sea epic.

As the tide receded we talked. My lack of a boat soon came up and it was then that the conversion project was born. Bill had his pension. He had been trained as a punt builder by his father and above all things, he said, he liked boat-work.

"I'd very much like to convert a lifeboat for you. Give me something to do and I don't reckon it need cost you much, about £70 for the boat and perhaps £150 for my work and materials. You say you've got the sails and this old boat of yours down at Rochester. Perhaps there is something on her we can use. Let's go and have a look at her, and while we are about it we could go and look for a lifeboat hull."

The project was launched, and a few days later we went off on our search. We went first in the direction of the East India Docks, where we had heard there were lifeboats for sale. In driving rain, in company with a wall-eyed individual who was a dealer in old craft, we climbed through a broken-down corrugated-iron fence, crossed a piece of waste ground, and alongside the slimy, noisome banks of the River Lea we found three huge and rather derelict-looking lifeboats. They were all about thirty feet long, and I had firmly fixed on twenty-four feet as my maximum. Bill examined the boats critically, had a brief conversation with the

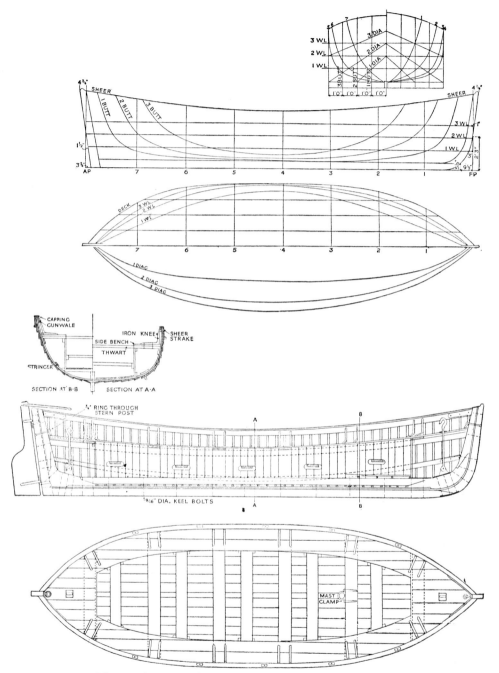

Lines and construction plans of 26ft lifeboat.

dealer and then said "That one will do", pointing to the most care-worn of them all. "Not for me, it won't," I answered nervously.

"No, that's not for you, that's for me. I don't reckon there is anything here will do for you, we'll have to go to Teddington for yours."

So by bus and rail and by devious routes we crossed London, and late in the afternoon we arrived at a Disposal of Small Craft Depot just above Teddington weir. It was a grey, misty dusk, with lights reflected in the river from distant street lamps. In a little backwater, moored up under a row of leafless willows, was a trot of lifeboats. I saw a nice little eighteen-footer that appealed to me.

"Too small," Bill said. "That one over there, that might do."

"That one" was practically under water and in the dim light looked enormous. We climbed over the trot and reached the one he had indicated. On its stern post was engraved "40 persons, 26.2 ft." She was rather larger than I had bargained for, but she seemed sound enough.

"She'll do you," Bill said. "Nice little boat, well timbered too, look, they are only about four inches apart." So on the closeness of her timbering, and even though we could not see her bottom, I bought her. A few days later she was delivered to Manningtree in company with Bill's monstrous craft. My boat was half full of leaf mould, so I spent a happy afternoon digging this out and finally washing her clean. She was as sound as the day she was built, and a lot of boat for the money.. This is the insidious thing about conversions: the illusion of something for nothing, or at least for very little.

We postponed our visit to Rochester until after Christmas. On a bitterly cold January day we found poor *Omega* in a state of desolation. However we salvaged six beautiful heavy brass opening portlights which alone would have cost new about twice what I originally paid for *Omega*, two deadlights and a rusty and quite useless old anchor. We returned to Manningtree with our spoils. The lifeboat was chocked up on the marshes. We had placed her on some old railway sleepers, taking some care to get her levels right, then covered her up and left her while Bill returned to Portsmouth to pack up his house and I sat down to draw my conversion plans.

There is something rather fascinating about converting boats. A lifeboat hull is a pretty uncompromising and rather unlovely thing. Straight ended and saddle backed, it is designed just to stay afloat and be rowed or to be able to blow downwind. I had seen some really terrible old "rise-ons", as they call them on the east coast, so I set about producing a design that would have a unity about it and

61

in which the boat's ancestry was fairly well hidden. And I felt the best precedent to follow would be fishing boats or nineteenth-century workboats. Whatever a converted lifeboat could be, it could not be a modern yacht.

The long, low hull clearly called for a two-masted rig, and with as unweatherly a hull as a lifeboat's a Bermudan rig would be wasted, so she became a gaff ketch. I had ideas of giving her a fiddle bow and perhaps clamping a counter on her as well, but Bill, who by the end of the winter had returned to Manningtree, talked me out of such extravagances.

It was just about this time, when he was about to start work on the boat, that the idea of writing a book about it came to me. So day by day, week by week and finally month by month, I kept a faithful record of the progress of the work. When I could I helped, but very much in the role of a boy who fetches the tools or holds the end of the plank, while the master saws or drills or does whatever else he has to. I learned a lot even by doing this, and by having to write it all down. I was beginning to serve my apprenticeship. It was a happy time and Bill was a happy man working away down on the marshes, right through a summer, a winter and another summer. He had rigged a tarpaulin cover under which he could work in all weathers. He was very slow, very thorough and the most honest man I have ever met. Each week I would get a detailed bill showing the number of hours he had worked (his hourly rate was 2/4d). One week he handed me a bill with "so many hours at 2/4d less eight hours." When I asked him what he meant, he said, "It was for thinking. I spent a whole day trying to puzzle out how to do that job—I can't charge you for that!"

For our spars we bought some spruce scaffolding poles from the local timber merchant. These poles, with their bark still on them, all looked very much alike to me but Bill and his uncle Dod spent a couple of hours trying out various poles by bouncing them up and down.

"I likes a bit of whip in my spars," Dod used to say. We had occasion to bless him for that whip more than once later on.

The next winter I completed my description and drawings of our conversion—but my publisher felt that a book on conversions ought to go beyond the description of a ship's lifeboat. So, by advertisement and other means, I contacted all kinds of "converters" who ranged from a Sapper Colonel to a schoolboy. It seemed to be an insidious disease, and apparently from the size of my correspondence there should be no dearth of readers for *Small Boat Conversion*. Only too aware of my limitations, I set about

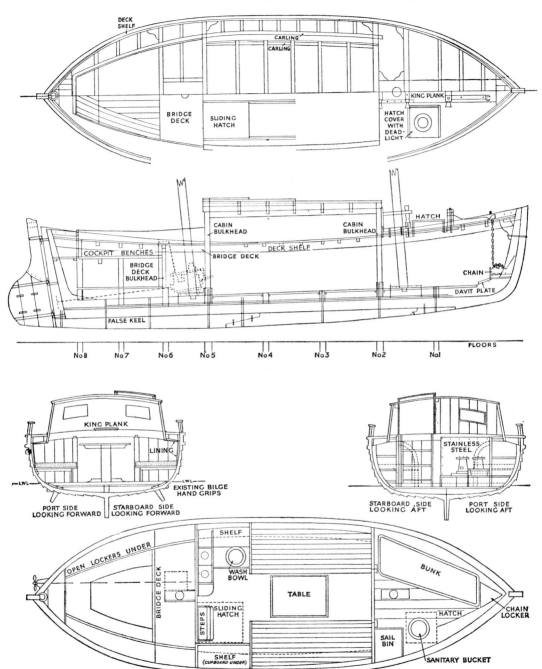

Construction plans of *Grace Darling*, 26ft lifeboat conversion.

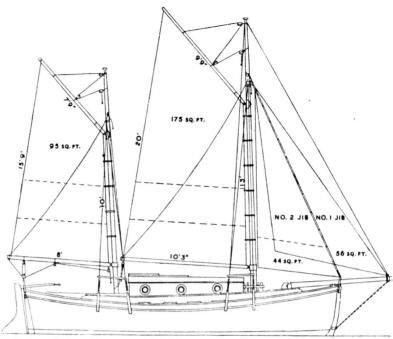

Sail plan of *Grace Darling*, 26ft lifeboat converted into a ketch.

assembling the details of conversions of other lifeboats, and of whalers, harbour launches, pinnaces and sailing dinghies. But the most ingenious conversion of them all was right on my doorstep. She had been christened *Calliope*, but because of her colour and her angularity she was known as the *Black Magic*. She was a barge yacht made from a bridging pontoon! Her joinery and other conversion work had a rather home-made look about it, yet I could not but marvel at the imagination of anyone who could see a sailing yacht in anything so box-like and unpromising as a pontoon. The converter had turned the pontoon back to front, taken out the square stern and wrapped the sides into a stempost. He had fitted chines and a deadwood and had made a jolly good little boat out of it. Her owner-skipper, a burly, black-bearded, pipe-smoking, duffle-coated Captain Kettle sort of figure, would stand in the *Crown Inn's* little snuggery discussing in the most modest way his unique craft. It was through no intention of his, I am sure, that his listeners were all convinced that he would soon be crossing great oceans in her, or at least winning the Hook to Harwich race. Such

Dod Porter trying out the sails.

journeys would have been rather uncomfortable, for her accommodation was primitive, and I don't believe she ever quite reached the mouth of the river, but at least she sailed quite tolerably—and to windward at that.

My lifeboat conversion and my book were finished at about the same time. The boat was launched and christened *Grace Darling* after that redoubtable Northumbrian heroine, the Farne lighthouse keeper's daughter. She looked rather handsome, but she was an anachronism if ever there was one, with her turned oak fife rails, her massive blocks and miles of rigging. However, she sailed quite well, within about five points of the wind, and the rig was a pleasure to handle and she would do a sternboard! We never reefed, we just dropped a sail or two, and there was still plenty left up there to blow us along. *Grace Darling* was a pleasant little ship and we sailed her for a couple of seasons in and out of Harwich harbour and down to the Walton Backwaters. For the first time we began to explore Hamford Water, for a while keeping the boat at a little waterside hamlet called Landermere.

 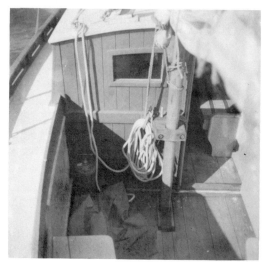

The lifeboat conversion.

Top left: bitts and fife rail. Top right: Bill Porter.
Bottom left: Griselda at the helm. Bottom right: Cockpit and mizzen mast.

Grace Darling moored at Landermere.

We had a few minor excitements and went aground time and again. With her nearly flat bottom she sat comfortably on the mud, except for one occasion when we dried out on the edge of a bank. There was half a gale blowing and we spent a few anxious hours imagining she was going to topple over, but she did not. On that occasion we got hopelessly embayed on a lee shore, and with anchors out from bow and stern we presented our whole length to the onslaught of wind and tide. After about thirty-six hours of this I had to get help to get us off.

Griselda remarked later that night, when we were comfortably moored off Landermere and the gale had blown itself out, "Sailing is painfully like going to the dentist, only nice when it's all over." Comparable observations must have been made by the wives of racing motorists, rowing blues and all-in wrestlers—but in none of those pastimes is the wife called upon to be more than a spectator. In sailing she's no spectator, she's right in the fight; not only does she have to endure all the discomforts of helmsmanship, watch keeping and sail changing, but usually has to be cook, dish washer and general hand as well. Her nails get broken fighting with stiff canvas, her hands get scorched by flying sheets, she gets covered with mud (at least she does if she sails on the east coast), her back is

Grace Darling on the saltings at Landermere.

nearly broken trying to break out the anchor, she is constantly being soaked by rain or spray. On top of all that she is expected to produce appetising hot meals and to look pretty as well. Not all wives will put up with it. If one thinks of it dispassionately, it is a marvel that any of them do.

Thinking back to those days, it fills me with amazement that with no engine and in as unweatherly a craft as the lifeboat conversion we did not get into any worse trouble than we did. She was certainly no rater, and I had a hankering for something with a better performance. So when the conversion book actually began to sell, I thought that from the proceeds of that and the sale of the conversion I could afford to have a new boat built, so I went and saw Kenneth Gibbs again. I had had a feeling of disloyalty to *Pequod's* builder since selling her after only a season. We discussed the kind of boat I wanted and I finally came up with the suggestion of an enlarged *Pequod*, with the same pretty Colin Archer stern.

I think I must have been a little vague, for what I thought I was going to order was a slim, sharp-nosed little sloop—but what finally emerged from our discussions was a tubby, apple-cheeked, full-ended ketch, and like most of his designs it was a pretty boat. Thinking I had a weakness for the rig, Kenneth suggested she should be a ketch and being quite convinced that he must at least know more about it than I did and having liked the rig on the lifeboat, I settled for that. The waterfront shook their heads when they heard that I had returned to an Upper Thames yard, where, they implied, the boatbuilders were fit only for building skiffs to be punted through buttercup-strewn meadows. But I had liked *Pequod* and I had visions of her larger sister slicing her way through the waves to windward rather than ambling along five or six points off the wind as the lifeboat did.

So at the end of our second season in *Grace Darling* I put her up for sale and the keel of the ketch *Far West* was laid down.

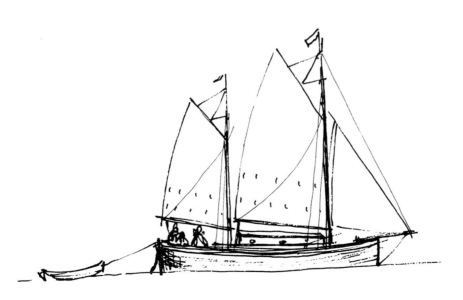

6

The building of *Far West*

She was named *Far West* by a little French girl who was staying with us, after *Annie du Far West*, the French version of *Annie Get Your Gun*.

During the following winter I made various journeys to the Thames to watch the progress of the new boat. It seemed foolish to repeat this stupidity and to leave an area in which boatbuilders are pretty thick on the ground and to travel half way across England to have my boat built, but there it was.

My first visit to *Far West* was on a sodden January afternoon. The boatyard was on the riverside, and I was struck then how river craft when laid up and needing a coat of paint look somehow more down at heel, more impoverished, than do their rugged seagoing sisters. Sodden lawns, dripping trees and flooded watermeadows seemed to be an inappropriate background for a seagoing boat. However, *Far West* was being built under cover in a brightly-lit shed which was festooned with power cables for electric drills, screwdrivers and riveters and hammers. Everything was done by mechanical power. It was a yard that was in many ways very advanced. At that time they specialised in alloy building and there was a wearisome clatter of metal on metal as some hard-chine five-tonners were being banged together. These unpainted craft in their unfinished state looked like large shiny sardine tins. In the middle of all these was the mahogany hull of my boat. I picked my way through the boatbuilders and tripped over their cables. *Far West* was already planked up and the timbers were being fitted. These timbers were both rather light and frugally spaced, so I remonstrated with the foreman shipwright, asking whether heavier scantlings and closer spacing would not be better. He just laughed.

"Timbers! they are just an archaic survival. In a clinker-built boat they only act as straps. Now if you had let us build your boat of sheets of ply on the stressed skin principle, just the way aircraft are built, we could have done away with timbers altogether."

"I don't want my boat to fly, I just wanted her to be strong enough to stand being banged into." And in went the little timbers, and how I worried about them. Would they be sturdy enough? Supposing she leaked? And that led me on to knees and breasthooks. *Far West* had none of these useful appendages. The lifeboat conversion had had heavy metal breasthooks at bow and stern and Bill Porter had festooned her with hanging knees and horizontal knees and upside-down knees all made from good English oak.

"Quite unnecessary!" the shipwright tartly replied, "her bulk-heads take the place of knees and her plywood deck is far more effective than any breasthook." Subdued by science, I went sorrowfully away, unconvinced and unqualified to argue.

Having boats built is a recurring disease. Once one has had it, it seems to attack one every few years—like malaria. And there doesn't seem to be any cure. If one must have a boat, one would think that the obvious course would be to buy one second-hand. Let other and richer men build to Lloyd's highest specification and fill their beloved craft with all the expensive gadgetry they can buy and then, after one season of wind and rain and the appropriate ultimatum from an exasperated wife, put their boat on the market at half the price it cost them. That's the moment for the wise man to buy. That would appear to be the sensible, logical thing to do. I even toyed with such an idea. I scanned the yacht agents' lists, and all I found at my price were boats so old, so hogged, so nail-sick they were beyond redemption; or boats so ugly and so gimcrack one wouldn't be seen dead in them. The hypothetical example that I looked for, built to Lloyd's highest specification, etc., even if she came my way at all and was knocked down to half what she cost, was still three times more than I was going to pay for the pleasure and privilege of building to my own desires. So I built.

This is not to say I didn't have any qualms. When I had got over the breasthook worry I began to think about her bilge keels, for *Far West* was somewhat ahead of fashion and was going to have these curious excrescences so that she could sit upright on the Manning-tree mud. Should they be deep and short, or long and shallow. What kind of profile should they have, and should they have an aerofoil section? I spent so long havering about this that the yard bolted a couple of nine-inch planks on edge on to her bilges and they worked wonders!

The next point at issue was the engine installation. I leant towards a centred one; but the designer was all for poking the shaft through her planking and clamping an A-bracket on her quarter. "It will have less effect on her sailing performance," he said. What perhaps he didn't visualise was my weakness for getting caught up

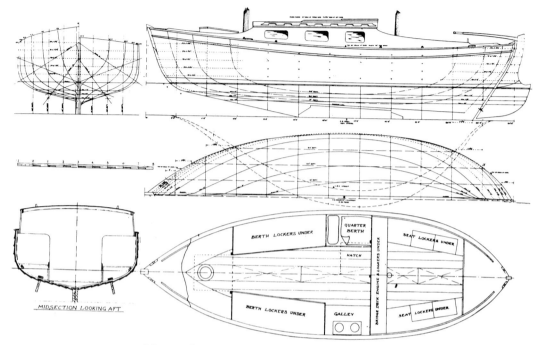

Lines and construction plans of *Far West*.

in mooring ropes, weeds, flotsam, jetsam, etc. On more than one occasion we have started out from our moorings under sail, cast the buoy overboard and sailed nearly our boat's length, to be pulled up all standing with the mooring rope having made a neat turn round the propeller or its blessed bracket.

On my next visit the point at issue was either opening brass portlights or windows. I professed a leaning to portlights.

"They'll cost you eight pounds each, £48 more on the bill." So we had windows. I should have settled for deadlights at thirty bob a go, but then the builder produced a special non-leaking window that opened at the top and was held shut by a little twig of a support. And they didn't leak! Not they! Water didn't seep or trickle through them, it poured in. In addition to this the plastic material with which they were made crazed so badly in the frost of the first winter she was laid up that we could no longer see through them.

Passing over these minor follies, I began to feel tolerably hopeful about the building of the hull. But when her cabin top was completed I began to feel less happy.

In spite of her pretty black-painted hull, *Far West* now had a rakish look—something of the riverside bungalow and a little bit of speedboat seemed to have crept into her appearance. She looked as if an industrial designer had got at her, all because of those windows. And in contrast to her hull, above the waterline there was a certain flimsiness about her coamings and fittings and what I can only call an immodesty in the expression of those windows. Building a boat or building a house or even taking a wife are all chancy things—disappointments are common enough. The thought of this does not prevent young people marrying, married people building houses, or old men building boats . . .

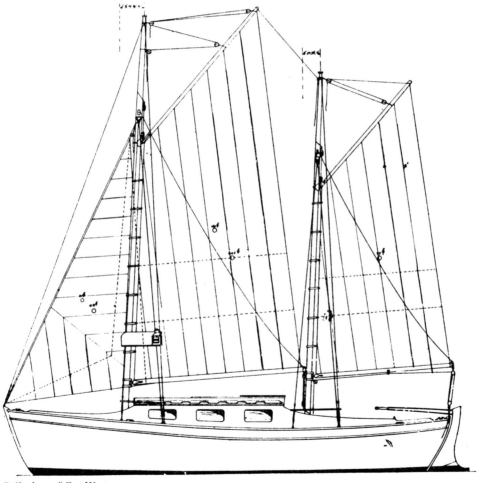

Sail plan of *Far West*.

THE DELIVERY OF *FAR WEST*

Far West was to be delivered to Manningtree by road. I was in bed with a streaming cold and Griselda was out when the boat arrived. From an upstairs window I directed the young Scottish lorry driver to the waterfront, where the longshoremen were waiting for him. I then returned to bed to cosset and minister to my cold. Late that afternoon Griselda arrived back from Ipswich, saying there was alarm and consternation on the shore, with the boat perched half on and half off the lorry. So, cold or no cold, I dressed and hurried down to the shore; and there I found my long-awaited, much-planned, brand-new boat lying with a large hole through her bilges! There were endless explanations of how she had toppled off her jack and much recrimination as to who was to blame. I felt sick and disheartened. Albert Porter put a temporary patch over the hole and laid her off on a mooring.

It was a sad beginning. Everything had gone so well, even the cheque for the sale of my converted lifeboat arriving the day before. And she looked a pretty boat, even in her hour of sorrow and in spite of those windows!

Trouble breeds trouble. The night after *Far West* arrived some unmentionable idiot discharged into the river a ton or so of used sump oil. A hard north-east wind was blowing all that night and this had driven the disgusting stuff all over the beach. The whole foreshore was filthy, boats were befouled and their warps were impregnated with oily slime. *Far West's* paintwork was ruined. Poor boat! Such was her reception at Manningtree.

After this rough start, two lengths of new planking were scarfed in quickly and her timbers were doubled at the point of damage. The fitting-out followed a normal course and by the beginning of June her two masts were stepped and her engine was given its first trial. After various backfires and explosions the engine worked—intermittently—and we circled round for half an hour. I didn't go far from my moorings because it gave me little confidence. Which was just as well, for that engine never ran for more than twenty minutes without breaking down.

A few days later Griselda and I took Dod Porter over to West Mersea to collect our sails from Gowen's. A sail loft is nearly always a pleasant place and Gowen's was no exception; the smell of Egyptian cotton, Italian hemp and beeswax filled the cool dark loft. An old, old man was sewing the seams of a Bermudan mainsail by hand. It must have been nearly fifty foot on the luff; there seemed to be acres of canvas in that one sail.

Our sails were produced and spread out for us to look at, and we were at once struck by their smallness. We checked their dimensions, which were according to the plans, and then packed them up. If small, they were at least colourful—an Indian red for working sails and a deep blue for the reaching jib.

The next day we bent on the sails and *Far West* was ready for her first trial. This coincided with the Manningtree Regatta. And as usual with east coast regattas it was not a very promising day. A hard north-west wind was blowing and the sky was filled with hurrying, rain-laden clouds. A thin line of bunting fluttered rather forlornly on the foreshore. Two little striped tents, for the Sailing Club committee and the timekeepers, were perched on the quay, looking as though they had been left over from some Crusade.

We were just pushing off the dinghy when Bill Porter came up to us. "Going to enter the race?" he asked.

"Good heavens, no!" I replied.

"Go on, you can touch 'em up in that little boat of yours. Just your weather. Only cost you half a dollar." After a bit more of this sort of talk I parted with my two-and-sixpence (12½p) and rowed off to *Far West*.

We set the sails, first of all with the staysail upside down. We righted that, dropped our moorings and *Far West's* maiden voyage began, to the raucous accompaniment of *The Skye Boat Song* from the loud hailer on the quay and a patter of rain on the decks. As we turned in to Thorn Reach the day darkened and the white horses suddenly became more noticeable—as white window frames do in contrast to drab brick on thundery grey days. However, we bucketed our way along under all plain sail. As we reached the starting line for our race, opposite the end of the Baltic Wharf, I hailed a competitor—the favourite for the race—asking how long we had to the starting gun.

"Five minutes or more," he shouted. So we came about just as the gun went off.

"There's the gun," Griselda shouted.

"That's only the five minute gun," I said, as we sailed back to Mistley. When we came about again the rest of the fleet were almost out of sight. We hurried off in pursuit. We set the larger blue reaching jib on the top forestay and dropped the working sail, for it was a reach all the way to Wrabness Horse buoy. The fleet drew ever further and further away from us and we never even looked like catching up with the slowest boat. However it was a splendid sail, *Far West* sailed upright as a Grenadier Guardsman and was palpably undercanvassed. Our first impression in Gowen's sail loft had been only too right and the ketch rig that had suited the

Far West sailing on the Stour.

lifeboat so well was terribly inefficient on this little buoyant hull.

The whole fleet passed us on their return journey before we had reached the Horse buoy. Here we came about for a close-hauled sail and ran into quite a lop, throwing a certain amount of spray aboard. I noticed that the mainsail was not setting too well and on going forward found that the gooseneck had slipped up the mast. As we clearly had no future in that race, I dropped sail and started the engine. It ran for a few minutes, faltered and stopped. So did *Far West*. I dived below and, remembering Dod Porter's advice, changed the plugs. With one turn she fired and was away. I was as surprised as I was gratified, though if I had realised how often that engine was going to die on me in this way in the future my gratification would have been tempered with doubt. Under engine, jib and mizzen we plugged along into the wind, but still failed to catch up with the rest of the competitors in the race. Long before we had completed the course the last of our rivals was safe ashore and probably at home having his tea.

By the time we had moored and rowed ashore, it was raining heavily. A few mackintosh-clad figures were scurrying up the street. The bunting flapped and dripped and the canned music still blared out pathetically. The foreshore was deserted. Even old Joe Lucas had left his saw bench. We walked home, wet and thoughtful.

TO LANDERMERE IN THE DARK

The following weekend we left Manningtree just after midday as the tide started to ebb. The cabin was practically filled with kitbags and baskets, tins, containers and cardboard boxes filled with enough provisions to take us to the South Seas. For this—our true maiden cruise—we had asked Dod Porter to come with us as far as Landermere. Lack of confidence in a new boat had inspired us to ask our old friend. Also I thought he knew something about two-stroke engines.

There was a fresh south-easterly wind as we dropped our mooring. We started under jib and mizzen but, the wind falling light under Mistley Quay, we set the mainsail. Griselda had produced some order in the cabin and then handed us out ham sandwiches as we approached Wrabness. As we sailed through the Reserve Fleet the wind grew more fitful.

"Better see if that little engine's running all right," Dod said, taking the tiller from me. "If this wind drops any more we shall need her, to stem the tide into Hamford."

I went below, uncovered the engine, switched on the ignition and petrol, flooded the carburettor and swung her. Nothing happened. I did this a dozen times, then came up for air.

"Won't she work?" Griselda asked anxiously.

"Give her a bit of choke," Dod suggested, taking evasive action as a liberty boat cut across our bows. I dived below again, "gave her a bit of choke" and cranked another dozen times. I was beginning to perspire and *Far West* to pitch and roll, for we were now clear of Harwich and making a long board over to the Felixstowe shore.

"Mucky plugs, I expect," Dod suggested, peering happily through his misty wire-rimmed spectacles. I retired below again and dismantled the plugs. They *were* mucky, so I cleaned them as well as I could in petrol and then tried drying them over a series of

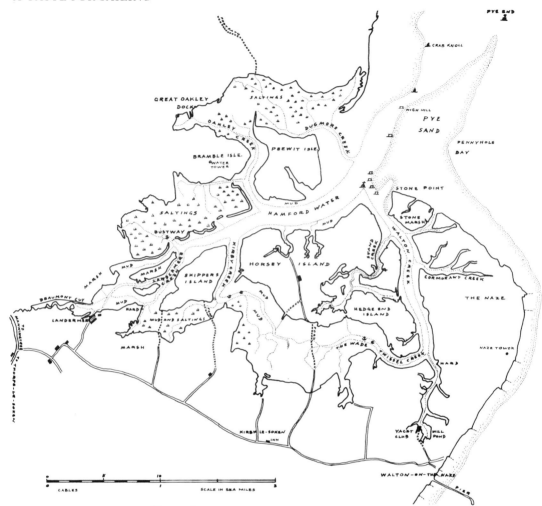

Chart of Hamford Water and the Walton Backwaters.

lighted matches. This did little except scorch my fingers. I replaced them, cranked again and, miracle of miracles, the engine started, ran smoothly for a moment, then let out a series of violent backfires, finally petering out with a rattle of chain.

After that each time I bobbed up for air Dod would suggest different remedies, such as, "Just you open them jets a bit," or "I reckon her timing isn't quite right." Finally I gave up, slammed the bridge deck door shut and climbed out on deck to see how *Far West* was behaving. The wind was against the ebb tide and there was a confused sea off Landguard Fort, but she slid over the waves, not taking anything aboard. My heart lightened.

"Goes well, doesn't she, Dod?" I said.

"Yes, nice little boat, she go all right, only she ain't going in the right direction. Couldn't expect it with this rig, she won't lay more than five or six points off the wind. You sure that motor won't work?" I assured him. "In that case we shall have to do the best we can and pray the good Lord gives us a slant to help us up Hamford."

It was roughish past the Pye End buoy, but as we got under the shelter of the Pye Sand the sea became smoother. Dod's deity must have been listening, for the wind backed into the south and then to the south-east, so we could just lay our course. It must have been about half past six and about an hour before low water when we passed the end of Walton Channel. We turned to starboard to enter Hamford Water when the wind swung right round into the west. Dod was at the helm and put *Far West* on to the other tack. A spit of mud was looming up in front of us.

"Better come about," I shouted.

"No, she's orlright, get what you can on this tack."

No sooner had he spoken than we came to a gentle halt.

"Back that jib," Dod shouted. "We'll have her off in a jiffy." I backed the jib and poked at the mud with the boathook, and all to no purpose.

"Oh, dear me! I've gone and put her on," the old man muttered. "I should have known better than that, all the times I've been up these waters."

"Can't we get her off?" I asked hopelessly.

"Well, you can try what you can do with that kedge." So I climbed into the dinghy and rowed the kedge off to the full scope of the warp; Dod gave a perfunctory tug on the kedge warp, shortened it in and made it fast to the bitts.

"Firm aground, nothing we can do till she float."

"When will that be?" Griselda asked hopefully.

"'bout ten o'clock, I shouldn't be surprised. Best thing you can do, Ma'am, is to get the kettle on, if that isn't putting too much on you." In a few minutes we were high and dry, but sitting quite upright. While I got the stoves going Griselda prepared kidneys and bacon and tomatoes. We were soon eating and stowing down mugs of boiling tea. The wind had now quite dropped away. After we had washed up I had another go at the engine, but to no purpose.

The evening was still and silent. The sun went down and we were still aground. At last the water came trickling up to her. The dinghy gave us a gentle nudge or two and then we floated, just before ten o'clock. There was still not a breath of wind so Dod insisted on getting into the dinghy and towing us. I stood at the tiller in what was now pitch darkness, every so often crying out to Dod to enquire if all was well.

"Yers, just you leave 'er to me." After about an hour of hearing nothing but the creak of rowlocks and the rhythmic splash of his oars, I heard him say:

"That'll do, you can drop your anchor now."

I scrambled on to the foredeck, cleared the dinghy painter and dropped the anchor overboard.

"Where are we?" I asked, as Dod clambered over the dripping, dewsoaked rail.

"Just off the entrance to Landermere creek, we'll lie nice and quiet here, no fear of drying out."

We made ready for bed—our first night aboard *Far West*. Dod had the quarter berth, and a hard bed it must have been with only kitbags and an army blanket for a mattress.

We awoke to a still, sunny morning. After breakfast I rowed Dod up to Landermere and found an amiable bookseller from Ipswich camping on the beach who said he would take him to a bus at Thorpe-le-Soken. Before returning to *Far West* I called on Bertie Lewes, a mechanically minded barrister who had one of the cottages at Landermere. He willingly volunteered to come back with me to see if he could sort out the trouble. When we arrived back at *Far West* Griselda had it all swept and tidied and was sitting on deck reading.

"Bertie has come back with me," I explained rather unnecessarily, "he's going to see what's wrong with the engine."

"I shouldn't waste your time, Bertie," she answered, "I should chuck the bloody thing overboard."

"That's rather drastic—these little two-stroke engines are a bit tricky, but we'll soon get her going."

The less said about the next few hours the better. I must have cranked that wretched engine a couple of thousand times before Bertie discovered that the carburettor was full of water. We emptied it, put it back in position and I cranked again. The engine started and ran smoothly for some moments, then stopped with a jerk.

"Why on earth did it do that?" said Bertie. "Good Lord, we've tried to climb the bank. I must have put her in reverse!" He peered over the stern. "The prop has carved up the mud like churned butter. Pity the tide's falling, but you'll be all right now. I think I had better get going before you dry out. I'd like to rejoin you for your return trip tomorrow. I'll bring my girls."

When I got back from depositing Bertie at Cardinal's Hard, the nearest landing place, *Far West's* stern was already about six inches out of the water. We ate our lunch rather silently, with *Far West* pointing downhill at an angle of about 45°. The beauty had gone out of the day and it had started to rain. We seemed likely at any moment to toboggan down to the bottom of the creek.

I looked out of the cabin window. All I could see was mud. Grey, glistening mud, primitive, untouched by man, a proper home for sidling, secretive crabs, lugworms and flounders. But what on earth were we doing here, stuck down in the bottom of a muddy ditch? As I pondered a flurry of hail blotted out the view, a halliard rattled against the mast and there was a sad little moan from the wind in the rigging. Griselda's silence had reached ominous proportions.

"I'm terribly sorry about all this, darling," I began.

"Why be sorry, it's your boat and you like it—or do you?"

"All right—I'll sell the wretched thing tomorrow."

"You won't do any such thing. Tomorrow will be a nice day and you will have forgotten all about this fatuous, miserable business."

Far West provided a diversion by sliding off the mud and into deep water as if to indicate that she'd have some sort of say in it. I put on my oilskins and climbed out into the cockpit. We were once again floating in the middle of the creek—our anchor had not been fouled by our backward dash up the bank. I wiped my glasses and looked around me. A steady downpour enveloped the whole landscape. Every few minutes a gusty squall swept over the creek, laying flat the marram grass and sea lavender.

Over on Skipper's Island four sad herons were perched, swaying in the upper branches of a scrubby oak tree. Rain-soaked creatures, they looked more like pterodactyls than birds, adding a final touch to the shiny, primordial watery mudscape. A violent squall drove me below again. Griselda was playing patience, a difficult one called "Long-tailed-tit." She looked up and smiled.

"Come and help me. I do believe it's coming out."

Whatever the weather was doing, the atmosphere inside seemed to have cleared. The patience did not come out, but it didn't seem to matter. *Far West's* cabin was cosy enough, even if water did stream through those patent non-leaking windows.

The next morning it was still overcast but no longer raining. I collected Bertie and his two young daughters from Cardinal's Hard and we were away under fore, main and mizzen by half past eight. The wind was light and southerly, giving us an easy reach down to the mouth of the Walton Channel, then we bore away to the north-east for High Hill and the Crab Knoll. Dovercourt Bay was a tumbled mass of grey-green waves. To the east, the hard clear line of the horizon was embroidered with a frieze of sailing craft, among them a ketch and a pretty old gaff-rigged cutter carrying a topsail and three jibs, in handsome contrast to the monotonous tall triangles of the modern Bermudan sloops. As we came up to the Pye End buoy a Harwich-registered fishing boat passed us, wallowing on its way to the Stone Banks.

When we picked up the flood into Harwich harbour the seas quietened down, and with a very light breeze we cleared the Stone Pier. We carried on to the Guard buoy, then jibed and bore up towards Parkeston Quay.

"How is the engine this morning," Bertie asked.

"I haven't tried her," I replied.

"Perhaps I'd better start her up, in case this wind dies away, though I expect she is all right."

Hollow words! No amount of swinging did any good—when we had dismantled the carburettor, we again found it full of water.

"I expect you emptied that water can into the fuel tank," Bertie suggested tactlessly. "Nothing much you can do except drain it." The wind, however, freshened slightly, backing easterly, so we shut the engine away and sailed on through the Reserve Fleet.

We ate our lunch as we crossed Copperas Bay. The sun shone fitfully, lighting up Holbrook Bay and the white clock tower of the Royal Hospital School. It was an easy "soldier's" sail and the little girls took it in turns to steer. As we approached Mistley and came into Baltic Wharf the wind died away almost to nothing. We ghosted past Free Rodwell's maltings and past two silent barges, and cleared Brooks' warehouses, where, as happens so often, the wind piped up and *Far West* heeled over and then fairly ripped along to the North Beacon. Coming out of Thorn Reach I took the tiller and Griselda and Bertie dropped the mainsail. We came up to our moorings under fore and mizzen. I had judged my distance badly. We sagged away to leeward, for a moment we were in irons, then the foresail was taken aback and we began to make a stern board into Freddy Woollard's *Silver Cloud*. Doubting we could stem the tide with only our jib and mizzen, shamefacedly I let go the anchor. If I had realised how often in the future I would have to resort to the same proceeding I mightn't have worried so much. We warped her up to the mooring, made everything snug and rowed ashore. The wind had completely died away, and as we beached the dinghy it started to rain again.

Well, our first weekend cruise in *Far West* had not been all it might have been. We had gone aground twice (once backwards). Her, or my, performance to windward was lamentable, she was very under-canvassed and I had spent a lot of time and energy on that unmentionable engine. But at least we had got to Hamford Water and back.

The next day I spent taking out the petrol tank and draining it to the last drop of its fifty-fifty mixture of petrol and water. I can only think now that the water resulted from condensation.

The engine ran better on its proper fuel, but it never gave me any confidence, having the most disconcerting habit of dying off after running for twenty minutes or so.

For our second little cruise Françoise, a pretty, plump little French girl, joined us. We had planned to repeat our journey to Hamford Water, but this time to sail right up to Landermere. On a rather dull Sunday we left Manningtree at high water and before a very light south-west wind we ran down the Stour. As we passed Harwich the wind fell lighter still, which meant that we should not be able to stem the ebb into Hamford Water. We made one long board over to Felixstowe Dock, then decided to turn up the Orwell. As we came out of Long Reach the wind died away to nothing. After some hesitation, and twice stalling, the engine reluctantly carried us over the ebb, in a dead calm, to an anchorage just below Pin Mill. The sky had cleared and it was a warm golden evening. We rowed ashore and paddled up the muddy hard. Two charabancs were unloading a crowd of trippers at the *Butt & Oyster*, so we walked on up the hill to a little inn called the *Riga*, presumably named after some Hanseatic trader. We went into the public bar, empty except for one old man, ordered beer and sat down on a hard settle. We had hardly taken our first gulp when a small, shaggy, very old terrier came into the room; looked round, saw us, sized us up and marched confidently over to me. He stood for a moment with his head on one side, barked, then rushed out of the bar.

"What a funny little dog!" Françoise said, "perhaps you reminded him of someone he doesn't like." I remonstrated with her, but before our argument could grow heated the door was thrown open and the little dog returned, carrying a large stone in his mouth. He dropped it in front of me, gave me a hopeful look and barked. I picked it up and went outside with the dog barking and leaping about with excitement. I chucked the stone as far as I could and, as I thought, probably out of its sight; but the dog, belying its age, went after it like a bullet, apparently straight through a chain link fence, and in a moment returned with the stone and dropped it at my feet. The next time I threw it even further and hurried back into the inn, shutting the door behind me. The woman behind the bar gave a wan smile and said;

"T'ain't no good shutting the door, 'e'll batter it down, that 'e will. Proper determined little dog 'e is. Ain't 'e, Joe?" turning to the old man in the corner.

"Always 'as been, since 'e were a pup."

As he spoke there was a bump at the door followed by a scratching, then a whine, then more scratching, a gruff bark and silence.

"He's given up," Griselda said.

"That 'e 'asn't," from the bar lady, "just you wait." We sat for a moment in silence, broken only by the old man blowing a dottle out of his pipe. Suddenly there was a resounding crack. "Oo, c'est marron! He has tried to burst the door," said Françoise, lapsing from her usually impeccable English. This bombardment continued until I could bear it no longer and capitulated. When both I and the small dog had had enough I returned to the bar to finish my drink. The old man pointed his pipe at me and said:

"If you'd bin 'ere high water, you'd have had to go down to the waterside—and I'll tell you for why—that little old dog, I reckon 'e's 'arf duck, I do. What 'e do like most of all is for you to throw a stone into the river. In 'e go, swims to where the stone drops, then 'e upends 'isself, and arse-up down 'e dives. And 'e don't come up till 'e find the right stone neither. Stay under water a quarter of an hour, that little dog can, and 'e's twelve year old." This was all said with such an air of conviction that we didn't dare dispute it. After more beer all round to toast the dog, we paid our dues and returned to *Far West*.

It was a very still, airless evening. Every boat in the anchorage was reflected in the glass-smooth water. We supped, washed up, then sat for a while on deck, the quiet only emphasised by distant voices. It slowly grew dark, reflections and trees merged into one blackness. It was time for bed, and then we came up against an unexpected obstacle.

Far West had three bunks, one on either side of the cabin and a third known as "the after-berth" which ran like a coffin, open only for a third of its length, under the bridge deck. Françoise was to sleep here. She undressed, put on her pyjamas, climbed into a fleabag and then started to get into the bunk. All went well for a

The *Butt and Oyster Inn*, Pin Mill.   *Photo: Butter Market Studio*

moment, then some gasps, and then "Oh, I think I am stuck!" Her most agreeable Gallic curves were apparently too bulky for *Far West's* spare bed. We tugged and we pushed and we pulled. After considerable efforts she at last came free. We then discovered that two baskets, three fenders and a large kitbag filled with clothes were also occupying the bunk. When these obstacles were removed she had just enough room.

We talked for a while, then one by one we fell asleep. Just before I dropped off, *Far West* rocked gently to the swell of a barge working down the river. An owl screeched twice and then I heard no more.

I woke early. It was a dazzlingly bright morning and I lay for a while on my back, watching the reflections dancing on the white

85

ceiling. I looked around the cabin. It was roomy, almost spacious because of the lack of side decks. She was a nice boat in which to live aboard, even if she was not much of a performer under sail. I could hear an occasional faint plop plop from a gurgle of water under the lands indicating a little catspaw of wind. Otherwise there was no noise at all. I looked at my watch. It was a quarter to seven. I did some laborious mental arithmetic trying to work out when high water would be at Landermere, how long it would take to get there and so at what time we ought to leave Pin Mill, and finally at what time we would have to get up.

After getting three different answers, I reckoned that the sooner we were under way the better, so I roused Griselda and Françoise, who both took their early awakening with surprisingly good grace, perhaps inspired by the sunny morning. The deck was already warm as I hung out the bedding in the rigging while breakfast was being prepared. There were few signs of activity on any of the

Far West's cabin.

other boats, but from an aged hog-backed cutter moored a few yards upwind came a smell of frying kippers. I went below to find the cabin surprisingly tidy and inviting. The combination of white paint, mahogany and shining brass made a pleasant setting for this Sunday-morning meal. Our breakfast of hot coffee, bread, butter and honey was somewhat less aromatic than the one I had smelt on the morning breeze. The one thing lacking in our boat breakfasts at that time was that we had not discovered how to make toast on the primus.

A shaft of sunlight playing on the breakfast table gave to the blue-and-white striped milk jug a more than three-dimensional quality. A wasp came in to explore the honey pot, then buzzed out again. Françoise turned the radio on. A tinkling rhythmic noise of a popular tune was being played on a zither.

"C'est *Le Troisième Homme*. 'Ow I love that man, that 'arry Lime." The wasp returned at that moment and dived into the honey pot. Griselda despatched it and started to gather up the dirty plates, even though we were still eating. Griselda is a do-er. She eats quickly and when finished likes to get on with the next job, which on the boat inevitably means washing up.

"What do you think of all this?" I asked Françoise, just as she was taking an enormous mouthful of bread and honey. Speechless, she waved her piece of bread at me, swallowed and said:

"I think the little boat is lovely, I think sailing is fun, except for that bed. I love to be here with you both—but I would not come in a boat for my honeymoon!"

"Oh, I don't know, there are more uncomfortable places and there is plenty of privacy."

"Too much I think. When I get married, for my honeymoon I shall want a very expensive hotel in Capri. After I have been married a lot of years like you, I shall like to come in a little boat like this." Griselda, who had been silent during this conversation, broke in with what was to be her constant *cri du coeur*.

"It's all right on a morning like this, when the weather is nice—but when the weather is nasty, it's not quite the same, and it is usually like that, no matter how long you've been married."

I did not pursue the matter but went on deck to set the sails.

When we got under way at about eight o'clock there was very little wind, so I set the second jib above the staysail on the upper forestay. We sailed gently through the Pin Mill anchorage, with only a few of the boats bestirring themselves and none getting under way. The reflection of the sun on the water was so bright that it positively hurt. We dropped slowly down the river. Just

Thoma II, mule-rigged yacht barge on the Orwell.   Photo: F. J. Armes

above Shotley a big clipper-bowed barge yacht was at anchor. She was the mule-rigged *Thoma II*, and she looked more like an old tea clipper than a barge. Harwich harbour opened up before us. It was unusually placid and with little activity on this Sunday morning. Once clear of the Stone Pier we turned south-west, and as the wind was now dead in our faces I dropped the extra jib and started up the engine, which fired only after much swinging and changing of her oily plugs. We motor-sailed as far as the Crab Knoll, then switched off to have a little peace. However, even with the flood under us, *Far West's* performance was very slow. I began to fear we would miss our tide to Landermere as we tacked backwards and forwards across Hamford Water, disturbing a family of shelduck which were accompanying us. As we approached the entrance to Landermere creek the wind fell right away, so after further plug cleaning I started up the engine again. The tide had already turned when we came up to Landermere. After some argument we decided to moor alongside the quay. We approached rather gingerly, with Griselda at the tiller and me at the bow with a boathook.

"Neutral," I cried.

"Neutral it is!" she said. Our speed did not slacken and the jetty reared up in front of us.

"Put her in reverse!" I screamed.

"She is in reverse!" she yelled back. With that, *Far West* leaped forward and charged straight into the quay. Trying to fend off, my boathook got caught in the forestay and I nearly fell overboard. The next moment *Far West's* bow—portly though it was—cut its way through the jetty. Massive baulks of timber were crushed like matchsticks before her onrush as, on hands and knees, I despairingly tried to lessen the force of our collision. We came to a sudden stop and the engine stalled. I climbed ruefully ashore and found that my visions of a crumpled bow had not been realised. Two slight scrapes were all we had to show for this assault, for the jetty was crumbling to pieces. It was as rotten as a Chinese egg.

With the help of some startled onlookers and a couple of bow lines we pushed *Far West* off and warped her along the quay and under the overshadowing walls of the *King's Head* to the top of the little cut. There we were provided with safe anchorage and with more water than in the estuary proper. With a couple of lines out from the stern fastened to posts on either bank we were secure, either aground or afloat. She became for a short time as landbound as a houseboat, and so we intended to use her for a day or two, stepping on to the marsh at any stage of the tide. This might seem an improper use for a sailing boat, but at this time we were enjoying living aboard her more than sailing her. And we had been lent an Uffa Fox 12-foot National sailing dinghy. This little boat we kept at Landermere, and it gave us a lot of fun. Perhaps also it taught us there was a bit more to sailing than just blowing along with a fair wind, which was about all poor *Far West* was fit for. She could get along all right on a reach, but before the wind she was under-canvassed, and into the wind she never even considered it. As for her motor! And her propeller, which was of a special reversible sort, but sometimes forgot to reverse! Hence our ramming the quay. *Far West's* engine was an unspeakable contrivance and is now long out of production. It looked nice, it had two shiny copper cylinder cases, it was very light and it must have been designed in about 1890. Its proper place was in the Science Museum. I was told some years later that its lightness was why so many yacht designers specified it. They could poke the wretched thing away anywhere in a sailing yacht without affecting a boat's trim. Whether it worked, or whether it could be got at if it didn't work, wasn't their worry!

Landermere anyway had much to recommend it. Though the tide is up for only about an hour and a half at either side of high water, it was a nice place to lie and we had friends living in three of the coastguard cottages. Arthur Ransome wrote delightfully about this inland sea in his book *Secret Water*. Including the Walton Backwaters, Hamford Water occupies an area of only about twelve square miles, but it has innumerable anchorages, some of them wonderfully secluded. Our favourite anchorage, which we discovered a week or so later, was known to the Manningtree wildfowlers as "The Bustway". Bill Porter had told us, "Going up Hamford, after you have passed the entrance to Oakley Creek you come to a break in the sea wall on your starboard hand—don't take no notice of that, wait till you are almost up on Landermere Creek, bang opposite Skipper's Island, and you will see another break, with some stakes sticking out of the water. That's 'The Bustway'. You go in there, there's a bar across the entrance, but with your draft, you'll be all right, and once inside you will lie safe and sound afloat all the time."

On our next visit to Hamford Water, we had left Manningtree early on a Sunday morning. It was grey and misty and visibility was little more than a hundred yards or so. We rounded the Dovercourt breakwater and almost immediately found ourselves threading our way through a number of lobster pot floats. I had to come about to avoid getting entangled with them. A motor fishing

89

boat loomed up out of the mist and we spoke to the two fishermen who gave us a friendly greeting, then guided us through this maze. The ebb was now against us and we made slow headway from the Pye End to the Crab Knoll buoy, but then our northerly wind freshened a little and *Far West's* plump bows began to push aside a tidy little bow wave. On reaching the most westerly of the buoys that lead into the Walton Channel we altered course up Hamford Water and hardened in our sheets. We had the water to ourselves, except for a flight of little terns that were plunging into the sea all round us, like so many albino swallows. An old heron flew creakingly across our bows. I say old, but herons look old from the moment they come out of the egg; he may well have been a mere boy—or even girl.

Oakley Creek opened up to starboard, Kirby Creek to port and then we were abreast of the broken sea wall opposite Skipper's Island. The wind had eased and we were ghosting along, just breasting the ebb.

"That looks like the opening," Griselda said.

I put the helm over and *Far West* came round and slid through a narrow opening between marsh on the Landermere side and a row of old stakes that were sticking out of the water on our other side. At first sight these weed-covered timbers looked like a group of old men bathing.

"I hope these stakes don't go right across," I said nervously.

"You will soon know if they do," Griselda answered. By the time she had spoken we were safely inside. We drifted up to the top of what amounted to a land-locked lagoon and dropped anchor in about thirteen feet of water. It was half-ebb and, though we did not realise it then, we had found the perfect anchorage. It could only have been about a couple of cables long and at high water barely a cable wide, at its widest point, but it was protected from wind and weather and there was no fear of dragging our anchor or grounding on the banks.

More of "The Bustway" later, for over the next seven years we returned there often. With fair winds and tides it used to take us almost four and a half hours to sail from our moorings at Manningtree to this little lagoon, and once there it was so isolated we might have been in the Outer Hebrides. We have lain there in fair weather and foul and only twice in those seven years did any other yacht attempt to invade our privacy—and on both occasions they went aground trying to get over the bar at the entrance.

Our cruising range over the next two years was limited to the Stour and the Orwell, to Harwich harbour, the Walton Backwaters and Hamford Water and to Butley Creek and the Aldeburgh river. It was mostly weekend sailing. Our summer holidays were usually working holidays spent rubbernecking in art galleries and libraries in France, Italy or the Netherlands. Yet such modest cruising as we did was fun and I feel that when I get too old and feeble to cruise abroad I shall return to such simple pleasures as just dropping down the river for the night. Maybe I shall do a little fishing. More likely, just potter about on the boat and watch the seabirds and the waders. Not the least of our pleasures was sailing past Parkeston Quay. I remember one day late in September that year. It was a dull, damp, grey morning with a light north-easterly wind. We slipped down Hamford Water on the last of the ebb. As we reached up towards the Dovercourt breakwater the Pye Sand was largely uncovered, for the flood tide had not yet started to run. We could see how narrow was the entrance to Hamford Water and the Backwaters and also what a menace the Pye Sand could be to anyone in this channel if the wind was west of north, but this would be nothing to its perils for a sailing boat coming down the Medusa Channel in an easterly blow. I only once grounded on the Pye and that was in someone else's boat; it was like hitting concrete. Fortunately there was no sea running that day and the original *Peter Duck*, once owned by Arthur Ransome, plucked us off. On this September morning there was a bit of a cross swell, but the seas quietened as we picked up the flood into Harwich harbour. There was a solitary angler on the end of the breakwater and a small boy shouted something—probably abuse—at us. The Zeeland shipping line's day boat to the Hook of Holland, the *Prinses Beatrix*, passed us outward bound as we came abreast of the old Great Eastern Hotel. Griselda kept *Far West* over to the south side of the river so that we could sail right alongside the steamers and packet boats. The two British Railways steamers, the *Arnhem* against the quay and the *Duke of York* in midstream, were resting quietly, awaiting the time for their nightly journey to the Hook. There were the elegant modern Danish *Kronprins Frederik* and the troopship *Empire Parkeston* and a couple of grubby, rusty little tramp steamers that had a neglected look as if they had arrived there long ago and their crews had gone ashore and no-one had ever been back to them. There was always a rather melancholy air about Parkeston.

The wind was on our beam but light, and even though we had both topsails up we were moving rather sluggishly. I tried setting the large blue staysail from the mizzen masthead and making the tack fast to a ringbolt to windward of the mainmast. I sheeted it in, and the effect was remarkable. *Far West* heaved herself forward like a fat housewife running for a bus.

"Got any more bits of washing to hang out?" Griselda asked.

"Well, we're not doing badly," I answered, "we've got two headsails, two topsails, main, mizzen and mizzen staysail—seven sails all told."

"I should have thought it would have been simpler to have just one, like the Arabs do," Griselda said, "though I suppose all these sails with their relevant little bits of stick and string give you something to do." She paused for a moment, looking up at *Far West's* collection of sails. "She's a pretty little thing, but isn't she a bit of a toy? You can't call this rig efficient—and as for that engine . . . " She stopped, stretched, got up and said "Here, you take her. I suppose you like her as she is. I'm going to get some lunch for us."

The oracle had spoken! *Far West* was a pretty thing, but really a pretty little toy. Her rig was far too inefficient, with all that stick and string, for the amount of windward work we had to do—and I still didn't like those windows—or the lack of side decks—and she was deadly slow, yet too light and buoyant to be comfortable in a seaway . . . and so on. By the time we had reached Manningtree I had decided either to sell her or alter her rig and change that unspeakable engine for something better.

The following winter we put her up for sale but had only one nibble, so I arranged with Fox's shipyard in Ipswich to install a new engine. My horizon—and possibly my finances—was still limited to petrol engines, but this time I decided on a two-cylinder Stuart-Turner. This engine was still, like the unmentionable one, a two-stroke, but there seemed to be so many of them in use that I felt I was on safer ground—as indeed I was.

On a misty morning in the second week of March, with Bill Porter as crew, we left our moorings and with a light westerly wind ran towards Harwich. The tide was at half-ebb, so we had to keep well into the channel. Under Mistley Quay Brooks' maltings blanketed our wind and Bill had to use one of the dinghy oars as a sweep to prevent us fouling a barge that was unloading grain. Once clear of Mistley we picked up our wind, and with it now dead aft we ran goosewinged—and it struck mighty cold on the small of one's back. At Stutton Ness we jibed the mizzen and turned across the river for Wrabness. A distant clock was striking eight o'clock and I began to feel hungry. Inshore of us we could see fishermen from Manningtree who were seine netting. Suddenly there was a great honking noise and a skein of Brent geese flew over us heading north-west. The tideline and the river were alive with birds. There were redshank and flocks of dunlin poking about on the mudflats. A heron was standing motionless in the shallows. Shelduck in pairs were flying fast and low over the water, and just as we came up on the Wrabness shore a flock of birds that I didn't recognise flew across our bows. They were a little larger than redshanks and had a white bar on the trailing edge of their wings. I might have guessed that they were bar-tailed godwits, but I had never seen them before. As far as Bill was concerned, birds were either ducks or ox-birds—a term that covered all the little waders, and as all the knots, little stints, ringed plovers and dunlins each have about four changes of plumage each year maybe it was not such a bad name.

As we neared Parkeston Quay the wind strengthened and veered a little to the north. I handed the tiller over to Bill and climbed down into the cabin to get a hot drink.

"Cup of coffee, Bill?" I said as I handed up a mug.

"Very welcome," he answered. Then, pointing with a very square finger to the north shore, "see those old timbers—used to be a proper farm landing place. I remember a year or so before the last war, I was on leave from my ship. It was a nice day, and Dad brought me and Mum down here in his old boat. We were going to anchor off Erwarton (he pronounced it "Harrington") for our tea, when Mum discovered we hadn't any milk. Poor old dear, she couldn't drink her tea without milk. Well, there was one of Paul's barges moored up to that landing place. As soon as she saw it, she said, 'we'll go and ask them if they can spare us a drop.' So we came right alongside the barge. The skipper was on deck. *Sold* us a tin of milk, he did. Not the giving away kind he wasn't. That's the last time I ever saw a barge there." His reminiscences were cut short by a naval motor launch cutting across our bows and leaving us rolling our side decks under. Bill muttered an oath, shook his empty mug at the ML which was now almost out of sight; "ought to be put on a charge, behaving like that."

We rounded the Shotley Spit buoy into the Orwell river and now had the last of the ebb against us. We made a little headway on each tack, dodging between the moored Shambles and South Goodwin lightvessels, for Harwich is the main Trinity House depot. After we had cleared Lower Reach we had the first of the flood tide with us, but we felt little benefit from it, for we had a dead "nose-ender" all the way up the river to Cliff Quay. There had been a bit of a lop in the lower reaches, and once or twice we took a little spray on board. However, with the wind in our faces and a bit of work to do making constant short tacks we kept pleasantly warm. A tug, a coaster and two nondescript motor craft passed us, outward bound. Pin Mill and Woolverstone looked quite deserted. Opposite the power station we had to make way for two outgoing colliers, both empty of cargo and towering high out of the water. Leaving Ostrich Creek to port, we finally ran aground just off Fox's yard.

During the trip I had pondered once again on the futility of this rig in so small a boat. Any lingering hopes that I had had about its romantic appearance were banished by Griselda, who had watched us come sailing up the river. She had said as we came ashore: "That boat looks quite absurd with those silly little sails above all that boat!"

That evening I telephoned a naval architect, J. Francis Jones, to ask him if he could advise me about a change of rig. We arranged to meet at Fox's yard the following Saturday.

7

The metamorphosis

The following Saturday I met Jack Francis Jones at Fox's yard. He went over *Far West* very carefully, then said: "She's got some rot in her cabin trunk sides."

"What's that mean?" I asked.

"Oh, taking off the cabin trunk and fitting new sides. The top is OK, but this is going to cost you a bit of money, particularly if you want to change the rig and fit a new engine. You might be better advised to try to sell her as she is and build a new boat."

"We've tried to sell her without much success, and I am quite fond of her."

"In that case, I will sketch out a new sail plan." At this point Henry Fox broke in:

"As the cabin trunk has to come off, why don't you shorten it by a couple of feet, so that it comes aft of the new mast position, and give yourself some side decks; I don't like these built-up topsides."

"Nor do I," I replied, "let's do that."

"All right," said Jack, "I will draw you out a new cabin. She'll look quite different. Rather nice, I think."

So *Far West's* fate was sealed. Before parting we argued a bit about the rig. Henry Fox wanted to make her into a Bermudan sloop. I favoured a high-peaked Dutchman's gaff rig and Jack Jones a gunter. We had a gunter! Two months later a virtually new boat was launched. She looked altogether a different craft. Her pretty hull could now be seen to full advantage. Griselda came over to Ipswich to see the transformation.

"That's more like it," she said, "I am glad you are getting that square-rig mentality out of your system. She's a different boat altogether. Let's re-christen her."

"It's meant to be unlucky, changing a boat's name."

"Rubbish! anyhow, she hasn't been particularly lucky so far; perhaps it will change her luck."

"Maybe you are right, what shall we call her?" We looked at her gleaming black hull and pondered for a while.

"Blackbird," suggested Henry Fox.

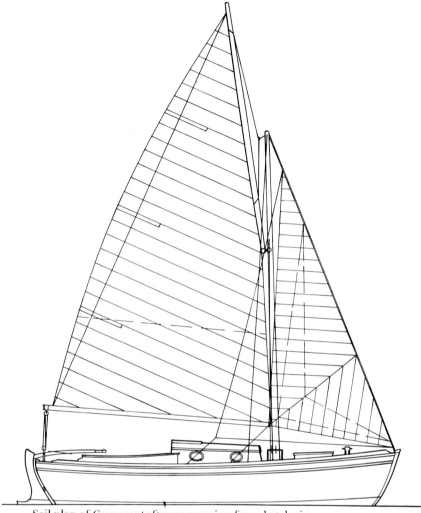

Sail plan of *Cormorant* after conversion from ketch rig.

"Why not Cormorant?" Griselda asked, "they are black enough, and there are plenty of them on the Stour. They might welcome another." So *Cormorant* she became.

I sailed *Cormorant* back to Manningtree next day, and could hardly believe it was the same boat. She thrust herself through the water in a far more purposeful way, and when the wind dropped away just below Mistley and we were bucking the first of the ebb, the Stuart, with its three-bladed propeller working through the stern post, fairly pushed her over the tide.

We had now got an almost ideal estuary cruiser or ditch-crawler. Her draft was only two foot, she would sleep three in tolerable comfort and she was very easy to handle single-handed. She was light and buoyant. For sheltered water sailing or for drying out on the mud, she could hardly be bettered. And now she was fun to sail. And that summer we found in an old friend, Anna Hadfield, an ideal sailing companion. She had before she was married been a McMullen, distantly connected to *Down Channel* McMullen. Brought up at West Mersea, she had spent her childhood crewing

Cormorant moored at Manningtree.

in her father's boat. Her pleasure at being aboard a small yacht and being once again able to explore the Essex and Suffolk estuaries was most infectious—and immediately communicated itself to us. Our weekend sails in the Stour and Orwell rivers, to Hamford Water or to the Aldeburgh river became that much more enjoyable. To add to our pleasures, we had bought from an affable chemist at Frinton a ten-foot sailing dinghy, fitted with a lugsail. She was a stable little boat and was easy to sail. Moored as we were so often in the Bustway or Kirby Creek, she gave us scope for exploring the tiny little creeks off Hamford Water. Sometimes we would leave *Cormorant* anchored in the Bustway for a day or so while we returned to Manningtree by road. On one occasion the three of us had to go back to some party or other. We were so loath to leave the boat that after returning to Manningtree from our party in the small hours we had changed into our boating gear and at 3.30 am had left Manningtree in a thick fog. It was just about first light when we got down to Landermere. The fog was still very dense and the dinghy was dripping with dew. I wiped it dry, loaded it up and we climbed aboard. There was absolute silence and we found ourselves speaking in whispers.

The tide was high and just on the turn. I rowed out from the shore at an angle of about 45°. The dinghy suddenly grounded— we had entered the channel proper. I back-paddled and let the first of the ebb carry me along. A withy loomed up; then, gently paddling in a straight line, we went from withy to withy until we reached a curious bent stick that I knew marked a southerly sweep in the channel. Here I crossed over to the opposite bank and, sounding my way along the cant edge, had no difficulty in finding the Bustway. It had turned cold, so we made a pot of tea, then turned into our berths and slept until mid-morning. People often asked us what on earth we found to do, anchored out there in those marshes. The answer was plenty. There is always something that needs doing on a boat. Lines to whip, ropes to splice, repairs, painting, brass to polish, decks to wash down and so on, quite apart from the other domestic chores. And if we got bored with the view we went exploring in the dinghy or else up-anchored and went somewhere else in *Cormorant*.

The beauty of the Bustway anchorage was that we were completely private, yet we could sail up to Landermere to see our friends the Huttons, the Leweses or the Spences. Basil Spence, a Scotsman who was soon to be famous as the architect of Coventry Cathedral, had bought himself a 16-foot Shetland double-ended boat that looked like a Viking ship. She was a beautiful little thing, though with low freeboard amidships she was not over-seaworthy. On one occasion he turned her over and nearly drowned himself. On another he came storming into the Bustway and, sailing round *Cormorant*, he got caught in a sudden squall and rammed us with his brass-capped pointed bow. One of our topside planks was split. The patch we put over the crack was always known as "Basil's dunt".

As we sailed back up the Stour under a light westerly wind Griselda was asleep in her bunk. Anna had said something about

Basil Spence with the Hutton twins and his little Shetland boat at
Landermere.

taking a movie of *Cormorant* under way, so I handed her my little
Bell and Howell camera and put her off in the dinghy. I tacked
Cormorant back and forth until Anna had exhausted the film, then
came alongside and picked her up. At that moment the wind piped
up. Anna was safely aboard, but the boom swung over and caught
the dinghy's shroud, for I had been towing it with the mast
stepped. Before I could do anything we had towed the dinghy
under and the mast was snapping like a stick of rhubarb. Within a
moment the dinghy was upside down. I tried to right it, succeeded,
but with the loss of an oar. It was impossible to empty the dinghy,
for it was awash to the gunwale. The only thing to do was to run
Cormorant aground, for the tide was flooding. Then, in our
underclothes, we waded ashore with the dinghy and emptied it out.
Only then did we discover that when it had capsized its anchor had
fallen out and we had dragged it halfway across the river, collecting
about a hundredweight of weed. Our final loss was the broken
mast, one oar, one bailer and two floorboards missing. Somewhat
chastened, we paddled back to *Cormorant*, made the dinghy fast and
sailed home to Manningtree.

It was rather a dirty, wet, windy summer, but we had our quota of
weekends on the boat. It was not until laying-up time that the
weather really improved. One afternoon in mid-October we put

Cormorant into her winter quarters. We saw an oyster catcher on the way up to the mud berth, and the water was as smooth as a looking-glass. That week would have been a perfect time for Hamford Water, with little wind and hour after hour of warm sunshine. The glass was set very fair, and remained so still that I thought it had bust. There was mist morning and evening. A coal stove would be a "must" for such late cruising, otherwise it could not have been faulted. So ended, as Bill said, the worst season for weather in living memory.

Cormorant in winter quarters.

LAYING UP

Cormorant was laid up in a mud berth by the railway bridge in a little creek that cut into the marsh between the north and south channels of the Stour. She only floated at spring tides and was reasonably protected by her remoteness from any kind of vandalism, though on one occasion she was broken into; nothing much of value was taken. She lay moored fore and aft by lines made fast to stakes driven into the marsh and was covered by two large tarpaulins, supported by a ridge pole.

Towards the end of March Bill and I punted up to *Cormorant's* winter quarters on a day when half a gale was blowing from the north-east, the river was covered with white horses and the sky was a hard metallic blue. We nearly swamped the punt before we reached *Cormorant*. We stripped the tarpaulins off the boat, took in the warps and then, with some pushing and heaving, brought her to the mouth of the creek. We anchored there, and while Bill folded the tarpaulins I refuelled the engine and bolted on the magneto. A little bit of fiddling about with the timing, then a couple of swings and she was off. We butted our way down the river, but I had to throttle right back or we would have swamped the duckpunt. These punts, which are such a delight to row, are brutes to tow, they snake from side to side and are in danger of broaching-to all the time.

We had decided to move our moorings from the Church mud to just off the old Fisherman's Dock, for the simple reason that I thought it would be nice to see *Cormorant* from our house. The mooring was made up of a length of heavy chain fastened to a ring on a swivel, set in a heavy lump of concrete, which was buried in the mud.

At low tide Bill had dug a hole in the mud for the new mooring and had marked its position with two stakes. We anchored on the Church mud a dozen yards or so from our old mooring and waited for the tide to drop. At last *Cormorant* was high and dry and sitting upright.

"Probably sitting on her anchor," I remarked.

"Oh, don't say that!" Bill replied, looking anxious. But sure enough, she was. It was surprisingly difficult to clear, but clear it we had to because the fluke was resting against the garboards, and we did not want to risk her bumping on it when she floated. We pulled and slipped and heaved. The anchor was caught by one fluke right under the keel and hitched out on the starboard side, the stock being on the port side. After various futile efforts to tug the anchor clear, Bill stumped off to the shore for a spade. While he did this I cleared the chain, which had also got caught under the keel, and I thought about the horrors of mud. How little we appreciate the firm ground, the garden path, the tarmac road, lovely slabs of concrete. Every time I heaved on that blessed chain my feet sank deeper into the ground, and then became firmly embedded. The frustrated misery of trying to lift gumbooted feet from the mud, when all that happens is the parting company of foot and boot, and sometimes sock as well. I had one consolation. I had remembered from a previous disastrous experience in the mud (that time it was digging for lugworms) to discard my oilskin coat, for a long wet oilskin collects the mud off one's boots and spreads it all over one.

Bill returned and we dug and heaved and cursed until we finally got it out. Then we had to dig out the mooring. When we had cleared the mud off it we levered a spike underneath it to ease any suction there might be, and then rove the anchor chain through the swivel. After that we sat and waited for the tide. As we floated we shortened the chain up to it until it hung vertically under the bow and then, as the tide rose, so the boat lifted the lump of concrete. Very slowly under engine power we moved towards the new place. Inch by inch we edged up to it; fortunately both wind and tide were now flowing the same way. The first time we missed it, so we rounded to and came up again, and this time dropped our concrete right in the middle of the hole.

The next day, a cold day with the wind blowing from due north, we towed *Cormorant* up on to the beach and chocked her up ready for fitting out. When the tide had dropped I noticed there was hardly any paint on her bottom. I pointed this out to Bill, and he said:

"It's always the same with paint, what you want is tar and turps—that'll sink right into the wood."

"What about anti-fouling? They say it won't take on tar."

"They'd *say* anything, it's only natural, that there Captain What's-is-name has got to sell as much paint as possible, you can't blame him."

So we decided that *Cormorant* should have her bottom tarred.

The next day Dod, Albert and I stepped *Cormorant's* mast. Bill was absent, nursing Mrs Porter, who, poor soul, was ill with dropsy.

"They drained off eight pints," Albert explained, "another half-hour and it would have covered her heart." I had visions of a fast rising tide. The sheerlegs were too short for the length of the mast, so we had to suspend the mast below its point of balance in order to give us sufficient lift, which didn't make it easier. However, after about a couple of hours messing about and pulling and pushing, and the expenditure of much emotion, it was safely stepped and the stays and shrouds made fast. It was then that Albert said:

"It would have been better if we had just taken one of the poles, fixed a tackle at its head and stepped it on a sandbag on the deck to give us extra height and stayed it with four guys fore and aft and athwartships. With that we would have had plenty of height and clearance." Just like an Irishman with a good idea after a bad one had been found wanting.

For the next ten days, in bright clear weather and cold easterly winds, Griselda and I rubbed down and varnished the cabin trunk, the coamings and all the rest. Then we painted the deck, the cockpit and the topsides. We had the satisfaction of making a good job of it; and conditions, in spite of chill winds, were almost ideal. Finally we tarred her bottom, bent on the sails and put her off to her new mooring.

This fitting-out and actually working on the boat oneself is not only the best way to get to know what condition she is in, but also greatly increases one's affection for her. And for two seasons we had hardly a barnacle on our tarred bottom; on the third we had a fearful crop—but so did the boats with anti-fouling.

With a boat eminently suited for the job, we spent the next two summers exploring our limited cruising ground. For anchorages in the Stour we had Stutton Ness (the west side) or Wrabness, depending which way the wind was blowing, or if we wanted complete protection, there was Holbrook Creek. The first time we went in there was on a bright blustery day in August, 1957. The boats anchored off Wrabness were all rolling about a bit, so about an hour and a half before high water we sailed down to below Wrabness, then we turned due north. It was not until we were well across the bay that we picked up first a can buoy and then a series of withies marking the port side of the channel that led to Holbrook Creek. With Griselda at the tiller and me with the leadline in one hand and binoculars in the other, we found our way into this tortuous creek. We anchored rather to the west of the channel, intending to dry out for the night on the soft mud up by the saltings. To go ashore, one should anchor further into the creek, which opens up into a small bight. It is an ideal anchorage for the craft that can dry out. Over the sea wall I could see the clock tower of the Royal Hospital School. As I was furling the sails a young man came rowing down the creek. On giving him "Good evening," he sculled across to see if we were all right. He said his name was Page and that he lived in the *cottage ornée* at the entrance to the Headmaster's house. He was a pleasant-spoken chap—a gardener by profession. He offered us the use of a mooring next time we came up there. I asked him if he fished.

"Nothing much, just go spearing for dabs; Bob Quantrill, he was the last man to fish here."

"Any relation to the redoubtable Jimmy Quantrill of Waldringfield?" I asked.

103

"Yes, his brother. Both of them characters—but I reckon these rivers, they breed characters, what with the Porters and the Lucases and the Woollards at Manningtree, the Quantrills at Waldringfield and all those Mussetts down at Mersea. Well, I must be getting back. Don't forget to give me a call if you want any help." He gave me a smile and paddled off to the crumbling old jetty.

We sat on deck, drinking whisky-and-ginger-ale and looking over the water, revelling in the evening. On the Harkstead side of the creek fields of ripe corn were glowing in the evening light. As night came on the wind dropped and there was no noise, except from across the fields the school clock striking the quarters.

In this estuary cruising one regulates one's time by the tides. They are all-important. Hence so many early starts. The dinghy wakened us next morning with a resounding bang on the quarter. It was ten past five and a bright, sunny morning. *Cormorant* was still aground, so I made coffee while waiting for her to swing to her anchor. Under the lightest of winds, we were away by six o'clock. As we sailed out into the river the wind strengthened. It was still due east. By the time we were opposite the farm landing at Erwarton Ness the tide was on the turn and we were tacking into quite a lop.

At Parkeston Quay the usual packet boats had been joined by a curious old-fashioned Mississippi-like steamer called *Mecklenburg*, tall and thin in the funnel. As we rounded the Guard buoy the seas became confused. A barge anchored off the Felixstowe shore got under way, with all plain sail set, for she was no auxiliary, but with her bowsprit still steeved up. The tumbling seas were a warm muddy colour. As we passed the Dovercourt stone breakwater I looked back towards Harwich. In the clear cool light its two old lighthouses and the group of Regency houses looked like one of William Daniel's aquatints in his *Voyage Round Britain*. We met a long swell (at least long for this place) coming in from the North Sea. We were now on a reach, but were rolling and wallowing our way southwards. Off the Pye End it was quite rough, but there was no vice in it for there was enough length to the seas. As we came up on No 3 port hand buoy the sailing barge appeared to be practically hull down on the horizon—I suppose because of the swell. We were now meeting the full weight of the ebb out of the backwaters, but with the wind now on our quarter we were making quite good time. As we turned westwards up Hamford Water we could only just see our barge, well on its way round the Gunfleet bound up Swin for London River. A blue motor cruiser came limping out of the Walton Channel with an odd dot-and-carry-one motion and a

Griselda and *Cormorant* in the Bustway.

marked list to port. Just beyond the entrance to Kirby Creek we put up a heron and a flight of ox-birds, otherwise the water was deserted.

Coming up Hamford Water the wind freshened and backed into the south, so I dropped the jib; and then as we came up to the entrance of the Bustway I dropped the throat halliard and peaked up the topping lift, thus reducing the sail area by almost half. The anchor was hanging from the stem head and as we approached our anchorage I eased it away and trailed it along the bottom (drudging, I believe the bargemen used to call this braking procedure). This effectively slows one up, then by paying off a little more cable you can let it bite. As we had turned into the Bustway, we sailed through a family of shelduck who all submerged in perfect unison. A tern and three cormorants were sitting on the giant timbers at the entrance, a redshank flew over us, and as we swung to anchor a heron heaved itself into the air and flew slowly away towards the explosives factory on Oakley Creek.

We lunched, and then sat for a while in the cockpit watching black-headed gulls scavenging our lunch leavings. It was sunny but windy. Great cloud banks were building up to the north. The wind was now south-easterly. The towering cumuli advanced towards us, then retreated without obscuring the sun. There was a bite in the wind, so we retired to the cabin. The sun-dappled water, muddy banks and windswept grass made a pretty picture seen through one of the cabin ports.

In the afternoon we lay on our bunks and listened to the BBC Symphony Orchestra playing Rimsky-Korsakov's interpretation of *The Arabian Nights*—his *Scheherazade*—music appropriate for listening aboard a yacht, with its tale of Sindbad the Sailor, its shipwreck and its lush extravagance. A musical counterpart to sweet rum punch.

As we sat down to a pre-dinner rum-and-orange three oyster catchers flew over us, piping frantic annoyance and excitement.

"The eternal triangle, I should think," Griselda said, standing up and looking out of the hatchway. I joined her and we stood for a moment just looking at the view. Blackheaded gulls hovered over the tide line uttering their raucous one-note cries, so much less evocative than that of the herring gull; yet they are graceful fliers, often hovering like a tern. Across the marshes a curlew called.

"I love that sound," I said.

"It always makes me feel a little sad," Griselda replied.

"Not as sad as a loon!"

"My heavens, no! That's a heartbreaking cry."

It brought back memories of a pair of great northern divers we had seen courting on a lonely lake in Northern Ontario. The sun had dropped behind a cloud bank. Suddenly it was cold and Hamford Water also seemed a lonely place. Griselda shivered and said:

"Let's get below. Light the lamps, let's get a good fug up."

"All right! We'll have another drink as well." I shut the hatch, lit the lamps and poured out our drinks. The cabin was a comfortable retreat in contrast to that austere landscape of creeks and marsh.

The east wind persisted for the next few days. It was typical Bustway weather, hard blue skies and a constant plop-plop-plop under the lands—with the noise much more noticeable in the cabin. We messed about on the boat. I polished brass—a soothing and a satisfying thing to do—and Griselda embroidered a chair seat. We read, we listened to the radio and we watched the birds. One evening in a quarter of an hour I saw four redshank and numerous blackheaded gulls, a curlew flying over Skipper's Island, a family of shelduck being told off by their mother for paddling too far away from her, a tern fishing and a pair of kestrels quartering the marsh towards Beaumont. In the distance two herons were lumbering across Horsey Island, and all the time the air was shrill with the cries of oyster catchers as they hurtled over the sea walls, chasing I know not what.

Later that same evening as I sat in *Cormorant's* little cabin I was struck by the magnificence of her sideboard and food cupboard, with its balustered railing along the top and its main glory the three panelled doors, built so lovingly by Bill Porter. The single door concealed the drink cupboard and at the bottom a Beatrix stove; the double doors, the dry goods or canned stuff at the bottom, the crocks above. On the top was a sideboard to carry the radio and various oddments, including Griselda's sewing. The doors, or their solidity, would have done credit to a Victorian bank. This massive piece of furniture was opposite the galley, which had originally been the quarter berth. A double-burner Swedish primus, surrounded by a fiddle rail, was bolted down on chocks on to zinc sheeting. The fine mahogany of the sideboard was rather let down by this utilitarian zinc. The galley looked a bit like a fish fryer, for this zinc sheet not only covered the galley platform but also the back to the shape of the boat. Its rather drab appearance was relieved by the sink, which was a gleaming stainless steel bowl from a surgical suppliers, intended for an operating theatre and costing 29/- instead of about £12 for a proper stainless steel sink, and without the waste pipes which can get choked up or, if the valves stick, perhaps sink your boat. That would indeed be a sink appropriately named. The zinc sheeting, incidentally, proved a failure, for it oxidised rapidly.

When we were anchored in the Bustway we would go for a sail in *Corny*, the little sailing dinghy, at least once or twice a day. In a hard blow, we would reef her little lugsail and go careering down Hamford Water on a miniature rough sea. She was a stable little boat and gave us endless pleasure, and she was a workhorse as well for any victualling or watering that had to be done. We sponged shamelessly on our friends at Landermere; the Spences and the Leweses were still there, and though the Huttons had gone Eduardo Paolozzi and his family had taken their place. The Bustway became *Cormorant's* second home, but sometimes for a change we anchored in Kirby Creek, or the need for more solid victuals than we could get at Landermere would make us sail up to Walton, or anchor in the Twizzle, off the Walton Channel.

During that week for just this reason we sailed round to the Twizzle. The Walton Channel and the Twizzle, compared to Hamford Water, were thick with yachts, including a very old clipper-bowed steam launch. She was in fine condition, her varnished teak, Indian red and sage green paintwork and polished brass looked an absolute picture. Most of the yachts in the Twizzle were fairly antique, including one very pretty smack yacht. There was a hard, quite a good landing place, on the east side of the Walton Channel just above the entrance to the Twizzle. From there it was a walk of about a mile along the sea wall into Walton. The little town was full of holidaymakers. We did our shopping, bought whisky, rum, bread and steaks and various other things, then walked back to the landing place. We returned to *Cormorant* and had our lunch. We could hear the sound of a radio from a nearby yacht and voices all around us. Then a rival radio broke in from another boat.

"Enough is enough," Griselda said, "let's go back to the Bustway!"

"All right, but shall we try crossing the Wade? That will take us into Kirby Creek."

"Anything is better than that din!" We washed up, checked the tide times and realised that it would be evening before there would be enough water for us to cross the mudflats behind Horsey Island. However, to get a little further away from the radios we motored up to the head of the Twizzle and anchored. We climbed into *Corny* and went off to reconnoitre.

The Wade is a road crossing from Horsey Island to the mainland on which at low water we had seen first a motor-cyclist and then three children on ponies. We brought the dinghy up to the road and scrambled out and spied out the channel that wandered across the mudflats to join the creek from Kirby. We estimated how high the water would have to be on a certain withy before we could get across.

"Better shift that rock," Griselda said, indicating a boulder on the edge of the road. "Might start a plank if we bashed into that. Come on, I will give you a hand." We went over to it and together gave a heave. It rolled over to one side to reveal a swarm of small crabs. Crabs have always had a fearful fascination for me—curious insensate creatures—but in this scurrying mass they were a loathsome sight, like turning up a stone in the garden and finding a myriad of woodlice or centipedes beneath it. In our horror we dropped the boulder back, then, remembering the purpose of our moving it, we heaved again and rolled it off the road, leaving the crabs once again exposed. They all scurried away except for one that was crushed, I suppose by the stone falling back upon it. Two little ones kept rushing up to it and away again, in distraction and despair, it would seem. Though I disliked the creatures, I would not willingly have inflicted hurt on the big one or bereavement on the little ones. We felt quite upset.

As we rowed back to *Cormorant* we heard the sound of church bells from across the marshes. It must have been the bell ringers of Kirby le Soken, over a mile away, practising a change. It was a very still afternoon and the sound came over clearly. There was a grey haze so that the marshes, the mudbanks, the water and the sky became a symphony of greys. There was a warm grey for the sky, a greeny grey for the water and a raw umber grey for the mudbanks and the marshes.

The tide at length flooded sufficiently for us to attempt a crossing of this shallow backwater. We started off cautiously with Griselda up in the chains swinging the lead. Though at times we had precious little water under us, we ghosted over the Wade, through Horsey Mere and finally anchored in Kirby Creek, near a race buoy. This is a good and well-protected anchorage, as we were to discover twenty-four hours later.

The next day the wind was westerly and, in Hilaire Belloc's phrase, the "waves garrulous". After breakfast we set off in *Corny* to explore some more of Hamford Water, sailing round Skipper's Island and from Cardinal's Hard taking a southerly route to Landermere, and very nearly sticking on the mud, for the tide had turned and there was little water over the mudflats even at the top of the tide. We stopped at Landermere and Freda Paolozzi gave us not only drinking water but cups of coffee.

As we walked past the *King's Head* a very pretty young Siamese cat came dancing out on its hind legs, clapping its paws above its head; it was chasing a butterfly. The day was warm and still. We drifted back to Kirby Creek, boarded *Cormorant* and changed into bathing things. The water was as warm as the Mediterranean. After our bathe we lunched, sunbathed and slept. The perfect day continued with shimmering heat over the water. As I climbed into bed I saw that the barometer had dropped from 30.03 to 29.80. During the night the wind began to blow and the dinghy kept ranging about and banging into us, until I tied a bucket to its stern—and then, apparently in a huff, she kept a respectful distance. The 7.55 weather forecast was full of gloom, with a deep depression coming in from the Atlantic and gale-force winds. Great gusts of rain blew across the creek, and the trees and the hills of Kirby le Soken were completely obscured. Griselda's head emerged from her fleabag. She sat up and peered sleepily out of one of the portholes.

"Good grief," she muttered, "what a prospect! You certainly get plenty of variety in this game. Let's have some coffee."

The glass continued to drop but we were snug enough in our little cabin. We lay on our bunks reading. I thought then, what a difference a bookcase makes to a yacht's cabin. *Cormorant's* bookcase was only a single mahogany shelf at the foot of my bunk. The books changed on each trip, but there were one or two constant friends. Roger Peterson's splendid *A Field Guide to the Birds of Britain and Europe* which really does make it possible to identify the seabirds and waders that occupy the marshes and the tidelines; George Arnott's three books on the Suffolk estuaries, Hervey Benham's *Last Stronghold of Sail*, Frank Carr's *Sailing Barges*, Cowper's *Sailing Tours*, a book on knots and splices, and lastly *The Pilot's Guide to the Thames Estuary*. These were all reference books. In addition there was usually something of RLS on board—on this occasion *Ebb Tide*, that stirring little drama of the South Seas. The shelf was made up with Colette's *Chéri*, Hilaire Belloc's *The Path to Rome* and Josef Conrad's *Nostromo*. The sight of such books added civilisation to our surroundings. They had a humanising, reassuring quality. After lunch the rain had cleared and though it was still blowing hard we took the dinghy up to Landermere, then on a further voyage of exploration up Oakley Creek to Bramble Island. Where the creek divides, we took the westerly branch past the old powder works.

The place had a forlorn and desolate air, and the muddy banks were scattered with old oil drums. The only sound was of a loose piece of corrugated iron flapping in the breeze. On our return to Kirby Creek we had a lengthy beat to windward. The reefed-down little lugsail was not a very weatherly rig, but in spite of the very rough going it got us there eventually. The evening shipping forecast gave gale warnings for Dover, Thames, Humber—Force 7 for Thames. The depression was forecast to be centred on King's Lynn by nightfall. We were in for a wet and windy twenty-four hours, and we had it all right. I was awakened at 1 am by a terrific storm, and rain was driving in through the hatchway. I leaped up and nearly decapitated myself trying to shut the forehatch. The rain was beating an ear-shattering tattoo on the cabin roof, but after about an hour it abated to a noise like the falling of pine needles. There were occasional violent gusts of wind and the rumbling of distant thunder. It was still blowing very hard in the morning, so we had a general clean up, scrubbing the cabin floor and reversing some worn rubber treads on the companionway steps. The sun shone intermittently, but as the tide rose so did the wind. Some intrepid character appeared from behind Skipper's

Island in a little white dinghy. She was well reefed down and went tearing up Kirby Creek and was passed by a fibreglass launch from the opposite direction. This craft had a party of four aboard. When it was about a hundred yards from us it nearly got swamped and soon returned home. The only other boat moored in this storm-bound anchorage was a handsome reverse sheer four-tonner, occupied apparently by one young man, perhaps of misogynist tendencies. She was anchored in the fairway of the channel and was sailing round and round her anchor. She must have drawn more than we did, for we were windrode the whole time. By midday it was a full gale and I thought we were dragging—so in pouring rain we dropped the kedge anchor well to windward. A couple of hours later that began to drag, so we laid it out even further across the creek. This time it held. The glass was still falling. There were intermittent bright intervals, but the wind blew with unabated violence. After some hours the drumming of the wind became a real bore.

The gale continued for another twenty-four hours before it showed any signs of easing off. The glass had stopped falling, then, rather tentatively, it moved up a point. The BBC forecast another depression hard on the heels of this one, but for some reason our spirits were lightening. Our misogynist friend was still there. Late in the afternoon of the third day there was a sudden lull. It was near low water. Griselda said:

"What about it?"

"We can at least go out and have a look." Earlier in the afternoon I had prepared *Corny* for the trip home. I had already taken down her mast and I had lashed everything down. With several rolls in the main and our smallest jib we tacked out of the creek and into Hamford Water, where the sea was relatively calm. The Pye Sand was quite uncovered—it was a spring tide—and so provided a good protection from any sea that was running outside. We saw a big double-ended ketch aground. She was a deep-draft boat, lying over at a fearful angle. She must have been aground for quite a while, for her crew were paddling round her in a most dispirited manner—I suppose looking for the channel. In our excitement we nearly went aground ourselves and had to bear away for deep water pretty sharply. Diligent plying of the lead showed us we might have shared the same fate. By the time we had reached the Crab Knoll there was quite a swell and the wind was still increasing. Once clear of the Pye Sand the sea began to build up and long before we had sighted the Pye End buoy we were running through the biggest seas I had ever seen on the east coast. They had

111

breaking crests, but they were reasonably long seas and we were swooping along quite happily. My only fear was for the dinghy, that she might take a sea on board. It was not until we had rounded the stone pier and were in less troubled waters, when our speed immediately increased and we began to roar along, that we very nearly lost *Corny*. She was being towed by a double painter and one of these parted with a noise like a pistol shot; however, the other held. Then it started to rain. It poured down and blew harder than ever. *Cormorant* was being pressed too much, so we put her head into the wind and, with a lot of slatting of canvas, I muffled the mainsail, stowed it, and then under jib alone we made for the comparative shelter of Parkeston Quay—and a short respite from the stinging fury of this summer gale. We had the wind right in our faces, but the flood tide was now under us. I dropped the jib and under engine alone we slowly butted our way upriver. There was some shelter under Wrabness and Griselda said:

"It's a bit quieter here, why not anchor here for the night?" But once started I was loath to stop. If I had had any sense I would have realised that there was not enough water to get up to our moorings at Manningtree for some hours, for the horse opposite Wrabness was still uncovered, which meant that there would be little enough water to Mistley and practically none beyond.

Once clear of such protection as the little cliff at Wrabness gave, we met the full force of what must have been a Force eight wind. *Cormorant* staggered gamely on. Coming up to Mistley in the darkening night we noticed a long spit of mud sticking out from the shore.

"I have never seen that!" I shouted to Griselda, who answered:

"Neither have I! Good God, look what's coming!" The factory at Cattawade and one or two lights near it had been our guiding marks, but as she spoke they disappeared. Swirling grey clouds were advancing across the water at a diabolical speed.

"Hang on!" I gasped as the first of the squalls hit us. *Cormorant* reeled, but the gallant little Stuart-Turner never faltered. We were both blinded and beaten back into the cockpit. The stinging, hurting rain seemed to be coming at us horizontally.

"Can you see the next buoy?" I gasped, "because I can't see a damn thing!" My spectacles were awash and my night vision—for all at once it was night—is nil.

"Can't see a thing either," Griselda shouted back, "keep going!" I did, but a resounding crash from the stern as the dinghy banged into us told me only too well what had happened. We were aground—and there we stayed with the propeller churning for

maybe ten minutes until at last we lifted and were off. For a
moment the rain squalls passed and Griselda said:

"I can see the starboard hand buoy. Good heavens, we're miles
off course."

Once back in the channel we were all right for a while, with
Griselda conning us from buoy to buoy. Soon another blinding
squall hit us, but at the last moment we had taken our bearings and
this time suffered no hurt, except for a further drenching and a
general assault on the nerves. That squall passed us as we were
coming up on Ballast Hill, just in time for us to avoid piling up on
that unfriendly hazard or taking the beguiling false channel that
lies to the south of it.

We altered course for Mistley Quay, whose lights loomed largely
through the rain.

"What on earth is that black and white object?" Griselda asked,
pointing to what was to me nothing but a huge blur in the darkness.
As we came up on it, it shrank to Marcus Horlock's motor boat
standing high above us on a mud bank.

"Masses of water, we shall be all right," I shouted, for in the
darkness the channel along Mistley Quay looked unusually wide.

"The mudbanks are uncovered, but there does seem to be more
water than usual," Griselda answered. It was only an optical
illusion. As soon as we entered Thorn Reach we ran aground.

"If I don't have a strong drink, I shall die," Griselda remarked as
she scrambled into the cabin. I flung the anchor overboard and
switched off the engine.

"Here, drink this," and she handed me a half-tumbler of Scotch.
I stood in the drenching rain and downed my drink.

"You'd better come on in out of the rain, I have lit the lamp, got
the stove going and put some soup on." I climbed down into the
cabin, shed my oilskins and changed out of soaking flannel
trousers. We both drank another gigantic Scotch, by which time the
soup was ready. Warmed by whisky and hot food, my optimistic
nature began to reassert itself.

"What's a bit of rain after all? I think we have done jolly well, we
might still be down in Kirby Creek."

"I never want to see or hear of that bloody creek again. And if
you think that blundering about in the dark and in the pouring
rain in this blessed boat on this God-forsaken river is my idea of
fun, you're mistaken!"

"Oh, darling, it isn't always like this!"

"Oh, no! we've had one nice day out of eight—and that's more
than one should expect, I suppose." After that I relapsed into

stupefied silence, interrupted by a great clattering of pans. At least she's taking it out of them, I thought.

"Don't take any notice of me," Griselda said in a calmer voice. "It's just the drink liberating what I imagine most sailing wives manage to bottle up."

On those comforting words I got back into my oilskins and went outside to see what I could see. The rain had stopped and the moon was shining through ragged, scudding clouds. The tide had come up quite a bit, so under quarter throttle we bumped our way along, sometimes grounding on one side of the channel, sometimes on the other. The gale had blown itself out, and when we finally reached our moorings the river was quite still. The lights along the Manningtree–Mistley road were perfectly doubled in their reflections in the water. On the north bank the BX factory looked like a giant ocean liner that had run aground.

TO THE ORFORD RIVER

I awoke at 3 am, subconsciously waiting for the alarm to ring. It was set for five o'clock. I was a bit premature. Looking down South Street from our bedroom window I could just see *Cormorant* through the morning mist. She had swung to the tide. The ebb had set in, so we would have to be away by six-thirty.

The church clock struck the half hour as we rounded the corner into the High Street. The dinghy was just afloat, but dripping with dew, so I paddled standing up. We boarded *Cormorant*, set the sails and cast off the mooring. The mist was thick on the river but the sun was trying to break through. We appeared to be sailing down a sun-speckled path that led to nowhere. Visibility was just enough to see from buoy to buoy. With a falling tide we kept to the channel, skirting Mistley Quay, which looked mysteriously beautiful in the morning light.

The gentle north-west wind strengthened as we opened up Harwich harbour and the mist began to clear. We ran to the Guard buoy, jibed over and made for the North-West Beach. At the Beach End we jibed over again, and with the wind on our quarter we sailed out into the Rolling Grounds. Hardening in our sheets a little we headed for the Cork lightvessel a bare two miles away. The wind was light and there was a bit of a swell. We sailed peacefully up the coast and outside the Cutler Sands, which lie off Woodbridge Haven. Leaving the North Cutler we edged in towards the entrance to the River Ore. We began to check off the martello towers that lie between Woodbridge and Orford River, but we could not reconcile what we counted with what was marked on the

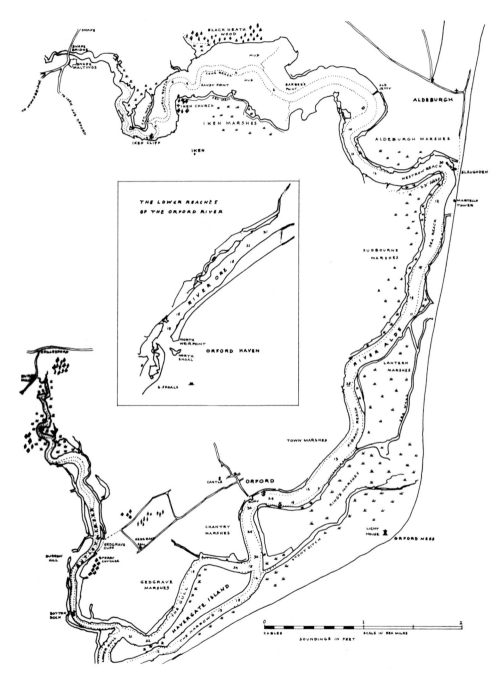

Chart of the River Alde, Butley Creek and Snape.

chart. Two porpoises surfaced noiselessly alongside us. As we drew level with Shingle Street I could see the leading marks, two "metes" set on poles that show white against the dark trees. It was some time before we spotted the little black buoy laid down by the Aldeburgh Yacht Club to mark the break in the bar.

We were now close-hauled and the wind appeared to have freshened a lot. We were making an undue amount of leeway and were about forty yards offshore, surrounded by breaking water. The metes were no longer in line. I was just about to put *Cormorant* about when we grounded, pounding on the shingle. The dinghy immediately started to make havoc of our topsides. Visions of breaking up, shipwreck and salvage flashed through my mind as I scrambled forward to drop the sails. The main came down with a run and I put a line round the jib. The gunter mainsail with its sixteen-foot yard is a cumbersome thing to deal with but Griselda bundled it up somehow.

All the while we were driving further on to the North Shoal. Not too hopefully, I started up the Stuart, and while Griselda held the dinghy off I put the engine into reverse. Nothing happened for a moment, then a swell lifted us and we roared off backwards with such speed that our stern touched another bank; I pushed the gear lever into forward and we were in deep water. I brought her almost up to the beach before bearing away up the river. Under engine alone we were making very slow progress, and only then did I realise that the ebb tide was still running out of the river. Once we were properly inside I put the sails up again, and as the ebb was soon played out we ran freely up Long Reach.

We had committed the unforgivable crime of trying to enter the river against the ebb, for though the tide was slack outside the ebb had by no means done. Fortunately this was not a spring tide, when it can run out of the entrance at a full five knots. It was a salutary experience. If we had grounded on a sandbank we would probably not have got off, but shingle is on the move all the time.

We were still in a thoughtful mood as we turned up the Lower Gull Reach, leaving Havergate Island on the seaward side of us. I dropped the sails again, for we were bound up the Butley River. The wind was dead ahead and there was little room to tack. The day had clouded up and the brick building on Boyton Dock looked forlorn in the flat grey light. There was only about seven-tenths cloud and a sudden shaft of sunlight lit up the grass-covered Barrow Hill. The sheep grazing on it looked whiter than white, as if they had just been painted.

We anchored by Gedgrave Cliffs short of the oyster beds and just twenty-four miles from our moorings at Manningtree. It blew a bit, rained a bit, then the clouds rolled back and all was bright and gay again, including our tempers. As I was finishing washing up the lunch things I noticed a great blackbacked gull behaving in an odd manner. It was dragging something down to the muddy bank of the river. It was an eel. The gull went through all kinds of antics, throwing the squirming creature about and banging it on a rock. The eel looked as if it had had its *coup de grâce*, and with three gulps the gull swallowed it. Its troubles were by no means over, for this must have revived the eel, and he started to squirm about inside the gull, who began to look most unhappy. He kept taking gulps of water, trying to wash down this lively and indigestible meal. It wasn't until half an hour had passed that he had the strength to fly across the river towards Orfordness, perhaps to tell his wife all about it.

The next afternoon on a rising tide we sailed the dinghy up to Butley. From Gedgrave Cliffs onwards the creek became more and more interesting. It was a sunny afternoon with an imposing array of cumulus clouds piling up in the north-west. We passed a little doll's house of a boatshed with a motor launch named *Loch Rannoch* moored alongside. The creek wound northwards, getting narrower all the time, past marsh and woodland, and finally through great reedbeds. A pair of Montagu harriers were beating the marshes, and all the way to the head of the creek we were accompanied by a family of shelduck who kept under the water most of the time. We reached the end of our little voyage at the last bend before Butley Mill, which has a nice eighteenth-century mill house set among the mill buildings. It was an idyllic scene, with to the east of us quite a high hill (for Suffolk) with a hanger of dark trees on the top and an overgrown sandpit halfway down its side. The wind was dropping, so under sail and oars we started our return journey.

"What *is* that noise?" Griselda asked.

I stopped rowing and listened. There was a whispering sound, and then quite suddenly all the reeds bent over in a southerly direction. We both stared in some bewilderment, and then Griselda smiled and said:

"Oh, I see what it is. It is the tide turning. But I have never seen it make such an abrupt about turn." The wind had died away but with the tide under us we glided along, helped by the oars. Soon the sky darkened and we had the benefit of a Turneresque-cum-Twilight-of-the-Gods series of effects, with shafts of sunlight dramatically spotlighting the distant hillside. We were safely aboard *Cormorant* before the rain came down in driving sheets; it

117

did not last long, we had only caught the fringe of the storm.

This was an excellent anchorage for a shoal-draught boat. For a boat drawing more than about three foot it is probably better to anchor lower down the river, off Boyton Dock. Though I do remember in a friend's boat when we had anchored there we dragged our anchor and ended up on the cant edge of the mud. Butley River is gentler, more civilised, than the marshy wilderness of Hamford Water, but it is certainly not the civilisation of bungalows and marinas. The only company we had were the cows and the sheep wandering on the skyline of Barrow Hill and the occasional fisherman seine netting who helped to humanise the scene, yet not to detract from one's solitude. Only the periodic roar of jets from the USAF at Bentwaters and the distant sounds of combine-harvesters reminded us that we were living in the twentieth century.

We often wondered if like Sutton Hoo there was a Saxon ship buried in Barrow Hill. It looked a most probable site.

The next morning was bright and cold, with a north-westerly wind and the glass steady. The ebb was still running as we turned into Lower Gull Reach and we took a little time even with a fair wind to reach Orford. The little town with its great Norman keep, its mediaeval church and odd jumble of houses of all ages made a pretty sight in the morning light. Its ageless appearance was assisted by the number of sailing boats moored near the quay, including two large Dutch craft, a red-painted boeier and a brightly varnished hoogarts, both magnificent ships with massive spars and tanned sails.

We went ashore and bought bread and milk, butter and sausages. On the way back to the quay we called in at *The Jolly Sailor*. By mistake we went into the saloon bar, polite with stuffed birds and uncomfortably stiff chairs. It was empty, so we moved next door to find the public bar solid with people. A pleasant-faced, grey-haired man made room for us on a settle. He was the owner of the hoogarts. I asked him how they compared with botters:

"I used to have a botter. She was a prettier boat than the hoogarts and we were very fond of her, but then I got bitten with passage making and bought a twelve-tonner. Three years of that was enough and I was back with a Dutchman."

"What sort of seaboat is she?" I asked.

"Splendid. They were used for fishing out of the Schelde and you can get shocking seas off that coast. I believe they even fished as far up as the Orkneys."

Hoogarts.

The Orford River. Water colour sketch.

"What does she draw?"

"Three foot six, or with the leeboards right down, over nine feet!"

"Seems to have the best of all worlds."

"Trust the Dutchman. There's nothing he does not know about shallow seas and the kind of boats for sailing them."

We drank more beer, talked for a while in the dark friendly little bar about boats and birds and the east coast and Dutch estuaries. Frank Harper (licensed to sell tobaccos, beers, wines and spirits) brought our conversation to a close with:

"Time, gentlemen, please."

We returned to *Cormorant* and after a belated lunch sailed up the river to Iken Cliff. Just below Slaughden Quay we found ourselves in the middle of a dinghy race—Lapwings I think they were; they looked like a cloud of cabbage white butterflies with one or two cinnabars among them.

The flood must only have started to run at about the time we left Orford, for the mudbanks were still uncovered below Black Heath Woods. We grounded in Church Reach, just to the west of Iken church. There was hardly any water in the channel ahead of us and the tide would have to run for quite a while before we could reach the anchorage below Iken Cliff. I dropped the anchor overboard and let out a few fathoms of cable. It was a grey and rather chilly afternoon. Griselda shivered and then said:

"Let's have a cup of coffee."

We sat comfortably on our bunks, drank our coffee and talked in a desultory way. We were both feeling a bit sleepy after all that beer at *The Jolly Sailor*.

"Luff, you fool, luff!" There was a clatter of blocks and further rude swearing. I awoke with a start and leaped up to see, a few feet away, the stern of a small sloop manned by two large gangling boys and a very little, precise old gentleman in a yachting cap. As they disappeared round the bend behind Iken church I could still hear him forcefully instructing his crew.

If there was enough water for them, there must be enough for us, so I ran up the jib and the main and heaved in the anchor. It was only about half a mile to the pool off Iken Cliff. When we got there we saw the little sloop sailing backwards and forwards with one of the boys, still under urgent instruction from the cockpit, getting into the mother and father of a muddle with a lead line. I headed *Cormorant* into the wind, allowed them to sail across our bows, then dropped the anchor and drifted backwards. As the anchor splashed into the water, the three heads on the sloop turned towards us as one man. Further orders were shouted. Once more they came about and finally anchored almost on top of us. Instructions in the art of sailing and anchoring and stowing sails and possibly other things useful for young men to know continued over the water until night had fallen. I switched the radio on. Stravinsky's *The Rite of Spring* effectively drowned that little old man's very carrying voice.

In the morning light Iken church looked most picturesque on its tree-clad promontory. The changing light on these rivers is not the least of their fascinations. We had seen Iken church against a backdrop of a thunderstorm looking most sinister, but on that morning it looked as pretty as a Victorian watercolour. During the morning we took the dinghy up to Snape bridge. Three small boys rushed forward to take our painter as we came alongside.

"Shall we take them for a sail?" Griselda asked.

"You take them," I replied, "I will go ashore and take a movie of you."

The children were delighted and I think enjoyed it a lot. I took my film of the cargo of eager Suffolk urchins and then walked down the road to get some shots of Newson Garrett's mid-nineteenth century maltings, to my eyes at least the most handsome industrial buildings in England.

Our sail back to *Cormorant* on the ebb tide and with a fair wind did not take long. The little sloop was still there, but no sound came from it.

"It's my belief," Griselda said, paraphrasing Eliza Doolittle, "the two boys have done the old man in." We lunched well. It was a still and hazy afternoon, so we sat about reading and listening to the test match on the radio. At home we had no TV and we could hardly be called radio fans, but on board our boats we have always had a radio, ostensibly for weather forecasts, but it is surprising how much it gets tuned to other programmes.

In this test match, England for once were faring well. That good cricketing parson, the Rev. David Shepherd, knocked up forty before Goddard, the West Indian captain, caught and bowled him. And then in came Graveney. Ruddy-faced Tom Graveney of Gloucester and England, with no more ado than if he were playing for Chipping Sodbury against Wootton-under-Edge on a fine Saturday afternoon and well filled with strong Herefordshire cider, began to knock those West Indian bowlers all round the gasometers. For this was the final Test at the Oval. It was at the Surrey ground when I was eleven years old that I saw one of the greatest innings of all time, by perhaps the greatest bat of them all, the immortal Jack Hobbs. While his partner, the Yorkshireman Herbert Sutcliffe, seemed hardly to score at all, on a wicket of appalling malevolence Hobbs, with exquisite grace and the timing of a genius, made exactly 100 runs before the Australian fast bowler Gregory sent his off bail flying fifty yards.

Our test match listening and reminiscing was cut short by the radio blowing a valve.

A couple of days later we picked up Anna at Orford Quay and sailed on downstream for the Butley River. We returned to the same anchorage and after tea went searching for mushrooms on Barrow Hill, which was reputed to be a good place for them. We found only a couple of rather small ones. Back on the boat, Anna and I sat on deck drinking our pre-dinner drinks while tantalising smells drifted up from the galley. The wind had dropped right away and there was not a sound except for the purr of the twin primus stoves and the occasional rattle of a saucepan lid.

It was a night with a full moon and there was not a cloud in the sky. The river was an oily ink black and mudbanks glistened like the convolutions of a brain fossilised in anthracite. I rowed the dinghy down the creek a little way and then for a while allowed myself to be carried back on the tide. *Cormorant* was shining blackly in the dark with the white letters of her name standing out on her bows. A curlew kept calling from down the creek, and once a redshank cried. Otherwise it was quite still and quiet. The trees on Gedgrave Cliff were silhouetted as if cut like lace from black paper. Towards Butley there appeared to be a gleaming light. When I trained the binoculars on it it was only a white notice board by the oyster layings reflecting the moonlight. I gently paddled back to the boat.

Cormorant looked welcoming, with a warm glow from the cabin lamps. We were loath to go to bed, and we sat on deck talking until at last a little chill in the air drove us below.

The calm of the previous night was still with us when we got under way early next morning. Turning out of Butley River, we found a little breeze in our faces and a foul tide, so with the help of the engine we bucked the tide and tacked down to the mouth of the River Ore. The breeze had hardened somewhat but there was no weight in it, so we were quite unprepared for meeting breaking seas on the bar and on the shoals off Shingle Street. The tide was flooding strongly and at one stage we were making hardly any headway at all. We tacked across the river almost on to the beach and at last began to make a little ground. With the leading marks in line I bore away for the bar buoy. Almost immediately we rolled our side decks under.

"Just the seas breaking on the bar," I shouted encouragingly.

"Must be a very big bar!" Griselda answered, "probably reaches to Holland, I should think." The sea was white capped as far as the horizon. With the help of the engine we wallowed and crashed along with the tide now under us, and an hour after leaving Orford Haven we were off the Deben. We came up to the bar buoy but none of us could see the leading marks. As the sea was in a fair old turmoil here, we thought the only seamanlike thing to do was to keep on for Harwich harbour. Both Woodbridge Haven and Orford Haven are tricky places with an onshore wind, but whereas the leading marks into the river Ore are fairly easy to spot, the ones into the Deben are often the very devil to see, as I was to discover more than once in later years.

With only the small jib and several rolls in the mainsail, but with the reliable Stuart still pushing his best, we tacked slowly past Felixstowe. The seas were quite deserted. The wind was blowing between Force six and seven and the hard blue sky was streaked with cirrus. Crossing the Rolling Grounds we took one wave of solid green water over our bows. We found ourselves being swept down on to the wreck of the *Simon Bolivar* off Landguard Fort, so I had to come about and make a long and very wet tack out towards the Stone Banks before the flood into the river picked us up and we came roaring in with the wind on our quarter.

Our sail up the Stour was a peaceful business after the buffeting outside, though the skies had clouded over. We were close-hauled and *Cormorant's* rather portly bow was chucking water all over the place. As we came under the shelter of Mistley Quay I dropped the sails. The tide swept us past a Dutch motor vessel and the old ironpot barge *Xylonite*. I refuelled and we motored up to our mooring. It was just half past one, and six and a half hours since we had left our anchorage in the Butley River. We felt a bit battered about the ears, but it had been an enjoyable few days.

Our sailing in 1957 ended with a patch of perfect weather early in October. We spent several days on the river, when there was little wind but the sun shone from dawn to dusk.

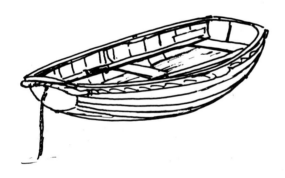

Part two

1 Going foreign

There is a lot to be said for gaining one's sailing experience in someone else's boat, and preferably in company with more experienced yachtsmen. As must be painfully obvious to anyone who has read as far as this, I was virtually self-taught and suffered from all the gaps in knowledge that that might imply.

I was just about ready for extending our cruising range from the Essex and Suffolk coasts and rivers when I got the chance of a cruise abroad. In the summer of 1958 Dr C. R. B. Welford, whom I had known since school days, invited me for a cruise to Holland. His boat *Dowsabel*, which he had designed himself, was a fairly powerful 32-foot yawl, with at that time an eight hp ex-industrial Stuart-Turner and a small two-bladed reversible propeller. This combination proved somewhat inadequate auxiliary equipment for a boat, of this size.

Dowsabel was an interesting craft and, living up to her name (*Douce et Belle*), was also a pretty boat, with a nice canoe stern. However, the combination of this stern, a mizzen mast and a shallow self-draining cockpit gave little room for handling the mizzen halliards and even less for handling the jib sheets. As her working rig included two headsails, when going about her cockpit became a bit like a rugger scrum, with at least three people falling over each other. Kit Welford had some fairly firm ideas of what he wanted in a yacht. Her cabin was spartan, with a narrow coach roof and deep box-bed-like bunks set below the side decks. These were designed for lying in at sea, and for nothing else. Under those conditions they were very comfortable. For sitting on, there was a narrow bench on the port side of the gangway, faced by a tip-up table hinged to the front of the starboard bunk. Her decks were uncluttered and, apart from a four-inch bulwark rail, had nothing to prevent one going overboard; no stanchions, lifelines or pulpit. When I once remonstrated with him about this, I was rather abruptly told by her owner that without such protection you were much more likely to hold on tight!

"Stanchions and lifelines are only for old maids—'It's ever so nice on the water, won't you take me arm dear?'" (he parodied a day tripper going for a jaunt round the bay). "On *Dowsabel* we do things differently. If anyone is fool enough to fall overboard, he can't expect to be picked up at sea," he ended rather tersely. These words came back to me most forcibly when, on a night watch a couple of years later, *Dowsabel* was hit by a sudden squall and I was nearly catapulted out of her cockpit and over the side.

I was given a trial sail one weekend, when we went from the Deben up to the Aldeburgh River, entering it in the very last of the daylight. We found the entrance much more by good luck than anything else. The only remarkable occurrence of that weekend was that we lost our anchor and twenty-five fathoms of nylon warp. This happened off Orford Quay when, even though it was blowing hard, Kit's sailing partner, an exuberant Irishman, felt an impelling need for beer. So we anchored and he rowed ashore. By the time he had slaked his thirst and was back at the quay again, carrying a couple of crates of beer, it was blowing so hard he had to get a 36-foot harbour launch to bring him off. The plastic cockleshell dinghy would certainly have drowned him.

The combination of a heavy CQR anchor and a very elastic nylon warp, no winches and an auxiliary out of action, and a five-knot spring tide proved somewhat daunting. No amount of heaving made any impression, so Kit said firmly:

"We'll sail it out." By now it must have been blowing a full Force 7 as under jib and mizzen we attempted this operation; and in less time than it takes to write this we had sailed round and round a huge Air Ministry buoy. There was only one thing to do. The Irishman got the carving knife and cut the warp. I will gloss over the subsequent arrival at Aldeburgh, with no ground tackle and apparently no vacant mooring. There were plaintive cries of:

"Where's Jumbo? I'm sure he'd give us a mooring!" Finally we spotted an unoccupied buoy. I was yelled at to grab it. I did—and nearly got pulled in half before thirty stone of crew fell on top of me as I lay across the gunwale. I could hear my ribs cracking. My skipper's only comment was:

"You want to get a bit more muscle on you!" Surprisingly, in spite of my sore chest and my lack of muscle, I had passed my initiation test. The invitation to join Kit Welford and his son Sebastian on a cruise through Holland arrived a few days later. We were to meet aboard the boat at Lowestoft on the evening of 11th July, which was the day of Convocation at the Royal College of Art. As a member of the staff of the College, as I was in those days, I had to attend this function. The morning of Convocation arrived, with the promise of a fine day. By eleven o'clock, wearing gowns borrowed for the occasion, we filed into the hall, which was also borrowed for the occasion from the Royal College of Music. It was a grilling hot day. We took our seats. In a nearby studio a soprano was belting out the Jewel song from *Faust* and one of our second-year students up in the gallery let off a fire-cracker. These sounds were drowned by an unmelodic fanfare of trumpets. As the speeches droned on I was far away, perhaps wondering a bit what I was in for on this, my first foreign cruise. At last the ceremony came to an end and we filed out into Prince Consort Road. A hurried lunch, and by twenty-five past two I was at Liverpool Street Station.

On an almost deserted platform an old porter walked painfully towards the barrier. He looked as if his feet were hurting him—then suddenly his furrowed face broke out into a beaming smile. I was glad he smiled—his smile went with the day. I had barely settled in my seat when the train pulled out. It was not a good train. It travelled fitfully, stopping at places like Ingatestone and Hatfield Peverel and Marks Tey that the more purposeful rush-hour trains would have scorned to notice. The afternoon grew hotter. A bald-headed young man next to me was reading a book about fishing. He fell asleep over Mullets. A lance-corporal in the Catering Corps slowly grilled himself to a turn in a very new battle dress. He scorned even to remove his webbing belt. Perhaps, I thought, he didn't know how to undo it. I sweated and watched the Essex countryside filter past us. Bits of grit kept settling on my sticky face. When at last we reached Colchester, the Catering Corporal and the Mullet got out and the carriage was filled with vociferous Nordic teenagers—young men and girls, fair of hair and pink of face, uttering strange glottal sounds. The Vale of Dedham opened up to my left. I buttoned my shirt collar, straightened my tie and put my jacket on as the train shambled to a halt at Manningtree station.

After hurriedly packing, Griselda and I set off for Lowestoft in the car. We found *Dowsabel* lying in the yacht basin. Kit and the crew were off at the boat; his wife was standing on the quay, trying without success to attract his attention. When at last they came ashore we went into the Royal Norfolk and Suffolk Yacht Club and had a drink—then our wives left us to our fate. After a few more drinks and a very good steak at the club we walked to the end of the pier, then turned in. No one washed. I had the portside bunk. Its box-bed form was cosy and gave some degree of privacy and it had its own bedhead electric light—for *Dowsabel* was well lit—wired by the skipper's son Sebastian and fed from a massive Nife battery.

We rocked gently from a light swell in the harbour. I turned and tossed about for a while, wondering what the morrow would bring. The bedding seemed a bit damp, but at last I fell asleep. I awoke at 7.30—the sun was already trying to break through the mist but no one stirred. A friendly young man who was only coming for the passage was the first up. He made some tea, and after we'd drunk it we dressed and went ashore for him to buy shaving things and some gumboots. Lowestoft was astir, the sun shone, but I was struck by the grubbiness of the place. A French or Dutch port, or even a West Country port, at this hour would have been brighter, more washed looking. Lowestoft was still rheumy eyed.

Back on *Dowsabel* we had a belated breakfast of fried chops and sausages, then prepared to get under way. As we were starting the mizzen topping-lift carried away. This took some ten or fifteen minutes to repair. However at 11.10 we cast off again and motored out of the harbour.

To begin with we could lay our course for Den Helder in North Holland, for the wind was in the south-east. It was warm and peaceful and pleasant. As the afternoon drew on, it became much colder. I took the helm from 7 pm–10 pm. To begin with I found it hard to keep her on course, for she tended to wander a bit, and she seemed a bit of a lump after *Cormorant*. A pigeon circled us twice, then landed on the crosstrees and settled there. The friendly young man took over at 10 pm as it was getting dark. He grumbled a bit, for the wind was heading us slightly and I should have hardened in the sheets. I partly undressed and climbed into my bunk. We heaved and crashed our way along and I began to wonder why I'd come. The wind was now getting up and suddenly it started to rain cats and dogs. I heard Kit taking over the middle watch at midnight, then fell into a troubled sleep. The next thing I heard was a voice saying "It's getting light, John, will you take her now." Kit was standing by my bunk in streaming oilskins. The time was 3 am. I pulled on as many clothes as I could over my pyjamas and got into my oilskins, but couldn't find my gumboots.

"Hurry up! The wind's changed, we're right on course, keep her as she goes." Kit was getting impatient, so I hurried out into the cockpit. It was not quite dark and very cold. I settled down to my watch, but found to my misery that my feet were already soaked. The self-draining cockpit was constantly awash—and it was raining again. With the wind on her quarter *Dowsabel* was striding along, rolling as she went. The pigeon that had roosted on our crosstrees had gone, but about 4 am as it began to get lighter two other tired birds circled the boat several times, then one pitched on the sea, lifting her tail up, as if to keep her skirts dry. The other flew away. I sat hunched over the tiller, looking over the awful solitude of grey waves, and I wondered again why I had come. The sheer desolation of such a scene. And the discomfort. Sebastian had succumbed to seasickness and nothing would shift him from his bunk. Both the others had vomited once or twice. Beyond feeling queasy all I got was a cracking headache which lasted throughout the day. We were doing three-hour watches and this seemed a long three hours. At six, shivering with cold and icy-footed, I awakened my relief and retired thankfully to my bunk. I continued to shiver, but at last fell asleep.

We were really travelling when I woke about nine, but I lay for a while still cold and still with frozen feet, when I heard someone shout:

"Land-ho!" I scrambled up on deck. We were right on our landfall, heading straight through the Schelpen Gat buoys. A big following sea had built up and we were carried along on this, doing a full seven knots. The waves piling up behind us made an impressive and intimidating sight. *Dowsabel's* freeboard aft seemed to have shrunk to a few inches, but here she was at her best, for she moved so easily and got going so quickly, leaving no disturbance behind her.

"Better hoist the Q flag," Kit shouted to one of us. Sebastian appeared up the companion way looking very wan and carrying a yellow flag and also a Dutch flag.

"What's that one for?" I asked.

Kit sniffed an expressive sniff, as if to imply that this was no moment for asking fatuous questions, and put the binoculars to his eyes. Sebastian, who was a polite boy and even when suffering from seasickness was as ready to impart gratuitous information as his father was reluctant, said:

"The Q flag is for customs and immigration clearance. Once we have that, we drop the yellow flag and hoist the Dutch flag as a courtesy gesture . . ."

The sea quietened as we came into the Texel Roads, and close under the shelter of the shore we rounded into Den Helder harbour. In this large naval base we had quite a job to find anywhere to tie up. We tried unsuccessfully to get a bridge to open that was never meant for such things. At last someone directed us into a little yacht harbour, filled with naval craft, a few Dragons and one or two other craft, including a magnificent great ketch,

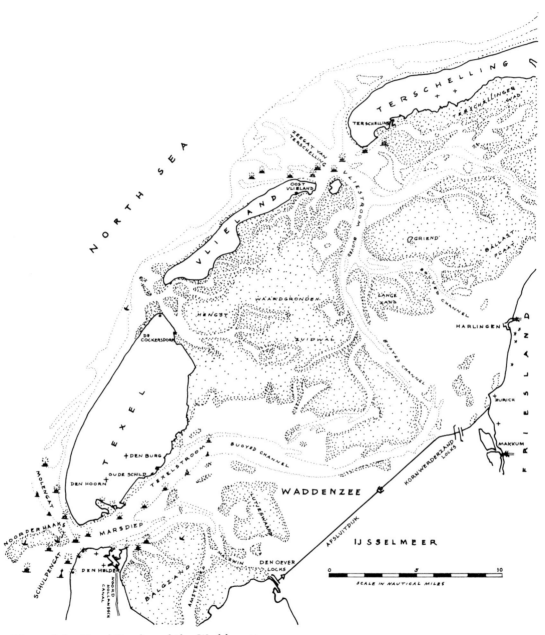

Chart of the Texel Roads and the Waddenzee.

which we discovered later was a training ship for cadets. We finally tied up soon after midday. Our time was 25 hours and 5 minutes from Lowestoft; the distance run was 110 miles.

The accuracy of Kit Welford's landfall astounded even him, for on the passage from Lowestoft to Den Helder there are no lightvessels after leaving Smith's Knoll, some twenty-five miles off the Norfolk coast, until one sights the Texel lightvessel some eighty miles on. *Dowsabel* carried no aids to navigation except for her compass and log line and an ancient sextant that lived a quiet and undisturbed life in its case under the skipper's bunk. As we stowed the sails and generally tidied up the ship we saw gale cones being hoisted, and for the next twenty-four hours it blew blue murder. We were lucky it had not happened a day earlier.

So my first North Sea passage was over. The experience at the time seemed far from agreeable. Boring to begin with, nothing to look at except the sea! Then the feeling of malaise—not actual sickness but just a general longing for green fields, a loving wife and home. And in the dawn watch, the sheer melancholy of those heaving wastes. Yet within an hour of arriving those feelings were already dimmed.

Den Helder (or to give the naval port its proper name, Nieuwediep harbour) is the most important base for the navy in Holland. The town of Den Helder is of no particular interest. We walked long and far on the hard brick roads in search of shops and pubs. The friendly young man left us in the evening to return to England by the Hook of Holland packet boat.

The next day, a Monday, the gale had blown itself out. We left Den Helder in the afternoon and had an easy sail over to Texel, the most westerly of the Friesian islands. Texel's one little port is called Oude Schild, with a harbour no bigger than a couple of tennis courts. Oude Schild's main customer is the ferry boat *Dr Wagemaker* from Nieuwediep harbour. It was a peaceful little spot, only galvanised into life when the ferry called, then falling asleep again, though once or twice during the night I awoke to the noise of boats coming in.

The next morning was quite windless, so we hauled Sebastian to the top of the mainmast to untangle the wimple. After this operation we breakfasted, leaving Oude Schild in a glassy calm. We motored right through the Texel Roads to the Zuider Zee dam. There was a lot of bird life about, oyster catchers, redshanks, curlews; and a flock of terns were flying about near the dam.

At last a north-east wind piped up and we had a close haul to Harlingen, the main port for Friesland. A bridge swung open for us to pass into the Haven. We moored alongside a Dutch hydrographic boat and had a friendly conversation with the crew. I went ashore and bought a fair-sized steak weighing 500 grammes, and 200 grammes of finely-cut bacon, all for 4.70 guilders (about 45p). After supper a succession of large fishing boats and shrimpers came chugging past our very busy anchorage. Kit decided we should put on shore clothes and walk up to the further end of the town in search of a pub. As we stepped down into the cabin, an oil barge let out five tremendous blasts. Kit turned to me and said:

"Do you know what those five blasts mean?" Before I could answer he went on: "Once we are in confined waters, you must be sure you know the rule of the road and what the various blasts on a ship's whistle mean." I nodded, I hoped intelligently, saying:

"Yes, I knew," but obviously I had not impressed him, so he continued:

"Better write it down . . . the rule of the road is keep to the right. At night passing ships going in the opposite direction—red light to red light. One hoot means a ship is turning to starboard, two to port, three he is going astern and five quick ones mean 'Get to hell out of it, I can't do anything except keep moving straight ahead'." Before we went for our drinks we tried our whistle, which answered with a hoarse croak, so some time was spent in trying to make it work, again hauling the now-protesting Sebastian aloft in a bosun's chair. A small boat is too small a place for three people with different ideas of what they want to do. Sebastian wanted to lie in his bunk, but was up the mast mending the whistle; Kit kept diving into the tool chest below the bench, apparently in search of tools and oblivious of the fact that I was sitting on the bench trying to change my socks. I was clear in my mind that I wanted beer. After Kit had trodden on my bare feet for the third time, I pushed my way out of the cabin in a rage, and with shoes and socks in my hand I climbed ashore. I sat on a bollard completing my toilet and was suddenly struck by the absurdity of the situation. By the time they had finished their chores I had regained my composure. The close quarters of a small yacht are a good breeding ground for friction and ill-temper. I was also discovering rather belatedly the difference between being master in one's own boat and being crew in someone else's.

Later when they joined me our conversation became animated and we talked about boats. Kit talked about what he thought was the ideal rig for a small yacht.

"There's a lot to be said for the gaff rig. You can drop it in a couple of seconds if it is properly designed. That's one thing I

131

wouldn't let any naval architect touch—I'd design that." After a lot more talk in this vein we wandered back to the boat.

I lay awake for a while thinking about the first day of my foreign cruise. As we had crossed the Waddenzee from Oude Schild, I had been struck again by the Dutchness of it all. It was like sailing through a seventeenth-century painting. A light, as clear as that in East Anglia but with wider horizons, and the pencil-thin skyline made up of a pattern of dykes and low houses and the sudden upward movement of a windmill tower or church spire. The whole scene was painted in tones of silvery grey. An archaic vessel, clipper-bowed, round-sterned with balustrades, and ketch-rigged with a vast collection of sails of different tones of white, grey and black, had ghosted slowly past us en route for Texel. One other yacht, a botter, which was trawling, two motor barges and two fishermen were all we saw the whole long day.

We had started too early for a fair tide and our progress was particularly slow. At one stage we were coming up on the fishing botter for over an hour without apparently getting any nearer. It was etched in a framework of withies and looked as if it were suspended in space. The Waddenzee can be treacherous and rough, but I shall never forget the serenity of that first sail over those placid waters.

The next morning, after going ashore to buy milk, we left Harlingen. A drizzling rain soon developed into heavy squally showers and there was a cold north wind. However, it was a fair wind and under headsails and mizzen we rolled down to the Ijsselmeer locks at Kornwerderzand. We followed behind a botter and came up with her in the lock. She was a pretty craft called *Joanna*, a hireling as we learned later. In her company we sailed out of Kornwerderzand for Enkhuizen. The botter was chucking a lot of spray about and we soon left her behind. Kit and Sebastian went below and I took the helm. I had the Zuider Zee to myself. Even under this reduced rig of headsails and mizzen, *Dowsabel* moved fast and easily. We found later that there was some sort of easterly set which took us a little off course. We arrived at Enkhuizen at half past four in the afternoon and anchored in the inner harbour, which was given over to fishermen and yachts. It was a spacious harbour, surrounded by green grass banks and brick quays. In spite of the driving rain, or maybe because of it, the place seemed to me to be of great beauty. By the evening the opposite quay to us had filled up with a number of fishing boats, black painted or tarred and picked out here and there with bright orange oxide. In the evening light these stood out as black silhouettes against the

Enkhuizen harbour with fishing boats moored on the north side.

brilliant green grass banks, the little brick houses and the leaden grey sky.

By morning the rain had stopped and the sun was shining fitfully. We went ashore to explore Enkhuizen, which is a nice little port, with tidy old brick houses. We at last reached the Zuider Zee Museum, which had a number of craft moored outside in a canal. It was a fascinating museum, though there was a fair amount of indifferent art and some not too exciting costume figures set in the most unnaturalistic settings. There was one room full of ship models and downstairs, in a large loft-like room, there was a display of simple models of botters, mounted on a glass sheet to represent the sea. Beneath this glass sheet could be seen their various trawls. The building as a whole was in courtyard form. The rooms were large and spacious—the house was sixteenth century, originally an East India merchant's warehouse. Like all Dutch houses of that time, it was well lit with magnificent great windows and much massive old oak, light in colour and pleasant against the

133

The botter *Joanna* moored alongside the greensward in the Binnenhaven at Hoorn.

white walls. There was also quite a lot of painted eighteenth and nineteenth-century furniture from Hindeloopen, including some pretty sledges. Regretfully we returned to *Dowsabel* and left Enkhuizen in the afternoon. Under short canvas we had a close-hauled, spray-splashed sail to Hoorn.

Hoorn was even more attractive than Enkhuizen. Our anchorage was on the edge of a small park of tall elms and short, very green grass. After sending Sebastian up to the top of the mast once again to clear the wimple we wandered along the quay for some beer. We found an interesting tavern where the publican showed us some pieces of Japanned ware, including a rather bulbous but pretty eighteenth-century coffee pot. Hanging on his walls were a number of moulds or patterns for cookies, carved in wood with figures such as Santa Claus, and a very large one of what looked like a portrait of an eighteenth-century admiral, intended for some mammoth piece of pastry. After supper we walked through the park to the outer harbour—between that and where we were lying was a little mere, deserted except for a single boat, a hoogarts. As we returned to *Dowsabel* the botter *Joanna* was being warped into the same quay. I stopped and looked at her. These botters are magnificently solid craft. That morning at Enkhuizen a friendly Dutchman from Arnhem had invited us aboard another one. She had not been altered in any way, except to have had all the tar scraped off her unbelievably massive oak timbers. The cabin, which was under the deck filling the fore part of the ship, had about four foot three inches headroom aft and about five foot six inches forward and no skylight—only deadlights; but what a cabin! The floor space was about twelve feet by ten feet. Right up in the bows a bulkhead had been put in for chain lockers. Against this bulkhead were two built-in berths, the one above the other. Otherwise, apart from an old circular iron stove with an iron chimney poking through the deck, there was a camp bed and a couple of stools, a case of beer and a brass lamp and nothing else. Yet it was the nicest cabin I have ever seen. It reminded me of a remark made by Weston Martyr in *The Southseaman*. Discussing cabins, he said: "If you wish to be comfortable and happy down there at all times, the place must be made as bare and clean as a hound's tooth." When sitting in this splendid cabin its low headroom was not oppressive and the warm colour of the oiled planks and timbers and the smell of Stockholm tar made one feel one was in a real ship. She was eighty years old and her market price, including a dreadful old one-lung diesel which had to be started with an explosive, was about £500; but to build her new (even in 1958) would have cost nearer £5,000. However, they said if we wanted one cheap we could have the one lying alongside for £20. She was ripe and rotten and would have been expensive at any price.

The *Joanna* had two skylights over her foredeck and when I looked through them I could see that the cabin had been partitioned off to make separate rooms. I preferred the open arrangement of the Enkhuizen botter. In both boats the great fish well was unaltered.

The following morning we left Hoorn under power. Though there was a nice breeze Kit had decided to do a bit of varnishing, so we motored all the way to Marken. In addition to varnishing the rail, he painted the tops of the stern bollards white, then went and sat on one.

There was a pearly-grey sky, hinting at a warm day to come. We passed one little five-ton yacht that we had seen at Hoorn; she was sailing very sweetly and doing almost as well as we were under power. A few minutes later a great white boeier crossed our stern.

135

She was under sail and looked very fine against the grey sky. By the time we came up to Vollendam the sky was clouding up, but still there was no weight in the wind. They were probably land clouds drawn up by the heat. Vollendam had a most picturesque skyline, with church spires, stepped gables and old oak trees, seen though a fence of botter masts. These masts with their wimples fluttering looked like a concourse of mounted horsemen with lances raised awaiting a mediaeval tournament. I wanted to put in there, but Kit had been there and expressed a wish to see Marken, in spite of my warning him that I had heard that it was tourist-ridden.

Streams of glass-covered launches ("Sixpenny sickers" Kit called them) passed us going to and fro into the harbour. We had to take avoiding action as one plastic monster started turning round in front of us. A becapped official frantically waved us into a little haven on the starboard hand. This was practically deserted, so Kit decided to swing round so that we could make a quick getaway.

He misjudged his distance or *Dowsabel* didn't answer the helm. We were approaching the wooden jetty at some speed. In desperation (for I was bowman) I heaved and fended off with the boathook; I succeeded only too well, to find myself acting as a bridge over an ever-widening gap between boat and shore; there was no chance of getting back on board and a big chance of falling into the water. I leapt for the retreating jetty and landed on the edge, poised unbalanced in a position of no security. Either I was going to fall back into the harbour or forward on to the jetty. The matter was in dispute for some seconds, then by a defiance of gravity I stayed with the land. In a moment Sebastian had thrown me a warp and *Dowsabel* was safely alongside. The skipper's only remark was:

"I felt the shallowness, that's why she didn't respond." I nearly said "why the devil didn't you put her in reverse," but thought better of it.

No sooner had we started our lunch than three of the youngest inhabitants, all decked out in the most elaborate traditional costumes, came alongside, presumably for our enjoyment and their due remuneration. We took no notice and eventually they went sadly away. After our lunch we went ashore in search of petrol. Marken was *swarming* with tourists—and what tourists: German, Belgian, English and even Japanese. They were a plain lot. Outside each cottage were young girls, middle-aged women and even some pathetically old men, all dressed up in their native costumes. One poor old man looked utterly miserable. I doubt if he'd ever donned the curious garb until he was too old to earn a living as a fisherman or a bricklayer or whatever trade he may have followed. Then, in his near dotage, his shrewish daughter must have said:

"Come on, Father, either you get into your coffin or you dress up and earn a few guilders that way."

We got our petrol, had a beer and pulled out for Amsterdam, only to find our course was leading us towards a great new dyke joining Marken to the mainland. This was not marked on our chart, which must have been a bit out of date. We circled the island, setting all sail, but there was hardly a breath of wind, so after an hour or so we dropped the sails and cranked up the motor.

Dowsabel was a thoroughbred under sail, but under her rather inadequate motor propulsion unit she was decidedly wayward. Our arrival at Amsterdam through the Juliana Lock was rather like a nervous widow trying to cross Horse Guards during the Trooping the Colour. Kit seemed unmoved, even when the Stuart-Turner, which normally behaved well, came to a stop with air bubbles in her fuel line. Ferry boats, liners, tugs and "cellophane sickers" were converging on us from all points. The bubbles were cleared, the engine restarted and after one or two near shaves we turned into the yacht haven, opposite Amsterdam's Central Station. Each yacht was allotted a little pen, divided by mooring posts and lines to the shore. It was a most convenient stopping place for visiting this lovely city (unfortunately the yacht haven no longer exists). As soon as we were moored, the Harbour Master hailed us and I was sent ashore to fill up our particulars both in a book and on a special form. Master's name, crew, tonnage, etc. Later we crossed the Waterway by ferry and walked round the Central Station to the Damrak. We walked for a while along canals, past tall narrow houses. We stopped to listen to a street organ and then turned into a bar and sat drinking and talking. It was a harmonious evening and we returned to the boat for a peaceful night.

I have often noticed on cruising holidays that if one decides to spend a day rubbernecking in a town it will be a perfect sailing day with a force three wind blowing in the right direction. This visit to Amsterdam was no exception. The wind was fair and the sun shone from a cloudless sky from morning to evening. After a belated rising, we had breakfast and I washed a shirt. We went ashore about midday and took a tram to the Rijksmuseum. Following the crowd, we found ourselves in front of Rembrandt's *Night Watch* which drew respectful noises from us all. The first time I saw this painting I thought it looked like an illustration out of the old *Strand Magazine*, but each time I have seen it since I marvel at it the more.

After that we looked at the Vermeers, de Hoochs and Ter

Helena van der Schalcke as a child by Gerhard Ter Borch.
Rijksmuseum
Amsterdam

Borchs. We were brought up all standing in front of the minute painting by Ter Borch of a little girl in a long white frock, wearing a cap and carrying a neat straw handbag over her arm. I saw that its title was *Helena van de Schalcke as a child:* fortunate little Helena to achieve such immortality. We looked at many lovely things. I could have spent a day looking at the Ter Borch alone. After our visit to the Rijksmuseum we went shopping and bought dripping, thinking we were buying butter (confusing "botter" with "room botter"). Well loaded with Geneva and beer we returned to *Dowsabel* and set off in the late afternoon for Ijmuiden. We soon left the factories and warehouses of Amsterdam behind and had a lazy sail through the meadows, past fishermen fishing, cows grazing, boys bathing, ducks flying—and what queer ducks there are in Holland, some as black as black kittens, some like piebald ponies. The wind had dropped and we motored along into the sun's path, helped a little by staysail and mizzen until at last we reached Ijmuiden, tying up alongside a gigantic barge. Kit was already preparing supper: a very excellent steak, well marinated and cooked with garlic and oil, with *haricots verts*, followed by delicious white peaches. After the washing up we went off to find the lock keeper, climbing ashore over three barges. We found a uniformed man who told us the lock we thought we were going through was out of action and hadn't been opened for five years. At last we found another lock keeper who directed us to the middle lock—a vast great basin. He was a tall, thin but jolly fellow.

"If you had stayed in that basin, I think you would have had to wait many years to get into the Noord Zee," he chortled good naturedly at the folly of the Engels.

If anything could have confirmed my belief in sheltered sailing, "creek bashing", or even taking up gardening, the happenings of the following day should have done so. After an early breakfast we locked out into the North Sea. As we put up the sails it was already blowing furiously from the south-west, the weather persistently ignoring the forecasts of fine weather and east winds. So we had a dead "nose-ender" all the way to the Hook. Not content with that, the gods (Thor and Wotan I presume) sent us thunder and lightning. I had suggested dropping the mainsail some half an hour earlier when we were suddenly caught by a fierce squall and laid flat. Sebastian and I under somewhat difficult conditions got the mainsail down. We were thrown about, buffeted up and down and generally made to feel imcompetent as *Dowsabel* crept miserably down that dreary coast. We still had both headsails up and the ship was unbalanced and labouring badly.

138

"Get that jib off her, Sebastian!" Kit shouted, peering shortsightedly through his rain-splashed glasses. Sebastian made no move. He was crouched up against the mizzen mast, for this was the only vantage point for handling the jib sheets. His father for a second time yelled at him more forcibly. White faced, the boy muttered:

"It's no go, I can't, it's not safe!"

"Out of the mouths of babes and sucklings," I privately thought, but Kit was giving more forceful expression to his opinions of this mutinous behaviour, ending up with:

". . . no more than I would have expected!" Then, turning to me, he said:

"Can you get that sail off her?" rather implying, I felt, that he doubted if I could. With ungainly caution I crept along the weather deck, reached the mainmast and clutched it as if it was a long-lost mistress. I freed the halliard, then, holding on to the forestay, dragged the sail down, getting thoroughly soaked in the process. I made a shapeless bundle of it, lashed it to the bitts and made my cautious way back to the comparative safety of the cockpit. The atmosphere remained strained, but there was still plenty of work to be done, for we were tacking back and forth. *Dowsabel* was sailing more easily, but making very slow progress. A small headsail and mizzen is about the most ineffective windward rig there is, even in as weatherly a hull as *Dowsabel* had.

We had the engine to help us, but it made little difference. Apart from the fact that *Dowsabel* had this wretched little variable pitch propeller, the 2-stroke was not powerful enough for a boat of that size. Also, that day, through a faulty petrol line, it stopped no fewer than sixteen times.

At one stage when I was at the helm we were literally submerged in a rain storm, so that in a few moments the two-to-three-mile visibility was reduced to a few yards. The only good thing to be said for the rain was that for a short while it flattened the sea down a bit. Steering under such conditions is difficult. Conditions such as these give one no particular cause for anxiety providing one shortens sail in good time, but they tend to be monotonous.

"Under a fair wind (which is the only wind to sail under), we'd have made this journey, with the tide under us, in four and a half to five hours," I remarked. Kit snorted:

"If you can't enjoy a good thrash to windward, you might as well have a power boat."

"Some thrash," I thought, "it has taken us ten hours and we are not there yet." Back and forth we tacked, with, at times, the engine dimly shoving, and we made our ground inch by inch. There was certainly a fair sea running and probably a Force six to seven wind in our eye. However, at long last (and with nothing to eat since breakfast time) we made the beastly Hook Beacon, and it took another three tacks before we could round it.

At last, with sheets freed, we could sail up the New Waterway. Kit had intended to take the canal south, marked on the chart as coming just after Buoy No. 6. When we got there we found that there was no canal. Our charts were clearly not quite what they ought to have been. First, at Marken, we had a polder when we thought there was sea, and now a canal that no longer existed. So we had to plug on, finally coming to rest at a place hideously and appropriately named Maassluis. This was on the north bank. Just as we were trying to get in there the fuel line took it upon itself to develop yet another blockage. However, the wind was behind us and we blew in. Warning cries from Kit to hang on to this or that barge with a boathook I disregarded, for that boathook was an abomination to end all boathooks. It was a murderous boathook. It had three horrid little shepherd's crooks on its end which became inextricably entangled in anything with which it came in contact. We finally tied ourselves up with our bows to a Shell barge and our stern to some wooden piles. By this time Sebastian and I were quite weak from want of food, for it was about ten o'clock in the evening, but his father said:

"Let's go and have some beer, all that salt's given me the hell of a thirst." Muttered mentions of hunger and supper were swept aside and off we went. To get ashore we had to scramble over the Shell barge, another tanker and a larger steamer. On the gunwale of the steamer I knocked my right kneecap right off (at least it felt as if I had), but by then I was past caring. We had some beers, the wrong brand, and then returned for an even more perilous scramble the other way and for the inevitable stint of potato peeling. I demanded another gin, and no sooner had I got it than I spilt it all over the table. We finished supper at midnight, when the skipper lightly said:

"Well, I will write up the ship's journal and you can do the washing up."

At that the crew struck. We stacked the dishes in the cockpit and retired to bed. Our anchorage was just by a low bridge over which the Hook–Rotterdam electric trains roared every minute just as if we were sleeping under the old El in New York.

After spending the next morning stripping the petrol line and apparently putting it to rights, we left after an early lunch. Our first attempt at getting out of the New Waterway was abortive—we

Dowsabel at Middelharnis. Watercolour sketch.

had gone up a blind alley where they were building an oil refinery. After wasting about an hour on this we found the right one and locked into the Hartel and Voorne canals. Most of the day was spent motoring down these muddy-banked canals through a pleasant flat green countryside, under great wide grey skies. A few Friesian cows, a fisherman or two and once a barge carrying some huge spaceship-like cylinders were all we saw. We had one hectic moment when approaching one of the locks: the variable prop seized and we as near as anything rammed the lock gates. However, by frantic fending off—which drove that aforementioned boat-hook right through my oilies—we avoided danger and passed neatly between the vast concrete supports of the lock and some massive piles with about one inch to spare on each side. The propeller had seized up through overheating. We had had the same trouble in *Far West* when we had rammed Landermere Quay.

After crossing the Haringvliet late in the evening we at last locked into the canal to Middelharnis. The town is about a mile up the canal. The little harbour takes the place of the town square. It is surrounded by houses, some old and pretty, some modern. Again I was struck by the fine dark green paint used by the Dutch for their front doors. These doors outlined in white frames looked very effective. There were only two other boats there, and as we were a bit unsure of the depth alongside the quays we tied up alongside an old Colin Archer yacht. That evening we ate in near darkness, for the battery was dying, then went ashore, climbing over the yacht to which we had made fast. We drank Amstel beer in a curious upstairs beer parlour. After the exertions of the previous day Kit, perhaps fearing mutiny from his reluctant crew, announced that we would spend the day in harbour—on condition we humped the Nife battery to a garage to get it recharged. In the morning we did just this, completed our chores and then we sketched. Middelharnis is a nice little place, and most paintable. It has a pretty grey and white mainstreet with a fine baroque gatehouse at the end of it. Later on in the afternoon we shopped, and had some difficulty in buying candles. I had had even greater difficulty in the morning trying to explain that we wanted the battery charged.

Early the next morning, after collecting the battery, we left Middelharnis. To begin with, with the wind free, it was an easy, fast sail, but by the time we had turned into the Hollandsch Diep it was blowing a very full Force 5 to 6 and we had no time to get our oilies on before we were all soaked. And soaked we remained for the next six hours.

A big, very short sea was running, with waves that seemed to be about a dozen feet in height and with precious little distance between crests. The rain drove down. Visibility had been reduced to barely a hundred yards when out of the murk a huge great tug came bearing down on us. On its mast were three black balls.

"Better bear away and let him pass," Kit said, when Sebastian suddenly shouted out:

"He's towing a barge!"

"Christ!" I shouted, "he's towing three barges!" and so he was, one astern and one on each quarter. "We had better get the hell out of this," Kit said as he put the helm hard down. At that moment, the tug skipper must have seen us, for he let out five furious blasts. For a moment the future looked bleak, for nothing could stop the way of the tug and her three charges, with a full ebb tide and several hundred miles of Rhine water behind them. We either got clear of that lethal spider's web or stood to be run down by the tug or the barges, or to have our decks swept clean by one of the steel hawsers. Another rain squall blinded us, and as *Dowsabel* plunged

The poplar-lined canal leading up to Goes.

forward we heard a further spate of hooting from the tug. Then a massive great lighter loomed up out of the murk, barely twenty yards astern of us.

"I wouldn't want anything nearer than that," Kit said, wiping his spectacles. The tug and barges disappeared into the gloom, and suddenly we were all happily talking together. It had been a humbling and salutary experience.

We finally locked into the canal that leads to Goes and had to wait there for a while until the tide had started to flood so that there was sufficient water for us to enter the canal. The lock was jammed tight with barges, fishing boats and yachts. While we were waiting we changed into dry clothes.

The canal up to Goes was lined with poplar trees. The town itself is pretty, with a very fine church. As a celebration we had supper ashore. We had a very filling if not very exciting meal, not realising that we were nearly next door to De Korenbeurs Hotel, which has one of the best restaurants in Holland.

The next morning we left Goes after breakfast and motored down the canal to the lock, which opened fairly promptly. The sail to Veere was again against headwinds, though we were spared the large seas that we had had in the Hollandsch Diep. It was tack and tack about down the Zandkreek. We could see Veere church and the Raadhuis tower from some distance. Each day I was getting more clumsy and that morning had practically knocked my other

The Grote Kerk, Veere.

kneecap off on the cabin door. At length we arrived at Veere, after some uncomfortable swirling about in the lock, in company with two vast barges. We were all tired and rather dejected and I was aching in every limb—perhaps as a result of the soaking the previous day.

Veere is an attractive place, with old houses with stepped gables and built of very small bricks. The church is a huge building, for long derelict but now in a state of repair, with one end covered in scaffolding. Wandering along by the fish market and the wharf I noticed an empty house where they were proposing to make a museum in memory of dear old Hendrik Willem van Loon, the Dutch-American historian. He had lived in Veere and had always loved the place, naming his house on Long Island Sound after it. In the windows there were notices in both Dutch and English appealing for money. It didn't look as if they had had much success. The yacht basin was to the side of the canal just inside the lock gates.* There were a number of craft there, some quite handsome, including a beautiful varnished clench-built yacht which Kit had seen building in Kampen at the Kroos Brothers' yard. But there were for once no nice traditional Dutch craft. The yacht basin was in a direct line with the Middelburg sewage farm, and when the wind was in the south-west one became well aware of

*It is now in the fishing harbour, as with the closing of the Veersegat the fishing fleet has moved away to Noord-Beveland.

144

Veere and the Raadhuis. The fishing harbour was still tidal.

its nearness. The fish wharf was filled with steel botter-like craft, but rather longer and less graceful than the botters.

We spent an idle day pottering round Veere, taking photographs and listening to Kit's Irish partner (who had joined us for the return passage) trying to rent a house, which he succeeded in doing in spite of speaking no Dutch. He was a man of some perseverance and initiative; in Italy during the war he had escaped after only thirty-six hours in the bag. That morning, using much the same initiative and having travelled over in the night ferry to Zeebrugge, he had come to Veere by means of a lift from an Anglo-Indian doctor and by the Vlissingen ferry, on which he had found two empty buses belonging to a party going on a tour of the war cemeteries. He had climbed into one of these buses. When the ferry reached the other side, he was joined by a crowd of Yorkshire miners. The one who sat next to him said:

"Thou weren't in this seat before, lad."

"Noo," he replied, in an attempt at the broadest Yorkshire, "ah was in t'other bus." After listening to a graphic description of the various war cemeteries, he had been decanted at Middelburg, a mere six kilometres from Veere. From there he had taken a local bus.

It had been blowing hard all day, and in the afternoon we had a look inside the church. It is a magnificent building, dating from the time of the Spanish domination, and stands like a great fortress. When Napoleon's armies were at Veere many of his troops had malaria. He put two floors into the church to house the wretched men. These floors are no longer there, but the great beams and tie-rods are still in position. The Dutch Government are slowly repairing the church, but it will never be restored to its original splendour. It crouches like some vast animal, glowering over the countryside, in marked contrast to the Raadhuis which spikes the sky with its fanciful, bulbous tower, looking like something out of the Kremlin.

In my log book I see the following note: "Kit looks distrait—the glass is falling." That afternoon the Veersegat was a tumble of white caps and on shore the trees were in violent motion. We all began to wonder about the return passage.

Four people (as we now were) in a boat of that size was a crowd, particularly as there was not much room to sit down. The arrangement of the cabin, though ideal for sleeping two at sea, was not ideal in harbour. All one could do was to climb into one's bunk and lie down. The foc's'le had one good built-in berth to port and a root bunk to starboard, which was normally folded up against the ship's side. When down it made the loo unusable.

I awoke once or twice during the night to the drone of the wind in the rigging and the sound of steady rain. By breakfast time the rain had stopped, but the clouds were hurtling across the sky. We had a discussion and decided to postpone our departure, which was just as well as by midday it was blowing Force 8. It continued to blow all the afternoon so, rather sadly, we decided to return by the British Railways night boat. We walked into Veere and found out about the buses and trains to the Hook. Looking at the skipper's passport, I noticed it was two years out of date. He seemed unperturbed. That evening, by bus and train, we travelled right round Zeeland to Hoek van Holland and went aboard the packet boat to Harwich.

In my bunk on the ss *Arnhem*, as we pitched and rolled our way through quite a respectable summer gale, I thought about *Dowsabel*, her skipper and her crew, and how we had moaned and grumbled as he had driven us through 250 miles of Holland, let alone 130 miles of the North Sea, all very much to schedule. *Dowsabel*, in spite of anything I may have said, was a fast, able sailing machine. As for her skipper, when tempers frayed I often had dark mutinous thoughts, likening him to the redoubtable Captain Bligh, though Sebastian and I made a poor *Bounty's* crew. Then I began to ponder again on the difference between being master in one's own boat and crewing in someone else's. Slowly, though much of this may be hindsight, I began to see the other side of the picture. Here was Kit Welford, with a hefty great boat with inadequate motor power for canal work, a somewhat inadequate crew and a tight, in fact far too tight, schedule. For he had to be back at his practice sixteen days after he had left Suffolk. There was after all another side to Bligh's character: the Bligh who brought the loyal members of the *Bounty's* crew in an open ship's boat from the neighbourhood of the island of Tafoa in the South Seas to Dutch Timor, a distance of 1,100 miles.

2

To the Woodbridge River

I returned from *Dowsabel* to weekends in *Cormorant*, either down in Hamford Water or to Butley Creek, Iken Cliffs and Snape. In the autumn of 1958 we moved from our much-loved eighteenth-century house at Manningtree to an old cottage set in water-meadows near Woodbridge, so *Cormorant* had to move her moorings from the Stour to the Deben.

For this last sail out of the Stour Dod Porter came with me, both for old times' sake and because he had been into the Woodbridge River many hundreds of times. It was a day early in October when we left our moorings at Manningtree. The Stour was giving us a kindly farewell. It was all a-glitter, and a great flock of swans came flying past us as we came up on Stutton Ness. It was a bright, cold morning with a nice little southerly wind. Harwich harbour was unusually docile but there was a bit of a swell once we were clear of Landguard Fort. The ten-foot sailing dinghy was towing nicely, on a nylon warp hooked on to a shackle half way down her stem.

Just off Woodbridge Haven, Dod handed me a remarkable-looking brass telescope.

"Made by Dollonds in 1846, used to belong to the Mistley pilot. Over a hundred years old, she is, that'd surprise them to think that's still working. See if you can pick up the bar buoy or the leading marks."

I imagine that on shore, firmly based on a fixed tripod, the Mistley pilot's telescope might have been a useful instrument. Trying to use it aboard *Cormorant* I practically poked my eye out. However, visibility was very good and we soon picked up the bar buoy, or at least what we thought was the bar buoy.

"Do you see those metes yet?" Dod asked in a quavering voice. "Khaki coloured they used to be, just keep them in line."

The wind had fallen light and was heading us, so I started up the engine. I strained my eyes but all I could see was a martello tower, a few houses and a row of beach huts. Then suddenly another black buoy loomed up in front of us. This of course was the bar buoy, the other must have been the Haven buoy.

"Didn't know they had no second buoy," Dod said warily, and held *Cormorant* to her course. The sea was beginning to boil round us. Quite suddenly a great bare shingle bank heaved into sight a few yards off on our port bow. At that moment the engine faltered and died. And still I could see no metes. However, the good south wind came to our rescue, which we certainly needed for we were meeting the ebb out of the river. We kept bravely on, and in a few minutes were in smooth water. The bar was behind us and there, right in front of us when we were only a biscuit's throw from the beach, were the metes. No wonder we had not seen them; they were painted not khaki but white, and sited on the skyline amid a row of white beach huts. A pair of white boards against a white sky, set among white buildings, made one think they had been put there to satisfy the deep-seated wrecking propensities of the locals and not, as was the fact, by a benevolent yacht club.

Though I had been sailing on the east coast for nearly a dozen years, this was the first time I had sailed into the Deben in my own boat. It was a river in marked contrast to the wide silvery Stour, for apart from its lower reaches it was narrower, with a beautifully wooded north bank. It was a much prettier river, I thought, but with a pang at my disloyalty to the beloved Stour. At the entrance to Kirton Creek a heron stood fishing in the shallows and a flock of redshanks, uttering shrill cries, flew across our bows. A little black bird surfaced near us, then quickly dived. A moment later we came on a flock of them. In a panic they flew off.

"Little auks, that's what they are," Dod said. To clear up any doubts about the proper use of aspirates, he spelt out "A-U-K—auk."

The river was rapidly shoaling and we finally grounded just above Kyson Point. We laid the anchor out and rowed up to the quay. The next morning I took *Cormorant* up to her new moorings under the shadow of Sutton Hoo, and there she rested under the care of Frank Knights. That she and I were shortly to part company never crossed my mind.

OPERATION DRY ROT

In November *Cormorant* was laid up. Frank Knights had lifted out her mast, removed her ballast and brought her ashore on a trailer. I had never seen her from below eye level before and she looked rather handsome. My pleasure was somewhat dampened when I climbed aboard and found under the floorboards a fungus as big as a pancake. It was of a grey-purple colour and rubbery in texture.

The timber on which it was growing looked sound enough, so I thought it might be some food fungus. Anyhow, this needed investigation.

The next morning I met Jack Jones in Woodbridge and told him of my fungus. "Food fungus?" His eyebrows shot up and he said sceptically, "might be—let's go and look at it."

He collected his tools and we made for the quay. We climbed aboard and down into the cabin. Jack sniffed and grimaced. He then got down on his hands and knees and put his nose to the offending fungus.

"That's it all right," he muttered.

"That's what?"

"Dry rot, of course. Merulius lacrymans to give it its proper name."

"What's to do?" I asked disconsolately.

"Go to Boots, buy a couple of pounds of Sodium Fluoride, mix it up—a pound to a bucket of water—and watch out, because it is very poisonous—then paint every bit of the bilge with it. Burn off the bottom of the floorboards and I will come back on Saturday and give her a proper inspection." I followed his instructions and on the Saturday watched him do his inspection. It was thorough and very depressing. He sniffed and poked and prodded at every bit of the boat's surface and his inspection revealed a lot. Every floor forward of the engine bed had to be removed.

"Funny thing," Jack remarked, "you never get this kind of trouble round engines—but she shouldn't have had elm floors; if cheapness was the object, far better to have used deal."

Both bunks had to come out in order to remove the floors.

"I should scrap that water tank, while you are about it," Jack continued, "they are always a source of this sort of trouble." He continued his survey. "There's rot in this bulkhead. That will have to go. Planking is all right, as far as I can see. The hog seems all right, and so does the deck and the carlines, but that laminated beam looks a bit rocky."

And so the tale of destruction continued. Outside on deck things were none too good either. The canvas had rotted in several places and the plywood deck beneath showed signs of delamination.

"Strip off all that deck canvas. Leave the coach roof, that looks all right. Then we will get a coat of epoxy resin paint on the deck, after Frank Knights has made good any bad spots."

We climbed down on to the quay.

"While we are about it," I said, "what about those planks?" I pointed out three of the port side strakes that looked rather

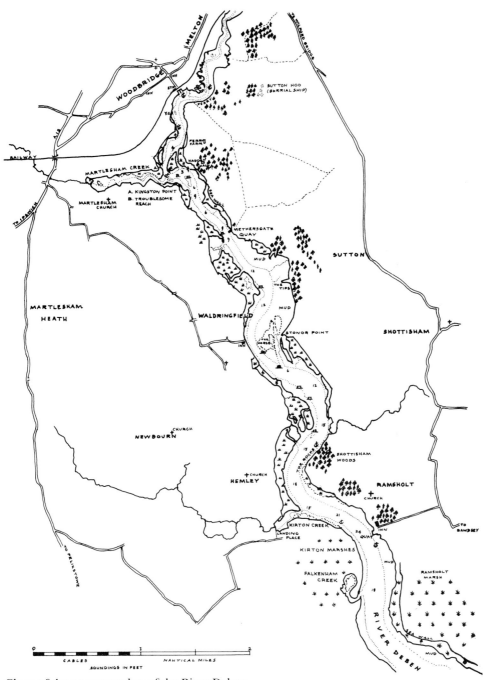

Chart of the upper reaches of the River Deben.

motheaten along the lands. Jack prodded these with his spike.

"Sapwood," he said laconically. "Let's have them out."

We were standing under her stern. Jack looked at it and said:

"Kenneth Gibbs has given her a pretty stern, as pretty a Colin Archer stern as I have ever seen." He peered at the propeller. "Have you any electrics on board?" I shook my head. "Well, there is a sign of electrical discharge on the prop," and he pointed out various discoloured patches. "Probably got the earth connected up to the positive instead of negative terminals."

I must have been looking very depressed, with visions of my boat reduced to a pile of matchwood, because he said:

"Oh, it might have been worse. I will have a look at that deck when Frank has got the canvas off it. But he had better start on those floors one at a time so that she doesn't go out of shape."

The work proceeded through the winter. The deck wasn't too bad, the delaminated areas of ply were cut out and pieces of mahogany were scarfed into place. The new floors were in position, the sapwood planks had been replaced, and all seemed to be going well until the fore bulkhead was being put in, when they found that the beam to which it was fastened, a laminated beam, was rotten in its top lamination, which was of British Columbia pine. Now *all* the beams in *Cormorant* were laminated; further inspection showed they were made up of a variety of woods, including British Columbia pine and various African mahoganies, which are all subject to dry rot. Philip, the boatbuilder who had been working on all this reconstruction, said:

"Forgive me for speaking up, but if I was you, I'd sell her!" I must have looked a bit shattered, for he continued: "That's not to say she isn't a nice design, she's a very nice little boat, but this rot has got right into her structure. You can never be sure when it won't break out."

My first reaction was "What, sell my *Cormorant*, after all this trouble—never!" I went home heavy-hearted and thought it all over. The moment of truth came when I began to wonder if another boat might not be more suitable for "going foreign"—a boat that would do both for creek bashing and for North Sea crossings. I suppose that settled *Cormorant's* fate.

The repairs to *Cormorant* were completed and she was sold with a full surveyor's report for about half what she would have fetched without this pedigree of trouble. I believe that under her new owner she travelled through the canals to the Mediterranean and back, but after that I lost trace of her. Maybe we had cured her rot; I hope so. It was a salutary and expensive experience.

3

The building of
Patient Griselda

Cormorant was sold in March, 1959, and I started immediately to plan the new boat. It was a delirious experience, as is the beginning of any design project. It is only when one's ideas are being translated into reality by either boatbuilder or house builder, or even printer, that there comes the rub.

My ideas about this boat were fairly fluid, but there were certain conditioning factors. I was well aware that a boat at least of *Dowsabel's* size (of about thirty-two foot overall) was a better proposition for North Sea work than anything of *Cormorant's* size (twenty-four foot overall). I was also equally aware that I could not afford either to build or maintain anything of that size, so I planned a heavier replacement of much the same size as *Cormorant*, approximately twenty-four foot overall by eight foot six inches maximum beam and a shallow draft of, say, one metre—which was just a foot deeper than the old boat. Having had three boats with pointed sterns, I thought I would like a broad transom, so I did a little drawing. The hull, broadside on, was a bit like one of Laurent Giles's *Vertues*, and I gave it a sweeping sheer. I had had enough of built-up topsides, with *Cormorant* in her original form. This time I wanted wide side decks and a foredeck with plenty of room, so the coach roof was to stop short of the mast.

Then I started to think about coach roofs and deck houses. It seemed to me that in modern boats, particularly small boats, beautiful hulls were often marred by intolerable superstructures; usually the result of putting quarts into pint pots and accepting a demand for standing headroom practically the whole length of the boat. If I could get standing headroom under the hatchway and in front of the galley I would be content. So the maximum height of the cabin had to be aft.

I drew out various versions, but the answer didn't come to me until I was next in Holland. It was as a result of looking at a nice little Dutch scow built on traditional lines that I found my solution. This had a cabin, with a roof line that swooped up aft in a hollow curve but in section was like a baroque pediment. The Dutch had been using this form of cabin on boeiers and Friesjachts and even Royal Yachts for the last three hundred years. It seemed to have stood the test of time all right. Its profile blended beautifully with the sheer I had planned. The ogee curves of the section gave maximum height in the middle of the cabin, yet brought the sides down to an acceptable height. I did another drawing of the hull, put the cabin on and added a well-raked mast. Then I looked at it again and thought about the rig. I wanted a lowering mast, so that put Bermudan out of court. The idea of working under bridges with about forty foot of mast poking out over the stern didn't appeal to me. The English gaff rig to be effective needed a topsail and a lot more string than I wanted. I was about to decide on a gunter like the one on *Cormorant*, yet I was not in love with the idea of a seventeen-foot yard flailing about up there. I looked at the little sketch again, and I looked at her Dutch cabin; I drew a curved gaff and of course it looked right.

The age-old Dutch rig, used on all their flat-bottomed boats, a very short curved gaff with a loosefooted sail on a tall pointed mast and a large overlapping headsail, matched the cabin perfectly. Well, it looked all right, but that was not to say it would work. The statement that "the boat that *looks* right *is* right" is at best only a half truth and certainly does not apply to boats intended to win races. But as this boat of mine was intended for anything but racing I did not worry too much, but I could find no precedent for any conventionally hulled yacht using such a rig. The nearest modern boats using such a rig were Tholen scows and A. F. Gunning's hard-chine steel yachts. At that time I had seen neither. Having got this far, I went off to see Jack Jones. I thought that as an architect of some severely modern reverse-sheer yachts he might laugh me to scorn, but I remembered that he had designed some yachts on traditional lines, including Philip Allen's very fine Whisstock-built twenty-six-ton cutter *Corista*, which had a topmast that housed and a bowsprit like a Bristol Channel pilot cutter.

I handed Jack my sketches. He was kind enough not to laugh at them. He took them as they were and very shortly produced a preliminary profile of the boat. As she ultimately developed, she was largely my conception above the waterline and Jack's below— and of course he did all the difficult part, from drawing the lines and setting out the table of offsets to the detailed construction specifications, drawings and sail plans. At the very beginning he

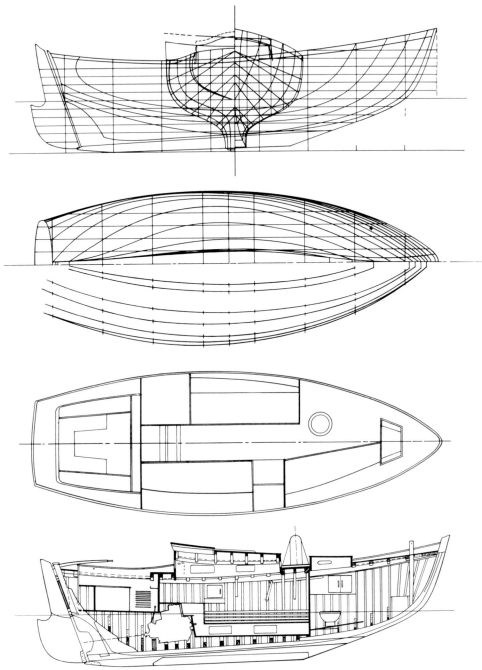

Lines and construction plans for *Patient Griselda*.

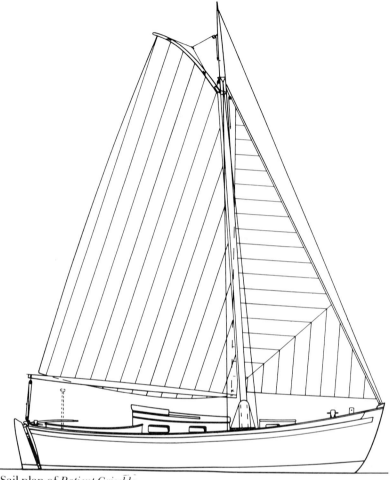

Sail plan of *Patient Griselda*.

came up with a clever idea for the shape of the keel. I wanted a draft of only one metre and I wanted most of the ballast outside the boat. To achieve this end, he suggested an eighteen-inch-wide iron keel, weighing something over 2,000 lb. This wide lump of iron was faired off at the stem into a wedge shape, tapering off up to the waterline, to give not too blunt an entry. We had already been down to the quay at Waldringfield to look at a similar keel arrangement on a boat that he had designed some nine years earlier. The owner of this boat had told me it seemed to make her very close-winded.

The planning discussions continued off and on for some weeks.

As the new boat was to be a heavier, sturdier version of my last boat, she would have to be carvel planked. The obvious difference between carvel and clinker (or clench) building is that with carvel the boat's planks abut one another, edge to edge, presenting a smooth topside, whereas with clinker building the planks overlap, giving a ridged surface. The most fundamental difference in the actual building is that for carvel building the timber framing is set up first and held in position with ribbands; the planking is then fastened to the timbers. In clinker building the boat is completely planked before the (much lighter) timbers are put in. Finally, in carvel building the seams between each plank have to be sealed either by the age-old method of caulking or with thin splines of wood which are glued into position.

At length the designs were sufficiently far advanced for us to go and find a builder. We decided on a small yard, thinking that with fewer overheads it might be cheaper for a one-off design. Jack Jones suggested we might visit a yard at Wivenhoe in Essex that was building a boat for him at that time. This was the Colne Marine and Yacht Company Limited, a small firm used to building largish yachts. The firm was run by Guy Harding and his wife Joan, and the bulk of the building was done by a family of shipwrights called Kerridge, helped by four other chaps answering to the names of Fred, Stan, Bob and Taff.

Wivenhoe lies on the north bank of the River Colne a few miles below Colchester. It has an intriguing waterfront, which is a jumble of eighteenth-century cottages and warehouses, with the square, squat tower of the church rising up behind. We found Guy Harding, a fair-haired, blue-eyed man wearing a naval duffle coat and gumboots, looking rather doubtfully, I thought, at the stern of a large motor yacht.

"What's the matter?" Jack Jones asked him, after he had introduced me.

"Plenty; your chum, the owner of this boat, has just been on the telephone. He has decided to put in a couple of engines about twice the size of the ones the boat was designed for. We shall have to take off the whole of the cabin trunk to get them in. Yachtsmen!"

Jack was reduced to silence. Having got that off his chest, Guy Harding took us into his office, which was at the top of a rickety stairway above his spar-making shed. He cleared a lot of iron-mongery off two chairs and invited us to sit down.

"Well, gentlemen, what can I do for you?" Jack spread out his preliminary designs for my boat and said:

"I wondered if you would like to build this little boat for John

157

Lewis?" Guy Harding looked at the sketches for a moment.

"I like her sheer—twenty-four foot six by eight foot nine; good beamy little old boat. What's she draw?" He peered at some figures on the drawing, but before he could decipher them Jack cut in with:

"Three foot three—one metre—that's all."

"Centreboard?" Guy Harding asked.

"No, fixed keel and a pretty thick one—about eighteen inches wide amidships with about 2,000 lb iron on it."

"Phew, you're going to need a pretty hefty backbone to carry that."

"Well, why not? She is planned to be a fairly rugged little craft, intended not only for the east coast rivers but also for knocking about in Dutch estuaries, canals and locks."

"I should think knocking about is the operative word for those locks," Guy Harding replied, then, stretching across the desk, he pulled a curtain back from his window and pointed to a large white yacht that lay at a mooring on the other side of the river.

"See that boat over there? We've got to do some major repairs on her, got squeezed between a couple of 500-ton barges in a lock at Flushing."

I felt it was about time I said something.

"What I really want is something more like a workboat than a yacht, with a thick rubbing strake round her and practically no bright work outside, except perhaps her bulwark rails—and I want real bulwarks against which one can brace a boot without fear of slipping overboard. And as far as the inside goes, all I want done is for the engine (the 8 hp Stuart Turner from my old boat) to be installed and the bunks, the galley, the wc and a coal stove to be built in."

"A coal stove," Guy Harding laughed, "now you're talking, boy. Winter sailing, ice on the water and icicles in your eyebrows—and ducks so tame you can pick them off the water. Yes, I reckon we'd very much like to build your little boat. I take it you don't want us to finish off the inside because of er . . . cost?" he ended delicately.

"Precisely," I answered, "I haven't got a fat lot to spend on her and what I do spend, I want to go into the structure of the boat."

"How right you are. That bloody boat you saw when you came in, the cost of the cabin joinery is about twice the cost of the hull; what with refrigerators, drawers, patent folding tables, glass racks and plate racks and dress hangers and trouser hangers and inlaid panelling, concealed lighting and Lord knows what else, including leather upholstery—it's more like an apartment in the Albany than a boat's cabin. Not that we can't do that sort of work, but what a waste of a boatbuilder's time."

We talked about timber. Jack took up the discussion with:

"Pitch pine planking on Canadian rock elm timbers, oak stem and stern posts and oak floors, and I should think for that wide keel a lump of elm. Decks: marine ply, painted."

"That sounds all right," Guy Harding answered, "providing we can get a good big grown crook for that stem post. Pitch pine, are you sure you wouldn't prefer iroko? You will never hide your seams with pitch pine. It's always on the move."

"No, it's pitch pine I want," I said, "I gather that's a wood that is unlikely to rot—and that is something I feel rather deeply about."

"You're right there," Guy Harding answered, "and I have got a beautiful log which will just about plank up your boat and long enough so you should have practically no butts."

"When could you start on her?" I asked.

"As soon as we can get that thing out of my shed. About six weeks' time, I should think, and let's see, it's December now—oh, she should be ready by the summer, yes easily." I remembered those prophetic words later. Within a couple of weeks a contract had been drawn up for the boat, including hull and spars, bunks and bare cabin fittings, etc., to be built for quite a modest price. Then I started to compile lists—a most satisfying occupation. I often do this for jobs that have to be done. Once one has completed such a list, it's almost as if the actual jobs were done! My first list was headed "Try floggers for . . ." and consisted of:

Water tanks.
Water cans.
Petrol cans.
Nife battery.
Galvanised bins (for chain locker and coal).
Stainless steel sheet (for galley).
Aeroplane tyres (for fenders).
Fire extinguishers.
Navigation lights.
Boathook.
Anchors 25 lb CQR and 20 lb fisherman.
Shock cord (for tiller lines, etc.).
Tin opener.
Rope (coir for kedge warps, Italian hemp for halliards, cotton for sheets).

Then I made another list which I headed "Fittings":

159

wc 2nd hand (*unused* ex-wd would be nicer).
Cooking stove 2-burner Swedish primus or Taylor paraffin ? gimballed.
Stainless steel operating-theatre bowl for galley.
3 Dunlopillo mattresses? rexine covered.
Cabin coal stove.
Tray and chimney for same.
Anchor chain 24 fathoms 5/16th. Hawse pipe.
Pump. Whale?
Bailer, broom and mop.
Lifebelts, boom crutch, ring bolts, wooden cleats (? make these).

Then, as the Boat Show was just about to open, I made another list of things to look at:

Galley layouts and lockers.
Sideboards and bunk lockers.
Clothes lockers.
Cabin flooring (treatment).
Light fittings.
Mattress coverings.
Halliard winches.
Sheet leads.
Cabin steps.
Cockpit flooring.
Position of cleats for sheets.
Cockpit lockers.
Opening and fixed portlights.

I then went to the Boat Show. There was not a single boat there that bore any resemblance to my conception of what I wanted in a boat, so I just went and drank a lot of Guinness and ate too many potted shrimps and forgot all about my lists.

By the beginning of February I thought something ought to be happening, so I drove over to Wivenhoe. Guy Harding told me that Jack Jones had promised him the lines and table of offsets that very week. To keep me happy, he took me down to the shed to see my pitch pine, which had come from Honduras or Nicaragua. The planks were in 28 ft lengths and looked to be flawless. He had also got an ex/wd *unused* wc for me, which we dutifully admired. When I got home, I rang up Jack Jones. One of his draftsmen answered the telephone.

"He is working on your lines, hoping to finish them tonight." On the strength of that I sent Guy Harding a cheque for the first instalment. Another three weeks passed before Harding rang up to tell me the lines were on the loft floor.

"She's very beamy and she's got a terrific sheer—but she's going to be all right. She's full of character and it's no good doing things by halves."

On seeing the lines on the floor, I felt that she was smaller than I had visualised; the chalk lines on the black floor looked to me less like a boat than the lines on a plan.

Jack Jones seemed satisfied with the lines, though she seemed to have grown by an inch in length. There was some pondering on her fullness aft. Guy Harding interposed:

"Well, we've just built two ships both down by the stern—it will be nice to have one down by the nose!"

It was not until the beginning of April that the big motor yacht was launched.

"I wouldn't have spent all that money on that thing," Guy Harding said to me when I got down to his yard. "She's as noisy as a cement mixer."

I thought, "I hope he will have a better opinion of my boat by the time she is launched." The mould for the keel had been made and a vast grown oak crook had arrived, but it had been cut the wrong way by the over-helpful timber people so that there was either not enough width at the top, which had to be fourteen inches wide inboard, or not enough length at the bottom. So they had to try to find another crook. Looking at this massive piece of timber, it struck me as being of a fantastic size for a little boat like mine.

By mid-April the sail plans were complete and I went down to West Mersea to see Paddy Hare at Gowen's to discuss sails. We talked about "tanned" terylene or 9 oz. Egyptian cotton and decided on the latter, to be cutch-tanned. We also planned a little storm jib. While we were talking tea was brought in and we were joined by Kim Holman, one of the most successful designers of offshore racers in this country.

We studied the plans of my boat again.

"She's got a lot of character," Holman said, "but I wonder why Jack Jones has married a dreadnought stem on to a tubby little Dutch hull. But I expect she will work all right."

"Probably my fault," I answered.

We talked on, one thing leading to another, and someone mentioned her colour, which at this stage was to be black.

"What is she planked in?" Kim Holman asked.

"Pitch pine."

"In that case, I certainly wouldn't paint her black. I had a boat that was pitch pine planked and we had to run a blow lamp over her before any paint would hold on her—she was so resinous. I think grey would suit her. Black is bound to draw the heat. You will have endless trouble with your seams."

As I drove away from Gowen's sail loft I looked across the Blackwater. Several tankers were at anchor below the Bench Head, and across on the Bradwell shore the atomic power station brooded balefully over a zircon green sea looking, in the haze, rather like the great church at Veere, seen from the entrance to the Zandkreek.

The next few weeks we were abroad, and it was not until halfway through May that I got down to Wivenhoe again. In the middle of the boatbuilding shed, where my boat should have been almost completed, lay two oak crooks, one partially fashioned, and the mould for the keel.

A very dejected Guy Harding joined me. We both stood silent and sorrowful and then he told me the full tale of woe, which hung on this massive stem that my boat was supposed to have. The first grown crook, as I have related, had been cut wrong. After much trouble they had found another which had looked a fine piece of timber. After several days' work with adze and saw, old Bert Kerridge had stumped up to Harding's office and announced that it wouldn't do.

"What do you mean, it won't do?" Guy had asked him.

"Rotten, that's what she is, plumb rotten, right in the centre. Sapwood!" Harding concluded:

The building of *Patient Griselda*.

"A bow fit to crush Polar Ice".　　　The moulds in position.　　　Fitting transom to deadwood.

"And there she lies, alongside the other crook, filling up the shed and doing no good."

"What on earth are you going to do, then?" I asked rather peevishly.

"I've been on to the timber people, they haven't got another crook of anything like this size. Bert reckons we could use the first one if we scarf a piece into the top."

After some more delay, that is just what they had to do. So, at long last, at the beginning of June, about when our boat should have been launched, the wooden keel was laid and her stem and stern posts set up. When a boat is built, templates (moulds, they call them) have to be made at various points of her cross section. These are set up on the keel and held in position by braces fastened to a beam set maybe six feet above the intended deck level of the boat. At last, with moulds and ribbands in position, I could get a three-dimensional idea of what the hull was going to look like. My boat looked, I must admit, a rather curious shape. I began to have nervous doubts about not only her looks, but whether she would sail at all! This nervous state was to recur again and again until the boat was finally launched. I imagine this to be a fairly normal condition for anyone building a boat.

At the end of June I joined *Dowsabel* for my second trip through Holland. Apart from visiting Terschelling and Vlieland, two of the Dutch Friesian Islands, and being stormbound for three days in Vlieland's tiny harbour, with only a few stone barges for company, the cruise repeated in all essentials the previous one.

The only notable thing happening on this cruise was a damaged propeller. At 5 am on a drizzling misty morning, as we were passing through a large bridge just to the north of Haarlem, the engine stopped with a shuddering jolt. A cousin of Kit Welford's bravely went over the side and came up reporting a badly bent blade. After much discussion, I was put ashore and set off to get help from a shipyard at a place called West-Graftdijk that we had passed the previous evening. It was raining hard by the time I reached the yard. The manager, a bright-faced, bespectacled, fair-haired young man, introduced himself as Van de Beldt. He had very short legs and very baggy trousers. I told him our troubles and in no time he had roused out from an old barge a very little, very old man. Van de Beldt turned to me and said:

"This man has a tug. He will bring your boat here for five florins."

The tugboat turned out to be a shabby little launch powered by a huge Perkins diesel.

Dowsabel in the harbour at Vlieland.

In driving rain we chugged down the canal, collected *Dowsabel* and in a relatively short time had towed her to the yard at West-Graftdijk. We spent a lot of time pulling and hauling and helping to fix slings. At last her stern was out of the water and there was the badly bent propeller. Van de Beldt took it off, heated it, bent it and banged it about, then, after lovingly repolishing it, put it back on again. As soon as it was done we were off again. We had not gone far when there was another loud bang and the engine stalled. This time we blew back to the yard under a jib. The same operation of fitting slings took place, but at double quick time, for it was near the end of their long working day. Up came *Dowsabel's* stern, and there was the propeller, just as badly bent. Van der Belt scratched his chin, gave the propeller a little tug and the whole shaft slid outboard.

"So that is it," he muttered. He rushed off to his workbench and came back with a box full of assorted grub screws. "Soon fix her," and with a couple of hearty welts from a hammer he banged the blade straight, replaced the missing screw and we were off again, but not before Dutch gin had been handed all round.

Our troubles were not yet over. The next morning as we were passing through Haarlem, once again there was the familiar bang under the counter. This time the engine kept going, but with a nasty juddering vibration. We finally anchored for the night by the Rotterdam motorway bridge at Sassenheim, which only opens between 6 and 7 am. The next morning we limped through and a couple of kilometres below the bridge we came to Van Lent's immaculate boatyard on the Kaagermeer. Within an hour *Dowsabel* was slipped, revealing a propeller with only one blade and a missing stern gland. By mid-afternoon this immensely efficient yard had had a new propeller made for us in Amsterdam, had collected it and fitted it. While we were waiting for the propeller I wandered off by myself to look at the various boats moored alongside Van Lent's yard. As well as some handsome great motor cruisers there were one or two traditional craft. Looking at a little steel scow, I was struck by its graceful lines and by how the hollow curves of its coach roof blended so well with its sheer. There was no concession to streamlining or any other mid-twentieth-century fad. The windows were firmly rectangular, except for a slight rounded arch at the top, with fitted slides for bad weather. It was a little boat full of curves; even the towing bollards were made of curved crooks, backed with a sheet of brass. I made a little drawing of one of those bollards. It seemed it might serve as a model for those on my own boat. I also did some drawings of the tapering mast, and the curved gaff. The way the mainsail on traditional Dutch flat-bottomed boats is fastened to the gaff is of some interest, for the gaff has a flange to which a flat seam in the head of the sail is laced. All this was to come in useful later on.

We made our return passage from Veere, sailing out into the Roompot through the fast-closing Veersegat. The dykes were built and only two caissons remained to be put in position. Passing through this narrow entrance was like going up a weir, for the level of the sea outside seemed to be at least three feet higher than the level in the estuary. The next time I was to come to Veere the dyke was closed and the Veersegat had become a tideless lake.

I owe much to *Dowsabel* and her owner for introducing me to cruising abroad. I had learnt some important facts not only about cruising on the canals and estuaries of Holland but also about crewing. I had also learnt something about the differences between a boat used for estuary cruising and one equipped for "going foreign."

A couple of weeks later, and back from Holland, I went over to Wivenhoe. To my surprise, another boat was building alongside mine and was nearly as far advanced. It was an attractive little racing sloop. However, my boat had progressed. She was completely framed, with extra frames in the way of the mast, and planked up to the first six planks. Her shape was slowly revealing itself, and was better than I had thought it might be. I had a lengthy discussion with Guy Harding about various details and decided that the sheer strake (which is a rubbing plank to take any wear and tear on the topsides) should be of ⅝ inch pitch pine, which proved in fact to be too thin; for a sheer strake to be any use it should stick out proud of everything, including the capping of the bulwark rail. The bulwark rail we planned to be half an inch clear of the deck for its full length, to allow any water that came aboard to run away. It was to be supported by webbed angle brackets. Finally we talked about paint and colour schemes, and I decided for my topsides on that very dark green I had first seen at Middelharnis and that the Dutch so often use for their front doors and shutters. The rest of the colours were a dusty yellow ochre for the coachroof top, forehatch cover and insides of the bulwarks, white for coachroof sides and cockpit, and red ochre for the decks, this to be the non-slip deck paint the east coast trawlers use for their decks.

We climbed inside the skeletal boat and started talking about stringers; we decided on one wide one at the turn of the bilge in place of the two small ones on the plans, in case I ever wanted to fit bilge keels. While we were about it we also decided to increase the depth of the shelf, on which the deck sits, from 4 in. to 5 in.

"She's going to be quite a roomy little boat," Guy said as he climbed down the ladder, "I wonder how she'll sail. With that heavy keel I shouldn't wonder but she'll sit up on that! You want to be careful if she ever dries out that she doesn't sit for a while, then come crashing down on her bilges." He broke off for a moment and then said:

"By the way, will you collect the drawings for the gudgeons and pintles and all that for the rudder? We shall need those bronze castings before too long."

Jack sent me the drawings for the castings by the end of the week and I took them to an engineering works in Ipswich to have the castings made. When they were completed they were most elegant bits of bronze, looking like small pieces of modern sculpture.

Week by week I continued to visit Wivenhoe. Progress seemed very slow. By mid-August she was planked up and I found old Bert

Patient Griselda nearing completion. The Raymond Wall-designed
Tomahawk lies between her and the sea.

Kerridge whittling away at some oak floors. So far he had fitted
about eight, but they were not to be fastened until the ballast keel
was in position. I began to get depressed again, for I found the
slowness of the work very dispiriting. I even began to wonder why
on earth I had ever had the temerity to build yet another boat. And
then I had had a brusque exchange of letters with the yard about
costs, ending up with my saying to Guy Harding:

"I told you what I could pay for this boat, and that's all I can
pay."

"Who is asking you to pay any more?" he replied somewhat
hotly, "all I am telling you is that it is costing me more!" and for the
time being we left it at that.

Then, with a jaundiced eye, I began to look around me. The

yard was typical of so much of the present-day English scene. But at least here was good workmanship, even if done in slovenly surroundings. Apart from the junk that lay about, the things that offended me most were the permanent collection of old and dirty crocks sitting in a washbowl, apparently awaiting the day of judgement to be washed up—this in the shed where my beautiful boat was being built! I walked out on to the quay. It was raining, the tide was out and the piled mud along the quayside looked most offensive. A day's work with a dredger would clear the lot. Then I looked at the yard-boat which was awash with bilge water and had not had a coat of paint in many years. In contrast I thought of Van Lent's yard in the Kaagermeer, as immaculate as a West End car showroom—but after that I thought of the yard at West-Graft-dijk, and that was certainly no ladies' boudoir. One thought led to another and I remembered Hilaire Belloc's comparison of French and English gun batteries:

"In the ideas of the English service, a French field battery is extremely slack. The harness is dull, often old and pieced together, sometimes shamefully tied up with string. The uniforms are not over clean. There is nothing too smart about the pieces themselves, even when they are prepared for a review. The conclusion is immediately arrived at that these foreigners ought not to have guns at all, seeing they do not know how to treat them . . .

"The smartness of the English batteries I have always heard vastly admired by the French gunners, *but never in connection with gunnery* . . . [rather as] something having no relation whatsoever to the function of a gun and its gunners, which is to deliver projectiles accurately and rapidly rather than to look pretty."

Reason returned to me. What the devil did dirty dishes, a muddy quayside or a half-drowned yard-boat matter, if I was getting such quality of workmanship. I wandered back into the yard past the pretty little racing sloop and up to my boat. I put my hand on her warm pitch pine planks and looked at her massive stem. She was beautifully planked. Pride of possession swept over me. I began to love her.

By the end of August the deck beams and carlines were in position. I found Fred and the other lad lying on their backs, drilling up for the keel bolts—an unenviable job. I climbed aboard and was at last able to assess what room there would be under the side and fore decks. I had a bit of a scramble to get through to the foc's'le, for there was not much headroom forward of the coach roof. The mast sits on deck in a tabernacle and its thrust is taken by two galvanised steel supports, set athwartships about 27 in. apart.

While I was sitting ruminating in the foc's'le Guy Harding's head appeared in the companionway.

"How do you feel about knees?" he asked, somewhat inconsequentially. Thinking of the various pin-ups around the shed, I answered:

"Much the same as most chaps, I suppose, but why stop there?"

"Tut, tut!" he replied, blushing like a schoolgirl, "you know what I mean, hanging knees and lodging knees, and I don't mean Lodger's knees!" So we relapsed into technicalities and decided that before putting the deck on he would fit two large hanging knees and three lodging knees a side to stiffen up the side decks.

"What do you want for caulking?" Fred shouted from underneath the boat. Guy and I stepped down to the floor and looked at the topsides. She was completely planked up on the port side and needed only the sheer plank on the starboard side.

"What do you think?" After a bit of a discussion, old Bert Kerridge wandered over holding something that looked like dressing gown cord.

"Cotton will do all right for the topsides, but I reckon you ought to have oakum for the keel and garboards." That settled it, the oracle had spoken; soon Bob and Fred were hammering away at the seams. I seem to remember old Slocum, when he was rebuilding the *Spray* at Fairhaven, having a lot of advice on caulking, particularly on the nature of cotton and its tendency to "crawl". So, to placate the critics, he had put a thread of oakum on top of the cotton and it never "crawled"—nor did our cotton.

October came, the sailing season was nearly over and our hanging knees had been fitted. These solid looking, if not very elegant, supports were cut from two sheets of ⅝ inch ply, glued together and edge-faced with rock elm.

"A nice grown crook with a pretty grain to it looks nicer," Guy Harding had said, "but these are immeasurably stronger. It was a method we used when building MTBs in the war. Now you're here we ought to talk about your spars."

"Surely," I said, "but aren't the spar plans enough guidance?"

"The mast and boom should be all right, but I am damned if I see how you make that little curved gaff. And old Bert doesn't know, and if he doesn't know, I don't reckon anyone round here would have a clue either."

"I have a friend who has had one of those M. V. Gunning's steel hard-chine boats built in a small yard in Holland, a place called Langeraar. I could drop the yard a line and ask them if they would make one and how much it would cost."

"Yes, you do that," Guy replied, "and to save a bit of money, I think for your mast we may be able to salvage one of the spars from the old *Cap Pilar*. Nice to think your mast had been blowing down the roaring forties, even if then it was only a mizzen spanker boom or a topgallant yard." Romance was in the air. *Cap Pilar*, a three-masted Breton barquentine which Adrian Seligman had sailed round the world in the late nineteen-thirties, had been lying for some years in the River Colne slowly rotting away. She was now at last being broken up. We walked up to the deserted Wivenhoe Shipyard and examined a great pile of spars. It did not take us very long to realise that they were fit only for firewood, or at best for use as flagpoles. As we walked back to Harding's yard we decided we should make a solid spar (to save money against the cost of a hollow one) which would be made up of three pieces of Baltic pine.

That evening I wrote off to Valentijn en Zonen, the yard at Langeraar, asking them if they could make my gaff, and for how much. Three days later I had a telegram from Valentijn saying that they could make it for "seventy-five guilders off the yard". It would be delivered to Harwich. A couple of weeks later I collected it, after paying the freight and a very modest duty to the Customs. It was a rugged little spar with a curious cross section.

With it came instructions for making and fastening the head of the sail, which was, like that on the Kaagermeer scow that I had examined, to have no headrope but a double flat seam, like the hem of a pillowcase, pierced with eyelets. This seam was to rest against the flange on the underside of the gaff, which was drilled with holes at about six-inch intervals to match the eyelets.

I drove over to West Mersea and handed the spar to Gowen's. Paddy Hare pored over Valentijn's diagram, finally saying:

"Well, this shows that we don't know everything. Let's hope it will work."

I began to notice the repeating pattern of these pious aspirations about my various innovations, and once again I began to wonder. Anyhow, it was too late to back out now.

Over the next few weeks the building appeared to speed up. We tried a mock-up in thin ply of the cabin trunk, and increased the height from the plans one inch forward and half an inch aft. As soon as the cabin sides had been cut out of a fine clean-grained plank of iroko I drew in the windows in chalk, slightly squarer and placed further forward than on the plan, because as I like to have my cabin trunk sitting on the deck, the trunk had become the width of the carlines wider and longer than originally drawn. This method of fixing a coachroof, though rather more work than the usual English method, is completely rigid and watertight; it is American in origin. The cabin roof beams were soon in position, and in spite of a certain amount of head shaking over the difficulties of planking a double curve they found that the narrow cedar planks fell absolutely true. The whole job was done in an hour and a half. I somehow felt the Dutch, a romantic but practical race, would not have hung on to such a shape for so long if it had been all that difficult to build. The little cabin trunk looked absolutely right, as if it had grown out of the boat. Guy Harding's chaps now seemed to have the bit between their teeth, and we were hard pressed to keep up with them. We made mock-ups in ply and thin splines of wood of the bunks, sideboard and galley. We measured and produced a fair curve with a spline for the cockpit coaming, and worked out the exact size of the cockpit benches and the general layout of the cockpit. The bridge deck was made to overlap the cockpit bulkhead by a good six inches so that the compass could sit under cover. After a lot of sliding it up and down the apron, we stuck the wc in the foc's'le just forward of the port side bulkhead, at the head of the bunk.

The forehatch was framed up; it was only then that it suddenly dawned on us that when lowering the mast the front would come hard up against the afterside of the hatch. After a bit of head scratching, one of the chaps said:

"Why not cut an opening in the after hatch coaming and have a little slide. You could take this out for ventilation." And this is what we did. The reason for all this *ad hoc* juggling with such details was that my arrangement with Jack Jones had been limited to his drawing the lines, the table of offsets and the main construction plan. The rest was over to me—and we found it easier to plan the thing on the spot than to do elaborate drawings and then, through inexperience, find they didn't work. By early October the work on the hull was nearing completion. One afternoon I found the chaps fitting the bulwark rail and was struck by a "turned-up toes" look about it. Thinking of *Dowsabel's* serpentine coble sheer, which tends to drop away forward, I spent about half an hour adjusting a long spline along the top edge of the rail. Bob finally trimmed about three quarters of an inch off it at the forward end, and it looked far better.

The work on the cabin was proceeding, with the floorboards set hard down on the top of the floors so that they were two inches higher forward, but giving us maximum headroom and standing headroom aft. Guy Harding and I humped the coal stove aboard and offered it up in the position I had planned in the foc's'le. It obviously would not do, because there was not enough floorspace, so Guy suggested putting it in the cabin. As the port side bunk had been built we shoved it on the starboard side just aft of the foc's'le bulkhead, and there it sat very nicely—and still does to this day. This meant moving the starboard bunk a couple of feet aft so that its occupier's feet were against the bulkhead, under the sideboard. Now one could sit on the port bunk and warm one's toes. That coal stove has proved a comfort, particularly in autumn or early spring. During the summer we may not use it more than once or twice, but it is the only way in bad weather of really drying out one's clothes and clearing the general humidity from the cabin. The stove we use is a little vitreous enamel, cast-iron affair called an Artayco, and I believe originally designed for caravans. It burns anthracite, is easy to light, and thanks to a satisfactory chimney never smokes. We did a certain amount of pondering over the chimney, finally copying one from a large Harding-built, Freeman-designed ketch called *Ylva* that was berthed alongside the quay at Wivenhoe. The important thing, *Ylva's* owner, Air-Commodore Russell, told us, was to have above decks a double chimney, that is a chimney with an outer skin and an air space between that and the inner lining. On top it had a conical cap. The chimney was removable, and a wooden cap screwed down on to the short trunk that remained above decks.

The next day the two-burner Swedish primus stove arrived. It seemed to take up the whole of the front of the galley. Guy and I looked at it in some dismay, because we had planned that the stainless steel basin should be let in to the front of the galley, so that when lifted out we could have access to the large pots and pans cupboard that was beneath the galley. Guy rubbed his chin, then said:

"Do you really want it in gimbals?"

"No, I doubt if we shall cook much at sea."

"Why not fit it in slides then, so that when not in use it can be pushed right back under the side decks?"

This proved to be most satisfactory, and providing one holds on to it one can still boil a kettle at sea. Taff joined us and said he had finished the cabin hatch:

"All curves, man, but she's pretty as a plump little donkey."

I climbed up on deck and walked forward to look at the other hatch and practically scalped myself on one of the criss-cross beams that supported the roof of the shed. When I had recovered from the blow, I took another look at our vast forehatch. The reason for its size was to give some headroom in the foc's'le. I opened the lid.

It hinged on the forward end and looked as big as a squaresail. I could well imagine opening it in a gale of wind and getting it properly wrung and not being able to shut it again. So after a bit of a discussion we decided to make it so that it would slide forward.

By this time the mast and boom were finished, in spite of a false start on the boom, for the draughtsman had mistaken the radius for the diameter, and at his first attempt Taff had come up with a thing about the size of a quant pole. The mast and boom were coated in polyurethane, except for the mast above the hounds, which was painted blue. It looked a massive spar, and in fact was longer than the plans had indicated. Guy Harding had told him to raise the hounds by six inches, as he reckoned there was not enough allowance for sail stretch. Paddy Hare at Gowen's had said that these mainsails with vertical cloths do stretch quite a bit.

By the end of October the boat was painted. The dark green looked quite handsome, but I was not at all sure that it suited her. The bulwarks were in place and capped, and the taffrail was on. Old Bert Kerridge was still chipping away at her stern, below the water line, grumbling to himself about its fullness. Inside the cabin the bunks, galley, sideboard and engine box were all complete and the coal stove was in position. Bob and I offered up the oak table that Bill Porter had made so lovingly for the lifeboat conversion. It was too long, so we decided to cut six inches off it and to make it movable. That is, it was to have bolts with wing nuts, so that it could be unscrewed quite easily and, if need be, stowed in the foc's'le.

November came in with a patch of dirty weather and it rained for a fortnight. There was no future for sailing in that year, so we decided to leave the boat at Wivenhoe until the following spring. The little racing boat was complete, and was taken out of the shed and christened *Tomahawk*. She was a pretty little design by Raymond Wall*. With the front of the shed empty at last I could get a clear view of my boat. She sat at the far end of the shed breasting a sea of trestles, chocks and wedges and looking powerful, determined, and as if longing for the sea.

As I climbed aboard a young painter, whom I had not met before, said:

"She's a bonny little boat, sir, she'll take care of you. But look out, the cabin sides and forehatch are still wet." For once I had the boat to myself. The stern locker in the cockpit was in, with a nice varnished lift-up seat. The lift-out side locker doors were also in

* Her owner was Dennis Hall, who had been one of my students at the Royal College of Art. He was a redoubtable sailor and in *Tomahawk* travelled tremendous distances.

position, lacking only their brass "buttons". There was little more for the yard to do. The rest was up to me. I sat for a while, getting used to the light, or lack of it, though I thought in the open she would be plenty light enough. I stretched out on each bunk and lay looking up at the cabin ceiling and wondered how many times in the future I would look up and see, in some quiet anchorage, the reflection of early morning sun on its warm planking. I roused myself from these agreeable reveries and started to think of all the things that still had to be done before she was equipped to go cruising. I found a pencil and a piece of paper and started to make a list, first heading it with jobs the yard should do before we took her off to Woodbridge.

1. Foc's'le: a folding root berth or fixed berth?
2. Cabin: line galley with formica—stainless steel too difficult.
3. On deck: fit towing bollards, fore and aft.
4. And of course complete the rigging.

And for myself to do:

1. Order three Dunlopillo mattresses, covered with terra cotta red Lionide.
2. Clean off topsides inside cabin and finish and varnish with a matt varnish.
3. Fit out galley with plate racks, cup hooks, glass rack, pan battens; and make formica-covered splashboard to keep grease etc. off the port side bunk.
4. Fit two oil lamps in gimbals.
5. Hooks in foc's'le for oilies, etc.

Just as I had got this far I heard a voice, and Paddy Hare's head, followed by the rest of him, appeared over the bulwark rail.

"To give old Francis (Jack Jones) his due, he can produce a handsome sheer. Very pretty, that's what she is."

"How do you think she will perform?" I asked.

"No question about it, she'll blow down wind all right," and with that I had to be content. Paddy sat on the opposite bunk and we talked for a while, then he said:

"We've modified those excellent Dutch instructions for your mainsail and given you shackles rather than hooks at peak and throat, otherwise it was as plain as can be—and no trouble at all. Now I want to see her under way—we've made plenty of curious sails in our time, but this is the first time we have made one of these."

By mid-November the boat had progressed from her berth at the back of the large shed on to a trolley which had been pushed to the front, as if she was trying to burst her way through the open doors. I climbed aboard and found Guy Harding on his hands and knees, vacuum cleaning out the foc's'le. He switched the machine off and we discussed various things. He had brought the Whale pump aboard; we offered it up on the starboard bulkhead of the cockpit and decided to fix it on two-inch-wide chocks to allow clearance for our knuckles. The towing bollards were still not in place, so I chalked their positions on the deck, the starboard side one just aft of the end of the shank of the CQR anchor. The bollards were to be of three-inch by four-inch oak. We climbed down from the boat and Guy said:

"You'd better come and see your old mast. She's finished now."

We walked round to the sparmaking shed and found Taff just putting the spike on which the wimple would swing to the top of the mast. He had given it a very nice taper.

"Pick it up man," Taff said, "no, not there, over here by the point of balance."

I gave a heave and up she came; she was quite a weight—my guess would be about 80 lb, but we never weighed her.

"Now here's your tiller. Does that satisfy you?" Taff asked.

It certainly did. It had a handsome curve, with a faceted knob that fitted one's hand perfectly.

By the end of November the boat was out of the shed, some twenty-nine months since planning had begun. She was to all intents and purposes, if not finished, at least ready for launching. She was sitting on the quayside on her trolley, a little down by the head.

"May she float more evenly," I thought, "but she's nice, a little comic but a dear little boat." Her curves that looked so exaggerated in the shed looked anything but exaggerated outside.

We spent some time messing about with the crane, trying to lower the mast into the tabernacle. It proved to be too tight a fit, so Taff got to work with a jack plane. When we had stayed the mast we bent the mainsail on to the gaff and boom and hauled it up. There was too much depth between hounds and throat, so the mast had to have six inches cut off her bottom. This time the drawings had been correct, and the yard wrong. At last we had it right and the mast that had looked so huge in the shed seemed to sit very happily above the full-bodied little hull. The curved towing bollards were in place, and chocks had been fitted at the corner of the taffrail for the quarter blocks. She looked a proper little ship.

On the last day of 1960 I went down to Wivenhoe. For six weeks my boat had been on the slip, well wrapped up in a large tarpaulin.

The day of the launch.

I climbed up the rickety ladder and found the Hardings gloomily working on their ledgers. After perfunctory geetings, I said:

"I have come to settle up. How much do I owe you?" Guy looked even gloomier and told me.

"Heavens!" I exclaimed, "that's about six hundred pounds more than I thought I had to pay."

"Yes, I know that," Guy answered, "but we can work back from there."

"No, we don't," I replied, "we start at the price you quoted for the hull, and which I accepted."

And so, very solemnly, we worked our way through all the details, pricing each job as we came to it, finally reaching a figure fairly near the contract price, excluding about £15 for wire rigging and the installation of the stove.

"That is legally what I owe you," I said. Guy's face became even more rueful. Joan looked out of the window and, tactful girl that she is, said nothing. The silence became pregnant and I said:

"What do you think it should be?"

The Hardings put their heads together, both peering at another list of figures, and then Guy said:

"Before you came in, we had been working back from the figure I gave you and had taken into account the time and labour wasted over that rotten stem post, which was no fault of yours, and had decided to knock £250 off that figure."

I thought for a while about my own financial position and finally said:

"Will you accept £350 off?"

Joan replied: "We had hoped for something a little nearer our costs!"

I did some sums. I had just about £450 left in my bank account. Adding that on to what I had already paid met them half way. I told them the position and made my offer, and this they accepted most gracefully. On paper they had lost quite a bit and I had paid quite a bit more than I had budgeted for. Which only goes to show what a very difficult thing to price is a one-off boat, which has to absorb not only the costs of making all the moulds, etc., but also has to cover all the trial-and-error factors that must go with every new design; factors that are ironed out in series production after the first boat is built.

We then repaired to the pub and drank a pint apiece. We parted friends and have remained friends ever since.

On 18th March, the boat was launched, and named *Patient Griselda* after my dear wife's long-suffering namesake. Dennis

177

Kerridge had carved the name most elegantly across the transom, using David Kindersley's "Tarquinius" capitals which I had drawn out for him.

It was a typical March day, blustery and rainy, with grey scudding clouds. Griselda failed to break a half-bottle of champagne on her bows, and after her second failure, as *Patient Griselda* slipped down the ways, Dennis grabbed the bottle and hurled it at the retreating boat. It bounced off her topside and, still unbroken, fell into the river.

"God bless us all," Guy Harding said, "it's a miracle, she floats as true as can be and just above her marks. Give the devils their due, at least one naval architect has got this one right."

With these words there came a blinding flash of lightning and, almost instantaneously, a mighty crash of thunder, and it started to deluge with rain. With one accord we rushed for cover, and in Harding's little office we drank champagne and toasted Griselda for bringing it and her namesake for being launched and safely moored alongside the quay. The sudden storm had stirred up quite a lop in the river. *Patient Griselda* moved restlessly to her mooring ropes, as if anxious to be away.

4

Tuning up and fitting out for foreign cruising

The summer of 1961 was spent in completing *Patient Griselda* and fitting her out for "going foreign". On our trip round from Wivenhoe we had found her a little tender, and very heavy on the tiller. With an extra 5 cwt of lead stowed under the cabin sole she became a different boat and pleasantly light on the helm. The more we sailed her, the more we liked her. She had one unusual attribute, and that was that before a following wind she would run goose-winged, with her staysail billowing out on the weather side with barely a tremor, as if it had been cut out of a sheet of tin; and this was without any boom or preventer stays. The only explanation that we could think of was that a current of air came through the quite wide slot between the luff of the mainsail and the mast and on to the jib. This gap between mainsail and mast is a characteristic of the traditional botter rig. The sail is diagonally laced to the mast with parrel balls taking the chafe. When the throat halliard is pulled taut, the luff of the sail is held firmly to the mast, but about six inches clear. The moment the throat and peak halliards are slackened off, all tension is taken off the parrel lacing, and because of the parrel balls it comes sliding down the mast without let or hindrance. It is a beautifully simple rig and can be handled with only one halliard. With a mainsail the size of *Patient Griselda's*, I thought that two halliards would help to spread the load a bit and give better control of the peak, so that when one is hoisting sail it does not get entangled with the runners. These runners, incidentally, were an afterthought, put on at Guy Harding's suggestion. They were certainly necessary when running before a strong breeze, otherwise they were a bit of a nuisance as the lee runner always has to be slackened off. No doubt if they had been fitted with tension levers on the side decks they would have been less trouble; as it was, they were tightened up with block and tackle.

For a dinghy I had bought a little plastic affair, like the one aboard *Dowsabel*, that would just stow on the foredeck. She proved to be a little unstable, as I was to discover to my sorrow later on.

We had our first little shakedown cruise to the Aldeburgh River. On an evening of silken greyness, with curlew, redshank and oyster catchers keeping us company, we sailed into the river and took the port hand channel round Havergate Island, for we were bound for Butley Creek. The banks were still uncovered as we made our way up the creek, past Boyton Dock, where the little brick building was now quite derelict, with its roof fallen in. We anchored about two hundred yards above the dock; we discovered for the first time that there was a horse there, by grounding on it at low water. Later we moved further up the creek, into deeper water (this was just below the oyster beds).

Our first night aboard *Patient Griselda* was most peaceful. We awoke to a lovely sunny morning, breakfasted and then really started to square things up. The foc's'le was given over to practical uses, with the bunk used for stowage, and coils of rope, the kedge warp, our oilies, a sack of vegetables and a string of onions all hanging from the deck beams.

"Looks a cross between a ship's chandler's and a greengrocer's shop," Griselda said as she hung up the old copper riding light, "but I like it. It's plain and workmanlike, and I must say this loo is an improvement on your previous arrangements."

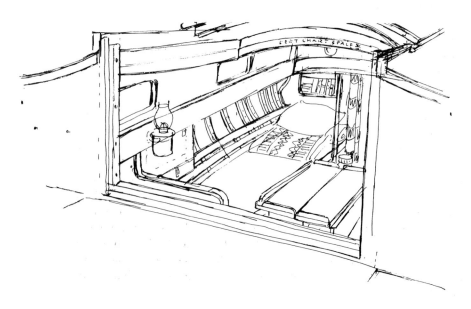

By the time we had finished sorting things out and generally cleaning up, the cabin looked most inviting. The absence of any paintwork is most agreeable, with the pitch pine planking, mahogany and iroko giving a pleasant warmth, aided by the red lionide bunks and the stripes of the brightly coloured Portuguese fishermen's blankets. The galley was a complete success. The white enamelled Swedish two-burner stove was both efficient and easy to keep clean and the stainless steel operating theatre bowl, doing duty for a sink, shone like a looking glass. We had by this time fitted plate and glass racks and hooks for the mugs.

We spent a peaceful ten days, sailing up to Iken Cliff and returning to Butley Creek. We read and listened to the radio, to programmes that ranged from a commentary on the Old Trafford Test Match with a fine innings by Peter May to Diana Holman-Hunt's description of her Pre-Raphaelite grandfather, "who scented his beard with sandalwood!" And we watched the birds. In those few days we saw among the seabirds and waders avocets from Havergate Island, redshank, sandpiper, oyster catchers, curlew, flocks of ox-birds, shelduck (father, mother and eight ducklings), mallard, cormorant, blackheaded gulls, greater black backed gulls, two herons, terns and little terns. Of land birds, we saw a pair of hawks (unidentified; they might have been marsh harriers), green woodpeckers, larks, meadow pipits and lapwings.

We were enjoying our return to the Orford river, so we decided to leave *Patient Griselda* in the care of George Brinkley. His cousin, our old friend Vic, had to our great sadness died the previous year.

"She's making a bit of water," I said to George Brinkley as we were leaving the quay. "I think it is through the stern gland, so keep an eye on her." He nodded gloomily as if he had only half heard us.

The next weekend I drove over to Orford to see if the boat was all right. I found George Brinkley in his launch.

"You should never have left a boat like that," he started off in a deep and gloomy voice, "leakin' I'll say she were. Bin aboard twice a day and there was five inches of water over her floorboards every time. My friend Walter he done me a favour and went off to pump her out last night. Right up to the tops of the bunks it was then. Still pouring in now, I just bin off to her."

I launched the dinghy and rowed out to *Patient Griselda* and climbed aboard. The water was nearly up to her floorboards again and it took a couple of hundred strokes of the pump to clear her. Then I started to look for the trouble. There was a slow drip from the stern gland, but that did not account for it. Then I saw, alongside her great solid stern post, a running stream of water cascading down as if from a tap. It appeared to be coming in from quite high up her stern post, almost at the water line.

I thought for a moment, then decided to try to raise her stern by ballasting her down forward. I had a fearful job getting the floorboards up, as they had swollen badly from the wet. Then I shifted about three hundredweight of lead pigs into the foc's'le. It worked; her stern had been raised by about three inches and the leak had stopped.

I drove back to Woodbridge somewhat worried. At Frank Knights' boatyard I found that Frank was abroad, but Philip, his second-in-command, was there and he agreed to come up to Orford with me the next morning.

I awoke at about 4 am to find the rain driving in on to the bed. There was half a gale blowing. I thought grimly of my poor boat, which was probably awash by now, perhaps even at the bottom of the river. Philip and I reached Orford by 10 am. Not only was it pouring with rain but spray was being blown right across the quay. George Brinkley said grimly:

"You'll never get out to your boat in that dinghy. I'll take you across in the launch and we'll tow the dinghy." Spray drove right over us as, huddled together in the launch, we butted our way down the river. *Patient Griselda* was at least still afloat. My ballast shifting had worked but now, with our combined weight in the cockpit, water started pouring in. We cleared the stern locker and had to cut a hole in the floor, as the locker had been built on top of the floorboards. Philip poked his head in, then came out saying:

"I can see where it comes from, and that is where the twelfth plank down butts the stern post—but it doesn't mean that it is the actual spot, it may be working through a scarf in the stern post."

"What's to do?" I asked, wiping my spectacles for the tenth time.

"Better get her up on the marsh, so we can tackle her when she dries out," he replied.

By the time we had broken out the anchor it was blowing hard. The river looked like the Portland Race. Under power we battled our way up the river, past the quay on the island to the bight beyond the old jetty, at the end of that oddly-named Pigpail Reach. When we were nearly on to the marsh among the sea lavender and marram grass, we anchored on a very short scope of chain. As the wind was blowing directly off the island, Philip rowed the kedge anchor ashore; we then hove up the CQR and he rather perilously rowed that ashore. He then picked up the kedge and rowed that out into deep water. Thus she lay, head to the marsh, but if the wind backed round she would be held off by the kedge.

Our row back was more venturesome than enjoyable. All we could do, with the wind behind us, was to guide the cockleshell across and try to keep afloat. This we did until we finally hit the marsh about a quarter of a mile above Orford. The seas were breaking over us and instantly the dinghy was full, but by then we were both ashore and, grabbing the painter, we dragged the dinghy after us. The quay was deserted, with sand blowing across like buckshot. It was indeed a desolate scene. *Patient Griselda*, grimly sitting it out on the opposite bank, was dimly visible through the mist and rain.

"What force, the wind?" I shouted at Philip.

"Eight at least, I should think," he replied.

"Yachtsman eight?" I asked as we climbed into the car.

"No, real honest to God Force 8. I've been in worse, though, during the war, in the Indian Ocean, Force 10. That was something, but at least we were in an aircraft carrier and not a plastic dinghy." I turned the radio on for the shipping forecast. Gales everywhere. At the Galloper lightvessel it was gusting Force 9.

A couple of days later, when the gale had blown itself out, we returned to Orford. *Patient Griselda* was aground. We rowed across to her and Philip got to work. With a caulking knife, he stopped up what might have been the offending seam.

"Let's hope that will do the trick," he said, "but I am still not sure. Better leave that ballast up forward until we can get her ashore and tackle the job properly."

On the following Monday I went up to Orford to put *Patient Griselda* off into deep water, ready for bringing her round to Woodbridge at the weekend. I felt sorry for my dear wife, who had gone to London for the day. It was a beautiful still July morning, without a cloud in the sky. I launched the dinghy, then, in shirt sleeves, for it was hot even on the water, I rowed across to *Patient Griselda*. She was afloat but the tide was already ebbing. The leak had, for the moment, been stopped. I sat for a while on the cabin roof, its hollow curve making a comfortable seat. The river was completely deserted and the only signs of life were a little tern that was diving for fish and a wisp of smoke coming out of a galley chimney on an old Norwegian pilot cutter. Looking up towards Aldeburgh the whole river was sparkling with the morning sun, with a shimmering heat haze on the water. It was a pleasant scene.

"I had better shift those anchors and put her off into deep water," I thought. As the anchor and cable would be coated with mud, and not wanting to get covered in filth, I decided to put on my thighboots. I climbed down into the cabin, almost blinded for a moment by the reflection of the sun from the steel washing-up bowl, and collected my long waders from the foc's'le. I climbed back into the cockpit, unlaced my ropesoled shoes and started to pull one of the waders on. It felt cold and clammy to my bare foot and I wondered whether to go below again for a pair of woollen socks, but I thought: "I'll only be a few minutes, I can't be bothered." Which laziness perhaps saved my life.

Properly booted and to some extent protected against the slimy cable and muddy CQR anchor, I rowed ashore, stepped out of the dinghy on to the marsh and freed the anchor, which I carefully placed in the stern of the dinghy. I then hauled myself off by the chain cable, pulling it aboard and piling it on the rather limited floor space of the dinghy. By the time I had all the cable aboard I was coated with mud. *Patient Griselda* had now swung to her kedge and was lying in deep water. In order to avoid the bower anchor getting mixed up with the kedge I rowed out towards the middle of the river, paying out the cable as I went. When I had reached the full scope of the chain I leaned forward to free the CQR anchor. It caught in the stern thwart; giving it a sudden heave, I found to my surprise that I was in the water, still holding it. I dropped it and made a desperate grab for the dinghy, but the tide had swept it just out of reach. As I sank below the surface, my last view of *Patient Griselda* was of her sitting on her reflection, just as some earnest amateur water-colourist might have painted her, with a kink in the middle of her reflected mast. How far down I sank I am not sure. The river must have been about twenty feet deep there. To add to my difficulties, my feet were above my head, for the air trapped in my boots made them lighter than the rest of me. However, this was not enough to bring me to the surface, and it occurred to me that unless I got rid of those thighboots I was not going to surface at all! Taking off those long waders was more easily thought about than done. I heaved and struggled and cursed in a frantic manner, but they showed no signs of shifting.

I don't know how long it took me to realise that I was probably going to be drowned. The whole of my past life did not flash across my mind. I was just filled with a blind fury at the fatuous way of my going. To be drowned at sea in some great gale would be unpleasant enough, but at least there would have been a kind of grandeur about it. But to be drowned like this, on a lovely, quiet, sunny morning, in what was for once a calm and sheltered river, all because I had put on those infernal thighboots just to keep my trousers clean—this was almost too much. I redoubled my struggles, but still the boots were glued to my legs by the water pressure. By this time I had swallowed a lot of water and was beginning to feel a bit unwell. For a moment everything went black. I remember calling on the deity to give me a hand; suddenly either He heard me or my boots had become full of water so that the pressure on them was released. Without further effort on my part they were plucked off my feet. I shot to the surface as if I had been blown up by a depth charge. Never have I been so glad to see the blue sky. I lay floating on my back, gasping and feeling very sick. But what did that matter? It was better than being down below, fighting those insensate boots. They had gone for good, anyhow— I had no wish ever to see them again. At last I looked about me and realised that a good spring tide was sweeping me down past Orford town at the rate of some knots. I also saw a dinghy being rowed towards me.

"Help!" I croaked rather feebly. As the dinghy drew near me, I heard a girl's voice:

"Are you all right?" I grabbed the transom of the dinghy, brushed my hair out of my eyes and then realised I was still wearing my glasses.

"Yes, thank you," I gulped, "but can you help me to collect my dinghy and oars?"

"Of course," said the girl, "funny thing was, I was cooking my lunch and I happened to look out of the galley window and suddenly I saw you shoot up out of the water. I never saw you fall in. Can you swim?"

"Yes," I replied, "but if you don't mind towing me into the shallows I would be grateful." So without further talk she bent to the oars and sent her heavy wooden dinghy scudding through the water. The dinghy came to a sudden stop. We were aground. I struggled up the mud bank and sat with my head in my hands and was as sick as a dog. My rescuer meanwhile was away and in a short time had collected my dinghy and oars. I must have looked a bit green, for she said:

"Are you sure you feel all right?"

"Good Lord, yes!" I answered, trying to keep my teeth from chattering, "and thank you with all my heart."

"Oh, that's nothing," she said, blushing rather prettily, "well, I'd better get back." And she rowed away.

I climbed dripping on to *Patient Griselda*, stripped off my clothes and gave myself a violent towelling. I was still shivering and feeling sick, but I managed to drink half a tumbler of rum and orange.

185

The comforting glow of that and warm dry clothes and the sun still beating down into the cabin restored me to something a little nearer normal, but I felt severely chastened. The memory of that July morning is still with me.

When I got ashore I went into the *Jolly Sailor* for another drink, for I was still shivering. I asked one of the watermen if he knew the name of my rescuer.

"What boat she come off?"

"The old Norwegian pilot cutter, with a blue rubbing strake."

"Oh, that's Mr So and So's."

"I'd like to send his wife a case of whisky for rescuing me."

"What did the lady look like?"

"She was a pretty girl, with dark hair."

"I should be a bit careful if I was you, sir, that's not his wife—that's the lady what he spends his weekends with!" So discretion got the better of me and my rescuer never got her crate of whisky.

There was another curious thing about that day. After I had driven home I thought it would be as well if I concealed all evidence of my near-disaster, so I washed my shirt and trousers, dried them as well as I could and was painstakingly ironing them when my wife burst in upon me.

"Are you all right?" then, seeing the flat-iron in my hand, she said: "What on earth are you doing with that?"

I am a poor hand at concealment, and soon she heard the whole story. But only then did it strike me as odd that she should be back so early, for among other things that she had planned to do in London on that day was to have lunch with an old boyfriend, and he was a man whose lunches usually went on until well into the afternoon.

"But why are you back so early?" I asked, "didn't you have lunch with Bobby after all?"

"Yes, I had lunch with him, at least half a lunch . . . " She stopped: "what time did you say all this happened?"

"I don't know, it must have been . . . " I looked at my watch. In spite of its being the kind that channel swimmers are reputed to wear when they go swimming, the inside of the glass was covered with beads of moisture and it had stopped. The hands, still dimly visible, had stuck at twenty past one.

"If that is anything to go by, 1.20 pm," I said. Griselda sat quietly for a moment, then she said:

"We were lunching at Scotts and I was halfway through a Sole Véronique when I was filled with a fearful foreboding and a feeling that something had happened to you. I hurriedly swallowed the rest of the sole, made my apologies to Bobby, who of course thought I was mad, and ran for the train. I actually left Scotts at 1.25 because I remember looking at my watch to see if I had time to catch the 2.30 pm train."

Later I thought a lot about that ducking. Investigation showed that the majority of fatal yachting accidents occurred with *dinghies* and not yachts. They were caused by a number of things, such as dinghies that were too small and too unstable, by overloading such dinghies, by boarding a yacht at night, perhaps after a visit to the pub ashore. Now, this little eight-foot plastic dinghy was a good load carrier—it would carry three persons, but its freeboard was then reduced to about a couple of inches; it was very light, so it was easy to lift aboard, but because it was so light it was pretty unstable. It had built-in buoyancy but, as I found to my cost when it turned upside down, though it didn't sink it offered little handhold apart from the two small lead skegs on its bottom, and these were out of my reach. I never used it again but sold it to a friend who wanted it for his child to use on a lake in his garden, which nowhere was more than two feet deep. I still had the old ten-foot sailing dinghy, which was a solid, stiff little boat, and for the rest of that season we towed her behind *Patient Griselda*. For our planned trip to Holland in the following summer I was not at all sure what we would use. I did not like the idea of towing a heavy dinghy across the North Sea, but I was perplexed as to what would be light enough and small enough to carry on deck and still be of some use in a seaway. Charles Hanson, who had planned to come with us, solved the problem by suggesting an inflatable Avon dinghy. But I am anticipating my narrative.

A few days later I took *Patient Griselda* back to Woodbridge and Frank Knights' crane lifted her out of the water on to the quay. The leak was not traced until one of the rudder pintles had been unscrewed, and behind that was the offending bolt hole, with no stopping in it. Five minutes' work sufficed to mend that trouble.

We continued to make improvements to the boat, but our cruising was limited to weekends. She proved to be a most docile and handy little craft, with a commendable habit of never missing stays when going about. The only thing I was not satisfied with was the engine. Fond though I was of the old Stuart-Turner, it was not man enough for really pushing the boat along. But the main objection was the amount of fuel we should have to carry for the two-stroke if we hit a windless North Sea crossing. The answer to the fuel problem was clearly a diesel, but whether it should be water-cooled or air-cooled exercised our thoughts for a while. Frank Knights finally made up my mind for me by saying:

"I have put twenty-eight Lister diesels into fishing boats and yachts over the last few years, and if your priority is reliability, I suggest you have one of these." For a long time it had seemed to me to be a nonsense to carry an auxiliary engine at all unless you were going to use it—and use it not only on windless days but to help bash a foul tide or even to enable one to lay a course. It took me a long time to learn that the use of an engine when going to windward may not push one through the water much faster but it helps one to lie a point or so nearer the wind. There may be times when this will save a tack or two, or even save a tide.

We continued to sail *Patient Griselda* until well on into November, but at last there came the time to lay her up and put into effect the various alterations and additions. The main addition was the 8½ hp Lister-Blackstone air-cooled diesel. As this was more than twice the size of the Stuart-Turner and had hot air trunking as well, it meant certain alterations to the galley as well as to the engine compartment.

We sold the Stuart-Turner and saw Frank Knights install it in a pretty old clipper-bowed shoal-draft yacht from Aldeburgh. This old craft was sitting on the Ferry Quay alongside *Patient Griselda*. Utterly different and at least half a century apart in age, they were both handsome boats, but to my eyes nothing can better a clipper bow. This old boat had a beauty which made me think she was American in design, though I believe she was built on the Thames some time before the first world war.

With the diesel engine installed in *Patient Griselda* the top of the new engine case had to be raised, which made a level platform and sideboard, and a larger step had to be provided, making a better seat for the cook. We lost the galley cupboard with the lift-up top, as this space was taken up by the hot air trunking. However, the space left in it provided us with a useful hot cupboard for storing soap powders, washing-up cloths, etc. In the cockpit, the port side forward locker now became a hot air locker, for the trunking discharged the hot air into the bottom of this. Philip made a new door with louvres and built a shelf perforated with holes above the trunking. This made a perfect airing cupboard. The objections to diesels in small craft are that they are much heavier than petrol engines of the same power, and if they are air-cooled they take up a lot more room. These objections are valid, but the weight did not worry us and we thought the loss of space was worth it. And in spite of being bothered by the rather offensive diesel smell when some of the fuel has leaked from the fuel line or filters, I would never willingly go to sea again with a petrol engine. And this for one reason only, and that is the confidence this diesel gives one that as soon as one presses the self-starter the engine will run, and go on running, come hell or high water, as long as there is fuel in the tank. To begin with, for temporary economy, we installed the engine without electrics but with a special cog on the flywheel to drive the dynamo if we ever had one. Cranking the engine up was a painless operation; it was like turning an old-fashioned mangle, for one cut out the compression by flicking back a couple of small levers on the tops of the cylinders. As soon as the heavy flywheel was spinning the decompression levers were pushed forward and she was off.

While the alterations were being made to the inside of the boat I spent some time drawing out and then making mock-ups of the pulpits, stanchions and lifelines. I noticed that many yachts had these useful aids to safety, but they often seemed to me to be of quite inadequate dimensions, and usually there was no stern pulpit. A lifeline that comes only about half way up the calf of one's leg is worse than useless and a stern pulpit is almost as important as one forward. From my designs Frank Knights made both stanchions and pulpits out of one-inch galvanised steel tubes. These stanchions, 27 in. high, fitted into sockets welded on to the webs that held the bulwark plank in position. The lifelines were of stainless steel wire with Talurit spliced eyes fore and aft. The whole affair inspired a feeling of immense confidence. I particularly liked our stern pulpit, for it really gave one something to hang on to or to lean against when steering. It also carried our stern light and lifesaving equipment, including lifebelt and lightfloat.

Our navigation lights were powered by a twelve-volt battery which was firmly chocked in the starboard side cockpit locker, below the fuel tank. The actual port and starboard lights were plastic-covered streamlined lights as used on aircraft, with festoon bulbs. These were placed on red and green boards mounted on the shrouds about five feet above the deck level. At this level and in this position there was no chance of their being blanketed by the sails. The stern light, a little chrome-plated brass cylinder with a screw top, was clamped on to the stern pulpit. The leads had waterproof plugs set into the deck and so far have never given any trouble. There was a light set under the overlapping shelf of the bridge deck, just above the gimballed compass. This was screened with a sheet of heavy dark-green plastic to cut down the glare. All these lights could be turned on or off by switches on the after bulkhead of the cabin, just inside the companionway.

Our electric lights inside the cabin were limited to reading lights at the head of each bunk and to a light above the chart table, which was made up of an Imperial-sized drawing board clamped at an angle of about 25° over the galley. For the comfort of their warmth and the pleasant light that they give, we use two small gimballed oil lamps; one of them is the original little brass lamp that I found in the ill-fated *Omega*.

A week before Whitsun, *Patient Griselda* was launched. The biggest visible change to the boat was her colour, apart from her pulpits and lifelines. At the end of her first season all her seams were showing, and from one or two of them she was spewing her caulking. So, remembering the conversation with Kim Holman down in Gowen's sail loft, I had the yard burn off her topsides, re-stop her seams, rub her down and repaint her a cool greeny-grey. She looked far better for it. Also, I seemed to have heard somewhere or other that green was an unlucky colour for boats.

Charles Hanson joined us for the Whitsun weekend. It was a cold and blustery few days and we were able to try the boat out both reefed and unreefed and with large and small headsails. Over the weekend we completed our fitting out and made plans for our cruise to Holland. In his Maurice Griffiths-designed *Veterata* he had taken part in the Hook to Ostend races with some success. *Patient Griselda* was about three foot six inches less in overall length than *Veterata*, but seemed to feel, so Charles said, to be of much the same size.

A day or two after he had returned to his job as a don at the University of Durham he wrote to me about the inflatable dinghy problem: "I think the question of a dinghy is quite the most difficult decision one has to make for a sea voyage. It could be argued that with a crew of three we ought to buy a ten-foot one, but presumably we should take it uninflated and I think it would be sheer wishful thinking to imagine that one could inflate a dinghy of that size by CO_2 or any other means on *Patient Griselda's* deck when it was blowing Force 8. I would rather accept the fact that we are taking it for psychological reassurance and buy the eight-foot Redstart without CO_2." He went on to say: "I think we must have the following equipment on board:

3 inflatable lifejackets.
1 can of red rocket flares.
1 small axe (I will bring one).

1 pair strong wire cutters.
1 light for throwing overboard if a man goes overboard at night (heaven forbid!)."

He concluded his letter with: "I hope you don't think I am being over-cautious, John, I've *never* had to use any of the above gear yet, but the ocean racing boys are no fools and it is a much shorter list than they have to carry on RORC races . . .'

We bought the lifesaving gear and the eight-foot Redstart dinghy and found that it could be stowed on the foredeck partially inflated (that is, without the bow compartment blown up) and still leave plenty of room for working her sails. Later on, after experimenting with the difficulties of pumping up the bow section alone under bad conditions, I took to carrying it completely inflated. Of course it got in the way, but it was reassuring to have it ready for immediate use. The Avon Redstart was a stable little boat, and easy to climb into from the water. But what Charles had said was perfectly true. Nothing short of a three-man liferaft with awning and survival kit would be much use if ever one had to abandon ship in very bad weather.

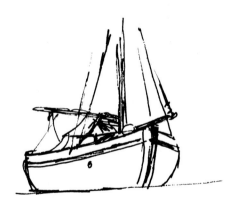

A Woodbridge boat: a Cherub-class yacht built by Everson.

191

5

To Friesland

Charles and I left Woodbridge on a Saturday in the middle of July and crossed the Deben bar some time after 11.00 hours. It was a sunny, warm day, yet with perversity; the wind, having blown from the north for the previous ten days, had gone round to the south-east, and there for the next twenty-four hours it blew gently but ever more firmly, exactly 135°—our precise course for Ostende. Any theories of dropping sail and motoring straight into the wind were soon to prove somewhat fallacious, even though the wind never exceeded Force 4. Under sail *Patient Griselda* will make 55° off the wind and with a Force 3, about 2½ knots; under bare poles and slap into the wind I doubt if she would do better than a mile or a mile and a half in the hour. The conclusions are obvious, so twelve hours after leaving Woodbridge we had returned to Suffolk and were anchored in the Orwell.

Charles, acting both as navigator and crew, had said so rightly:

"We can keep going, but who knows what the weather will be doing in another twelve hours; according to the forecast there is a cold front coming up."

The following day, as we lay under the shelter of Shotley, we listened to the wind and the rain and we congratulated ourselves. By evening the worst of the depression had passed over and on Monday morning the wind had boxed right round into the north. The weather forecast was fair and we were away by 0.800 hours. The wind varied between Forces 3 and 4 and for the first eight or nine hours *Patient Griselda* tramped along on a broad reach with a healthy hum from the spinning propeller.

About 17.00 hours the wind began to drop, so we started the diesel up and with it turning over quietly we motor-sailed for the rest of the way. We pottered along through the night with a glittering path to starboard reflecting a huge full moon. As the night wore on, with the diesel thudding away reassuringly, the sky clouded over and a heavy shower fell, which soon eased to a slight drizzle.

On this course to Ostende we were never long without the sight of a lightvessel. The longest spell of something less than two hours was between the Galloper and the West Hinder. We checked our position every hour by log readings and bearings on the lightvessels when we could see their lights. Due to the considerable set of the spring tides our course was a sweeping S. I soon learned that without making due allowance for these tides one could be badly out.

We picked up the Ostende light some eighteen miles out. It was a rather disconcerting pin-prick, with no previous loom. The wind was no more than enough to steady us as we slowly came up on the Belgian shore. In the first light, and when we were about two miles from Ostende, we dropped the sails and only then realised their steadying power, for as we came over the shallow banks we rolled in a hideous fashion. We passed through the piers and into the silent but crowded yacht haven. We tied up at the end of a trot of yachts, drank some soup from a Thermos and tumbled into bed.

At this time of year Ostende is not without a certain picturesque charm, and the harbour was animated by the constant movement of fishing boats. We idled through the next day, sent telegrams and postcards and lunched and dined ashore.

Thursday was a glorious day and a splendid omen for our holiday. With the tide under us we had an easy, sunbathing kind of sail to Zeebrugge. The wind was still in the north and it would have been useless for us to go any further, for we should have had the ebb tide running out of the Scheldt against us. It was a spring tide of some power, as we discovered next day.

We explored Zeebrugge, found an excellent yacht chandler's and bought the absolutely essential tidal atlas of the South Holland estuaries. After that we dined at the Noord Zee Yacht Club off a very well-cooked grilled sole. It had been a lovely day. On returning to *Patient Griselda* we found a pretty little steel sloop, named *Zeekaag*, moored alongside us. Her Dutch owner with a charming French wife and two nice children entertained us to Dutch gin until the early hours. This was my introduction to Bokma, the "oude Geneva" from Friesland.

Next morning began with half a gale blowing and with very poor visibility, but by midday when we had cleared the mole, in company with our Dutch friends, the visibility had improved and the wind had settled into a steady Force 4 from the south-east. With the tide under us we started to snort along, and in one period of twenty-five minutes we covered five and a half miles over the ground. We continued to make what were by our modest standards fantastic speeds, for there was no sea. At the beginning, in the lee of the land, it was glassy smooth. It was an extraordinary sensation to have a wind and a tide of that strength and barely a ripple to contend with. It seemed no time before we were in the mouth of the Scheldt. There was a lot of traffic and we had to wait our opportunity to cross to the north shore. We hove to for a large cargo liner to pick up her pilot and then crossed under her stern. She acknowledged our courtesy by dipping her ensign. As we made our way towards Flushing we were followed by a number of fishing boats coming in on the tide. They looked like Daddy-longlegs with their nets goosewinged from yards on either side of them.

We drew level with *Zeekaag* as we reached the lock entrance to the Middelburg Canal, barely two and a half hours after leaving Zeebrugge, some sixteen and a half miles away. The importance of working these tides hardly needs stressing.

We were delayed for a while at both the lock and at the road bridge, which was being painted. At last we were through and were motoring quietly along towards Middelburg. Arriving there in the middle of their rush hour, we were again delayed before another road bridge while some very mixed traffic passed across it, including a very thin curé, dressed in a cassock and a flat hat, mounted on a bicycle and leading a huge strawberry roan Percheron mare. This great creature, with its neck arched high, was trotting along behind her master like a sportive little dog. Finally the traffic stopped, the red and white striped poles dropped across the road and the bridge cantilevered open. We were on our last lap to Veere. On the horizon we could see the great church and the onion-spiked tower of the Raadhuis. At Veere we tied up to the staging near the lock, spurning the new yacht haven which now occupies the old fishing harbour, for since the Veersegat is closed all Veere's fishing boats have moved to North Beveland.

Veere on this, my third, visit still seemed a charming place, its architecture more Flemish than Dutch. On this particular evening it looked mellow and welcoming in the warm westerly light. We made for the restaurant in the old watch tower overlooking the entrance to the harbour. Here we drank Bokma and dined off excellent smoked eel and roast chicken. This restaurant is on the first floor of the Campveerse Toren and is a handsome high-ceilinged room with beams painted most effectively in red and green. The windows on three sides give one limitless views of the Veersegat. Inside these windows are shutters of a fine faded silvery oak. With its light and height and colour and the warmth of its woodwork, it is a room that could only be found in the

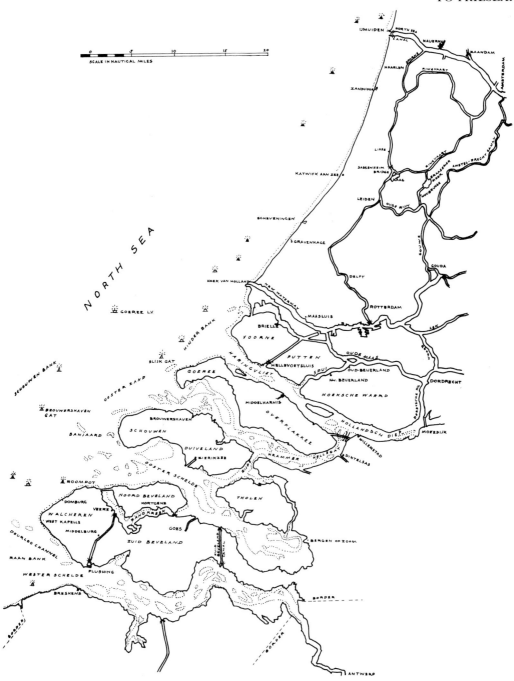

Chart of Zeeland and the coast up to Ijmuiden.

Netherlands. It was Charles's first visit to Veere and he was most clearly pleased by it.

We left Veere at midday on Friday. I made a thorough mess of passing our warps to the lock-keeper as a result of not having coiled them down properly. There is much to learn about handling boats in locks, and little opportunity to practise in English coastal waters. I had no idea how much way *Patient Griselda* carried or how much reverse throttle was needed to stop her, for she had never sailed or motored in tideless waters before. We learned quickly after a few frights.

The morning had started both wet and muggy, with a warm south-west wind, but as we passed out into the Veersegat the sky cleared, the sun beat down on us and we were to have an afternoon to remember. Soon we had stripped off most of our clothes, but it was too hot even for sunbathing. Though there is a fair amount of barge traffic, on a day such as this these waterways are unmatched for sheltered cruising. A shimmering heat haze raised the low horizon of trees, hedges and barns so that there appeared to be a strip of sky between them and the water. Coming up the Zandkreek we passed two yachts anchored close to a sandbank while their occupants splashed about in the water or sunbathed on the white sand. As we came level with a little church standing on the bank to port (it proved to be a place called Kortgene) a resonant bell chimed out three o'clock. A gentle breeze wafted us along. There was no urgency; I felt I would have been content for this to have gone on for ever.

At last we reached the huge lock at the end of the Zandkreek and by some inexplicable manoeuvre I succeeded in turning *Patient Griselda* back to front, and so we tied up as if we preferred it that way.

Once out in the Scheldt, we turned to starboard for Goes. The television tower at Goes can be seen for miles. We were soon up to the lock, where a friendly lock-keeper took our lines from us, then came aboard to discuss the weather and to take our dues. The canal up to Goes is very similar to the one leading to Middelharnis, with a line of tall poplars on the bank. We had one more bridge to pass. I practically burst our loud hailer before the bridge-keeper appeared out of a nearby tavern. The yacht haven lay to port, its entrance almost hidden by overhanging willows. It is a delicious little harbour with high tree-lined banks round it, and the whole place is a mass of roses. At the end of a little quay which divides the haven into two is a very small stone lighthouse, which rather unexpectedly proved to be the privy. As I tied up I noticed we were

Griselda joined us at Goes.

The harbour at Goes with lighthouse-privy.

Patient Griselda in the Hollandsche Diep.   *Photo: Doddy Kahn*

alongside a handsome converted lifeboat. It was *Sonnavaert*, with whose owner I had had much correspondence in connection with a book I was writing on lifeboat conversions. Goes seems to be the home of a number of these conversions. Wandering round the little harbour we counted at least seven or eight, and some of them very good-looking.

We walked into the middle of this very nice town, and there in the Grote Markt we found the *Korenbeurs Hotel*, where we had the first of two memorable meals. As Charles drank his third Bokma, he peered shortsightedly at the square green bottle and said:

"They make this stuff in Friesland, do they? Well, that is certainly a good enough reason for going there."

The night was still and warm and *Patient Griselda* looked rather a robust seagoing kind of craft in this rose-bower of a haven. The wind had dropped and there was not a sound as we climbed into our bunks.

Griselda arrived next morning, after a night passage from Harwich to the Hook. It was another bright sunny day, most of which we spent pottering about on the boat. *Zeekaag* came into the yacht haven in the afternoon; the last we had seen of her was at Flushing. All day in the Grote Markt there had been some sort of *Kermis* in preparation for a bicycle race. Whether it was a *tour de Holland* or something less energetic we never discovered.

Sunday morning was again bright, over-bright and very blowy. *Zeekaag's* owner called out to us:

"You won't get far today, you'd better stay here. We have both a bottle of gin and a bottle of whisky."

Resisting such enticements, we motored the three miles down to the lock. By the time we had got there it was obvious to all of us that it was going to be a very long, very wet sail to Willemstad. So we tied up to the staging by the dock and had lunch, and then went for a walk along the sea wall. The wind was now so fierce that we gave up the struggle and flopped down on the leeward side, where all was quiet and warm in the sun. We had a splendid view of the estuary, which must be over three miles wide there. Far out on the north side we could see a number of large yachts racing off Zierikzee. Charles focused my Ross 7 × 50s on them.

"My goodness! they are getting wet, even though they are under the lee of those sandbanks."

I took the glasses from him and watched with some pleasure someone else's discomfort. We would certainly have had a tumble if we had tried to make Willemstad. We lazed for a while, watching some men fishing in the shallows. A flock of oyster catchers came screaming overhead in an agitated flight like a troop of minor canons hurrying to evensong. They were followed by several curlew flying rather more sedately, while all along the water's edge terns were wheeling and diving. Rested, we walked along the marsh, protected from the wind by the dyke. Numerous Dutch families were picnicking in neat little tents, complete with chairs and tables and even in one or two cases rugs and carpets. Used to the winds and the variable weather of these shores, they were taking no chances.

In the evening we motored back up the canal to Goes. The wind blew hard all that night, but by breakfast time next morning it had dropped to a nice breeze. We left Goes in company with *Zeekaag*.

We were discovering the pleasures of sailing in company. After an easy sail up the Hollandsch Diep, we both dropped our sails as we turned into the cut leading up to Willemstad. We slipped up this narrow waterway and rounded the corner into the harbour. The last time I had been there was on my second trip in *Dowsabel*, when on a night of seraphic stillness near to midnight we had glided into an almost deserted harbour. The floodlights were playing on the Raadhuis and the windmill. The scene looked for all the world like a stage set. We found no such tranquil scene this time. The harbour was packed solid with yachts which had been racing at the Zierikzee regatta, or had decided that it was too windy to race and had remained harbour-bound. We tied up alongside *Zeekaag*. There were five boats between her and the quay, so we practically blocked the fairway. However, we were not the last in by any means. A huge boeier handled with superb skill by a professional skipper squeezed her way in just beyond us. At the sight of her massive bow, a space opened as if by magic and in a moment she was lying snugly against the quay. After drinks with the Kahns aboard *Zeekaag* we went ashore and dined well at *Bonds Hotel* on the quayside. After dinner we walked round this pretty little village. I made a resolution that the next time I visited Willemstad I would stay there for some time. On this occasion, just as on my previous visit in *Dowsabel*, we had to make an early departure to catch the tide to Dordrecht.

We had breakfasted and were away by 08.30 hours, again in company with *Zeekaag*. Sailing free we soon drew ahead of them, but as soon as we were close-hauled they came up with us. However, just as we were coming into the Dordtsche Kil we were both left standing by a little racing boeier that was sailing almost two knots to our one, and this on a fairly close reach.

From Dordrecht onwards the commercial traffic grew thicker, and as we came into the Lek—the main waterway above Rotterdam—we were beset on all sides by barges and tugs dragging three, four, five and even six barges. We kept on going hour after hour until, leaving the Rotterdam waterway and with my crew nearing mutiny, we drew into a little backwater at a place called Boskoop. We had been travelling for just over twelve hours. We tied up to a deserted lighter and the Kahns brought *Zeekaag* alongside for a farewell drink before sailing on to their home port on the Kaagermeer, some four hours ahead. Obviously they were made of sterner stuff than we were.

Next day we took our time, stopping for lunch at a waterside café and finally arriving at the Kaagermeer at about 18.00 hours on a grey, misty evening. The Kaag consists of a string of beautiful lakes that lie some twelve miles south-east of Haarlem. They are a little like the Norfolk Broads, and tend to be crowded. When we arrived there were a number of boats sailing about. We heard one sounding its foghorn, but it wasn't all that misty and there was no bridge in sight, so we took no notice. It was not until we saw someone in obvious pursuit of us that we realised it was *Zeekaag*. After a joyful reunion, we tied up in front of a café and were entertained most engagingly to Dutch gin and bacon pancakes.

We finally parted from the Kahns. Their holiday was over and they sailed off in the dark to their yacht haven, which was only a few hundred yards away. We remained where we were, disturbed for a while by the wash of passing barges, and then about midnight by a somewhat tipsy party of Belgians going aboard a boat that lay just ahead of ours. After that all was quiet and we slept.

We awoke at 05.30 hours to the irritating noise of the alarm clock. This early rising was to enable us to pass through the Sassenheim Bridge at 06.00. At 06.05 hours the Brugwachter sleepily climbed up the steps into his cabin, stopped the traffic and let us through. The mist of the previous evening still hung low over the water and there was an October-like chill in the air. The mist slowly cleared to give way to low overhanging clouds. We tied up in the middle of Haarlem after going through four bridges, and went ashore to change travellers' cheques and to visit the Frans Hals Museum. Before we had reached the museum it had begun to pour with rain, and we got drenched. The gallery, which occupies a series of seventeenth-century almshouses, is usually rather empty. On that day it was packed solid with earnest steaming catalogue-consulting Germans who provided a damp screen of humanity through which it was difficult to see the pictures. The afternoon wore on, the rain came down harder than ever, so at length with courage inspired by boredom we made a dash for the boat.

We shut the hatches, changed our clothes and were just about to have a drink when I heard someone calling me by name—somewhat unexpectedly on a canal in the middle of Haarlem in a thunderstorm. It was Sem Hartz, engraver and type designer to one of the most famous printing houses in Europe, the Haarlem firm of Enschedé en Zonen. He propped his elegant green bicycle against a tree. It was a vehicle that looked a likely mount for an Edwardian governess, with its enclosed chain in an oilbath and string-guarded rear wheel.

"I saw this boat with a red ensign. I read the name on the transom and thought nobody but you would have a boat with a name like that." His witty, good-looking face sparkled with delight

201

as he examined our rather damp, very untidy cabin.

"She's nice, John. I am thinking of building a boat about this size. My old botter is getting too old, she costs a fortune to keep in good trim, and in Holland people like to keep their boats as if they were pieces of antique furniture. How big is she?"

I told him.

"Yes, that is a good size and one metre is a good draft. You won't want more in Friesland. I have been aground there with less!" All this was spoken in English so faultless that it made us feel very humble about our foreign language shortcomings.

After he had left us we put on oilskins and prepared for the next obstacle, the Spaarne railway bridge, which opens only at certain specific times. We circled in front of it blowing away on our foghorn, for we were under the impression that it opened at six o'clock. After about twenty minutes of fruitless activity I consulted the timetable again, to find that the six o'clock opening was on Saturdays only and the bridge would remain tight shut until 8 pm. We tied up to a filthy coal lighter and went below to have supper. At five to eight we got under way again and the rain redoubled its fury. We repeated our hooting and circling act, but this time we were acknowledged by the bridge-keeper, who told us that there had been some delay on the railway. Finally the bridge opened at 8.55 pm. We passed through. It was now practically dark. A mile or so below the bridge we tied up to a quayside that was marked on the map as a yacht haven. An affable man took our warps and then went in search of the harbour master, to see if we could really stay there.

The harbour master was a somewhat taciturn character. He told us curtly to move a few feet forward or sternward, I forget which, to establish his position of authority. Charles then startled us all by asking if he could have a bath in the clubhouse.

"Only a cold shower."

Any momentary desire for cleanliness that he may have had evaporated. We fixed up the awning over the companionway and retired to our beds, cold and damp.

By the morning the rain had eased to a slight drizzle. The awning had given us a dry night below. I switched on the radio for the shipping forecast " . . . Galloper wind Force 6, visibility nil, Tiree Force 7, heavy rain . . ." The weather was breaking up everywhere. At least we were in a canal, even if it was a very dirty one. We breakfasted and were away from this Haarlem yacht haven by eight o'clock and made good time in spite of a fifty-minute delay at the Krommenie railway bridge. The day cleared and gave promise of very different weather to that over the seas round the British Isles.

The Nauernasche Vaart, which runs due north from the North Sea Waterway into the Markervaart, is a fairly quiet canal. We had a following wind, so I cut the engine and raised the jib. We blew gently along, but as soon as we rounded out of the Markervaart into the North Holland canal we raised the main and had a glorious sail. As we came near to a great grey thatched mill the miller saw our ensign, waved hectically and ran to take the brake off his own wind machine. It was already spinning energetically as we sailed past. It continued to whirl away merrily as long as we were in sight. These mills are not only thatched on their roofs but on their sides as well. At a distance, the grey reed thatching looks like silvery cedar shingles.

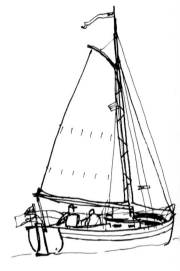

We left the North Holland canal at a pretty little town called Purmerend. Here there are five or six bridges, four of them under the same management, which consisted of an aged man equipped with a bicycle and a terrifying-looking old troll who might well have served as a model for the elder Brueghel. Here the Purmer Ringvaart joins the North Holland canal and there is a wide basin. We circled for a while, but as there was no sign of the bridge-keeper, we tied up and went to look for him. We had walked only fifty yards or so when he came pedalling along towards us. I paid our modest dues (25c per bridge) and he and his fearsome-looking female accomplice (for all I know she could have been his wife) let us through with no delay.

We were to learn later that from Haarlem the quickest way to the Zuider Zee is by the North Sea Waterway and through the Oranjesluis at Amsterdam, but the Purmerend–Edam route takes one through one of the prettiest canals in Holland. From Purmerend onwards it is a meandering reed-lined waterway sprinkled at the edges with yellow waterlilies. Practically the only other occupants of the canal were ducks and coots scuttling in and out of the reeds. At one point there was some commotion; then we saw a kestrel hovering overhead. It pitched twice, apparently after baby ducks, but with no success, and it wheeled away in disgust and flew off in search of less submersible prey. A moment later we saw a small disturbance in the water ahead. As we drew level with it, we saw it was a mole swimming in a very determined manner from one bank to the other, its nose scarlet with exertion and its large front paws whirling like a pair of paddle wheels.

We arrived at Edam in the late afternoon. As at Purmerend there are several bridges which are in the care of a friendly man

203

In the afternoon we were standing on the jetty looking out into the Ijsselmeer when a large old-fashioned cutter rounded into the harbour. She was *Dyarchy*, a 27-ton gaff cutter designed by Laurent Giles. Her draft of nearly seven feet, as her skipper later told us, was something of a problem in those waters. *Dyarchy* had been built in Sweden in 1939 for Roger Pinckney, Vice-Commodore of the Royal Cruising Club.

who led us to a perfect mooring in a quiet stretch of the canal which we had all to ourselves. It was flanked on one side by flower-filled gardens, at the back of what looked to be rather nice houses, and on the other side by a cobbled street with a grass verge shaded by lime trees. We made our bow and stern lines fast to two of these. Edam is a picturesque little town. We dined adequately at a simple café near the canal, then walked for a while through the winding narrow streets. On Saturday morning we shopped, then locked out of the canal into the Ijsselmeer. The lock-keeper spoke fluent English.

"I'm an old Navy bloke," he said, "and I married a girl from Chatham."

From Edam to Hoorn is only eight or nine miles. The sea was calm, the wind northerly and barely Force 2. We passed very few yachts, so were not prepared for the crowded state of the two harbours at Hoorn. We took a look at the outer harbour, where the yachts are moored in trots, and decided to try the inner. Twice we had to circle this before we could find a deserted yacht to lie along-side. On our first time round each time we tried to come alongside a boat we were warned away with cries of "Wet paint!" or "Your tyres will mark our varnish!" This was most untypical of Holland; most of the boats could not have been Dutch.

Sunday was spent quietly. The sun shone all day, many of the boats departed and we soon had a large expanse of the tree-shaded quay to ourselves. In the afternoon *Dyarchy* came into harbour.

Monday was another warm, sunny day. Under a light south-easterly wind we sailed for Enkhuizen. The harbour there was a bit crowded, but we found a vacant lot in the top left hand corner into which *Patient Griselda* backed herself with surprising dexterity.

The next day we were up early (by the standards of this leisurely cruise) and had left Enkhuizen by 09.30 hours. The sky was overcast and the Ijsselmeer quite deserted. We trailed the log, for we were en route for Friesland. With a fair wind, we covered just over four nautical miles in each hour. For ease of steering we tacked downwind. As we neared the Frisian shore the day brightened and visibility improved. We ran down the coast into Lemmer Bay. Ahead of us there were at least a hundred little white sails. It was, we learned later, the week of the Lemmer regatta. From this cloud of snowflakes a small flock of tan-sailed scows emerged, sailing close-hauled towards us at a surprising speed. We hove to, to let them pass across our bows.

We locked out of the Ijsselmeer through the Prinses Margriet-sluis and made for our first Frisian meer, the Grote Brekken, and our objective, a little village called Sloten. There are two ways of reaching Sloten from the Grote Brekken, either along the dead straight Langesloot at the south end or by the winding Kromine Ee at the north. We chose the latter, for it passed through what promised to be a pretty little mere; and we chose wrong. For some reason I was not feeling too well, but in honour of our arrival in Friesland I went below to put on a clean smock. At that moment, just as we were turning out of the Grote Brekken, we went hard aground. Charles got out the kedge and started pumping up the dinghy when Griselda shouted:

"Here's a motor cruiser, perhaps they will help." They did, most willingly, and after two unsuccessful attempts finally pulled us clear. By this time, three more boats had grounded near us, completely blocking the channel. We then somewhat tardily took a good look at the chart and saw for the first time the ominous phrase "N. oever ondiep" (N. bank shallow). In the deepest part of the channel there was only 1.2 metres and we were down on our marks. Somewhat chastened, we retraced our course down the Grote Brekken and into the Langesloot, up the Ee of Boomsvaart and so to Sloten.

We had reached Friesland and we thought it enchanting. The meres vary from a few hundred yards to several miles in length. They are joined by rush-lined rivers and cuts, much as the Norfolk Broads are. The vast skies shed a bright pearly light over this very horizontal landscape, with the horizon broken only by the large Frisian barns, which are combined with the farmhouses and usually set among clumps of willows. These barns are the winter quarters for the cows; each cow has its own window so that it can watch the changing scene of the wintry Frisian countryside from the comfort of a warm stall.

Coming up the Boomsvaart we were surrounded by clouds of terns wheeling and diving, among them the little black tern that we see so rarely in England. A heron peered at us with one glassy eye, then, stretching his great umbrella-like wings, slowly flew off. For a moment we had the waterway to ourselves, then a pair of swans with a family of cygnets came gliding round a corner in a regal manner. The afternoon was drawing on and the scene was bathed in golden light. All was quiet, for I had switched off the diesel. Suddenly the air was filled with shrill piping and five oyster catchers in line astern shot over us as if propelled from a gun. Whenever I hear this cry over our East Anglian saltings I shall remember Holland and this summer of 1962. Not a day since we had left Zeeland had passed without our seeing or hearing these

The jachthaven at Sloten. *Patient Griselda* is the second boat from the left of the photograph.

endearing, rather comic birds. As one approaches Sloten from the south the yacht haven lies to the west of the windmill. On this evening, as it appeared crowded, we left it to port and tied up to a little old scow a hundred yards or so short of the swing bridge. We were behind some rather mean cottages and several very old men appeared and took our warps. As soon as we had made fast, I turned to thank them, but with touching good manners they had disappeared, apparently into the ground.

Sloten is really an island and was once a walled town. The island is bisected by the Lindengracht, a pretty street with lime trees overshadowing the canal. There are fixed stone bridges at either end and a wooden bridge in the middle. On this bridge the old men of the village forgather daily to discuss all matters of importance.

Next morning, I awoke feeling that all was not well with the world and with myself in particular. Something seemed to have happened to my face. When I looked in the mirror, I nearly dropped it. A huge swelling had closed my right eye and made me look like the kind of monster Hieronymus Bosch so loved to paint. After breakfast, Griselda and I went in search of a doctor or a dentist, because I thought it might have been an abscess over a wisdom tooth. We found both doctor and dentist under the same roof at the further end of the Lindengracht. The doctor, tall, young and fair, took one look at me and said:

"I think it is my wife you should see." We had to wait for a few

207

minutes while his wife dealt with a patient. While we were waiting he told us something of life in Sloten and the particular advantages of marrying a wife who was a dentist.

"There is no dentist for twenty kilometres, so she has plenty of work. Me, I have not too much work, because in Friesland people are very well. Yesterday I was racing my boat at Lemmer . . ."

Our conversation was cut short by about twenty people emerging from his wife's surgery. He smiled deprecatingly:

"When one is in the chair, the rest of the family like to watch!"

Mevrouw Tjalma was dark and small. In a very modern surgery she set to work on me in earnest. She poked and prodded my mouth and hammered my teeth as if they were train wheels.

"It is not your teeth," she said briefly, and handed me back to her husband. After he had examined me he said:

"I think it is a virus infection," and despatched me into the world with penicillin and some noxious black ointment.

After returning to the boat, we moved it round into the yacht haven. There was no wind and the sun beat down on us from a hard blue sky. I lurked below while Charles spent the afternoon cleaning the topsides, with boiling water, detergent and finally steel wool, of the oil and coal dust that we had collected in Haarlem.

The Sloten yacht haven had been made only a couple of years previously by cutting the bank away and removing a small footbridge. It is fringed with silvery bat willows and overlooked by a handsome thatched mill. To the south the open, very green fields stretch with periodic interruptions of barns and clumps of trees to the gently undulating horizon. In the evening I came out on deck and we sat in the sun drinking good Frisian gin, which I found to be a tolerably effective anaesthetic. Six or seven pretty little open boats, all of the same design with leeboards and the traditional high-peaked curved gaff rig, came sailing by. They were like tiny boeiers with their fan-shaped leeboards.

Apart from two motor cruisers, *Patient Griselda* was the largest boat in the haven. Most of the craft were from fourteen to eighteen foot long. They were all fitted up with canvas awnings under which anything up to half a dozen young people could sleep.

After dark the young doctor and his wife came down to the boat and drank coffee with us. She was a South Hollander, a Zeelander, and he a real Frisian. They told us that both the Frisians and the Zeelanders were very suspicious of strangers. And with the Frisians there is no half way, they either love you or hate you. Dr Tjalma started talking about Sloten in wintertime:

"Oh, it is very quiet. No business, much rain and cold, then suddenly the rain stops, the wind drops and frost comes. All the meres and all the canals freeze. Then many people come and Sloten wakes up, just like the summer. For Sloten is one of the 'eleven towns' of Friesland. We have a great tour of these towns, all on skates. It goes on by day and by night, when the skaters carry flaming torches."

"Which are the 'eleven towns'?" Griselda asked.

"Now, let me see, there's Hindeloopen, Workum, Dokkum, Makkum, Ijlst, Leeuwarden . . ." he paused and his wife chimed in with:

"Don't forget Sloten."

"Yes, I know, but that is only seven. Oh! yes, there's Sneek, Lemmer and Bolsward. That makes eleven."

"No, it's not, it's only ten." They argued back and forward, but the eleventh town they could never think of, and to this day I don't know which it is.

We sat talking until late in the light from the two little brass oil lamps; the soft tones of pitch pine, iroko and mahogany and the rich red patterns of the Portuguese blankets gave the cabin an invitingly warm appearance. At last the Tjalmas rose to go.

"I have my surgery at eight o'clock in the morning." I made some remark about the earliness of this. "Not for my patients. They are all farmers (in fact they are most of them my uncles or aunts). They get up at four; by seven they have finished their milking and the milk has been despatched to the factories. Then they eat their breakfast and by eight o'clock they are ready to come and see me, without any interruption to their day. If I am lucky, by ten o'clock I am also free. Then I can go sailing."

It rained during the night, but by the morning the skies were clear and bright with a few high cumulus clouds ambling over the Frisian landscape. In deference to my face, we remained at Sloten for another day. By Saturday my appearance was, if anything more frightening. Dr Tjalma took one look at it and said:

"But your face is quite crooked, is it always like that?" I muttered "No." He shook his head: "I am not happy." I admitted I wasn't either.

"I think I will take you to the hospital at Sneek, I have a friend there."

After some telephoning this kind young man drove me the twenty kilometres to the town of Sneek where, in a very up-to-date hospital, I saw no fewer than four specialists. At last the ear, nose and throat man said:

"Your sinuses, your antrims, your nose, your throat and your ears are all all right. It is a virus infection of the facial nerves like people have round their middles. The name is *Herpes Zoster*." Herpes Zoster! What on earth could it be? In Holland the past and the present are pretty close. I had visions of the plague, of the Black Death and other mediaeval complaints. Yet a virus infection had a reassuringly modern sound about it. At length I was returned to the boat and to the care of my crew, with what amounted to a portable pharmacy and strict orders to keep out of the wind and to go home at once. Keeping out of the wind, particularly as it was gusting at about Force 6 that morning, is not a very easy thing to do in a small boat. However, we had a hurried lunch and were just about to set off when Captain Tjalma, the doctor's uncle, appeared beside us. He was a charming old man with a great love of England. He had served in the Dutch merchant navy, sailing out of Newcastle during the war. He bowed formally, then set himself up for a speech.

"I have a proposal to make. As you know I am a captain in the merchant navy, and I know about navigation and the Noord Zee and all that. You are ill, I would like to help you sail your little boat home. I am ready to come now if you say the word."

We were almost overcome by his kindness, but explained that we had planned to leave our boat in Holland and come back for her later. We said our goodbyes and set off through the winding Frisian waterways, which I saw mostly through the cabin windows. We reached Stavoren at about six o'clock. This was to be our point of departure for Enkhuizen. There was a nice anchorage alongside the quay inside the lock. We tied up there and then found that the lock remained shut for the whole of Sunday, so having no wish to be held up for another twenty-four hours we had to lock out into the harbour where there was a bit of a swell. The only restaurant we could find was one alongside the lock. Here we drank a lot of Dutch gin. What we ate I cannot remember. Towards the end of the meal, I lightheadedly (being full of Bokma) suggested we made the trip to Enkhuizen during the night. The wind had dropped to a nice sailing breeze and my crew immediately took me up on this.

In gathering darkness, we slipped our mooring lines and at 21.30 hours streamed the log. We could lay Enkhuizen on a westerly tack. This was Griselda's first night sail, and she was at the helm for most of the way. The wind began to fail when we were about four or five miles off Enkhuizen, so it was under sail and motor that we finally made the north end of the dyke that protects the harbours. For anyone entering by night for the first time it is rather confusing. We found our way in by using the dyke as a handrail and keeping within twenty yards of it. The entrance to the yacht haven is about a mile inside the dyke. One passes the northern harbour first, then makes for the bright white light that stands on the port side of the entrance to the yacht haven. This harbour was used by fishing boats as well as yachts, the fishing boats keeping to starboard and the yachts to port. We circled the sleeping haven but could see no vacant places on the port quay, so, loath to tie up to anyone in the small hours of the morning, we came alongside the fishermen's quay where the botters unload their eels; and it smelt like it! Griselda heated up some Scotch broth and we drank this as dawn was breaking, then climbed into our berths. The right side of my face felt as if it had been hit by a trip hammer.

I slept fitfully, dreaming I was going to my own funeral and finally waking to the sound of church bells. It was Sunday morning and through my remaining eye I could see beams of sunlight playing on the cabin roof. The others slept soundly. I climbed stiffly out of bed and peered into the looking-glass. It would have been better if I had not. Hearing me moving about, the crew rather reluctantly bestirred themselves. We combined breakfast and lunch. As with some difficulty I ate some food, I noticed that they both studiously avoided looking at me, and that they spoke in slightly hushed voices.

It was another bright day but with a lot of cumulus about as we sailed out of the pierheads and southwards alongside the dyke. Enkhuizen was suddenly illuminated by a shaft of sunlight. Seen against the sombre green cloud-shadowed sea, it presented just such an appearance as it must have had when richly-laden Dutch transports from the East Indies rolled their way home over the last few shallow miles of the Zuider Zee. There is a lot of the past to be seen in Holland, but in moments like this the past becomes indissolubly linked with the present.

We spent the night outside the Edam lock and by 08.45 hours next morning we were inside the gates. Once inside, the kindly lock-keeper and his English wife persuaded us that it would be much quicker to go to Haarlem by the Ijsselmeer and Amsterdam, than through Purmerend, the way we had come. So we turned about and, though the lock was only a couple of feet wider than *Patient Griselda* is long, we were able to swing her round using a stern spring. Our journey to Haarlem was uneventful and we reached the Spaarne railway bridge with fifteen minutes to spare, for it was due to open at four o'clock. As we entered Haarlem it started to rain heavily.

"Does it never do anything but rain in this damned place?"

Charles asked rather querulously. He was looking a little weary, and as my face had reached a kind of numb stage I took over from him. The rain continued to pour down, and by the last Haarlem road bridge we were kept jilling round for over half an hour before the bridge-keeper left his little glass box. He then hailed us alongside and accused us of not paying at any of the other bridges. We refuted his charges stoutly, but I doubt if we convinced him. As we had been most punctilious about dropping our 25c pieces into the lowered klompen we were somewhat annoyed.

We motored along through Heemstede and the steady downpour showed no signs of letting up. Our plan was to reach the Sassenheim motorway bridge and to tie up there for the night. Just as it was getting dark, and Griselda was at the helm, the infallible diesel coughed, spluttered and died. We had allowed it to run out of fuel! I hastily poured a couple of gallons into the tank and Charles cranked, but all to no purpose. I guessed an airlock had formed and had no idea then of how to clear it. All this while *Patient Griselda* was quietly going on her way, for Griselda had hauled up the jib the moment the engine had failed. We were about two and a half miles short of a little place called Lisse. The rain was falling almost vertically and we had only a very faint following wind. Anyway, we had steerage way, and in the darkness we ghosted silently along. In Lisse there is one bridge, and we approached it very slowly indeed. The bridge-keeper kept it open for us for quite ten minutes as we crept up to him. Charles, with some foresight, shouted:

"Is there a Jachtwerf near here?"

"Een honderd metres rechts" came the reply from above our heads. This proved to be a very Irish-Dutch hundred metres. It must have been ten times that distance before we reached the yacht yard. By this time the wind had increased and there was an absolute cloudburst of rain. We rounded up to the quay with head to wind and made fast. We then set the awning up over the hatch and dived below to a welcome meal of hot soup, new potatoes and the finest underdone cold roast beef I had ever eaten.

A broken-down engine, darkness, heavy rain, the cruise cut short and Herpes Zoster might have been conducive to some lowness of spirit, yet I felt strangely happy. The sensation of gliding down that canal in the rain and the darkness was far from disagreeable. Charles's plan for getting us to a yacht yard was for them to fix our engine and to lower our mast for us so that we could pass under the Sassenheim bridge, whose opening time we would inevitably have missed.

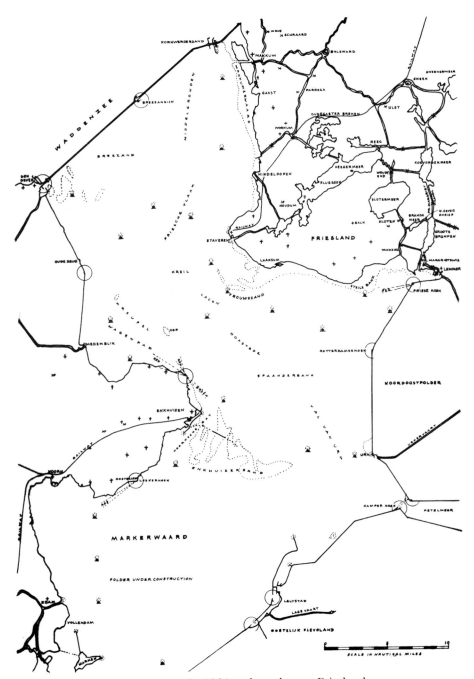

Chart of the Ijsselmeer as it was in 1964 and south-west Friesland.

I woke feeling bloody. By 07.30 hours Charles had been ashore and had returned with a mechanic, who set to work on the engine. After a moment or two he grunted the Dutch equivalent of "Air-lock". In twenty minutes the Lister was running as sweetly as ever. Meanwhile I could hear footsteps overhead and some argument between two of the boatyard men, one apparently bright, the other somewhat chuckleheaded, who were lowering the mast. In spite of their periodic disagreements they had completed their job and made everything secure in just over half an hour. The bill for the whole operation, including eight gallons of fuel, came to nine guilders.

It was still raining, it was cold and it was now blowing very hard. We had a hurried breakfast, then I retired to my bunk and Charles and Griselda took us on our way. We shot the Sassenheim bridge, skirted the Kaagermeer, and then as we came up to the Braassemermeer the wind began to blow at gale force. Now this is only a shallow lake, some two miles or so in length. On this morning seen through a porthole it looked like the Pentland Firth. The water really began to fly.

"You go below," Charles shouted to Griselda, "no point in us both getting soaked." But at that moment the awning, which they had left up as a spray hood, began to come adrift. It was quite impossible to unship it, so Griselda crouched on the bridge deck and held it down by practically lying on it. The wind was now gusting very strongly, the trees were in violent motion and the reeds were being blown almost horizontal. *Patient Griselda* butted her full bow into these short, steep little waves and threw sheets of spray into the cockpit. At one moment Charles thought he would have to turn back, because he could not see the buoys marking the channel. As we came to the southern end of this turbulent mere, the seas quietened. This had been something of an eyeopener to one who had never sailed on inland waters before.

We left the Braassemermeer behind us and approached a place called Woubrugge.

"There's the yard!" Griselda shouted, "we'll tie up to that botter." It looked to be a beautifully-kept yard. Griselda went in search of the proprietors Van Wijk en Zoon and found them, father and son, in a very modern office. They made her very welcome and young Van Wijk returned with her aboard *Patient Griselda*. He appeared to like our boat and told us that though they earned their livelihood by building boats, their pleasure was in sailing them; his father had just been on the Fastnet Race and he had been taking part in the Flying Dutchman championships. In no time we had fixed up with the Van Wijks that *Patient Griselda* should rest there for the winter.

We caught the night boat back from the Hook and by nine o'clock next morning I was in my doctor's surgery.

"Heavens alive! what on earth is the matter with you?" he exclaimed. He examined me and then said: "It is clear enough, you have got a severe attack of shingles."

"Shingles?" I asked, "they told me in Holland it was something called Herpes Zoster!"

"It may sound more impressive, but I am afraid that it is exactly the same thing—and probably just as uncomfortable under either name."

When I got back from the doctor's surgery Griselda gave me the sad news that my old lifeboat-conversion friend Bill Porter had been drowned while sailing. Bill and his wife had been on a long-awaited holiday in his lifeboat conversion *Trader Horn*, the lifeboat he had bought on the sleazy bank of the River Lea. Returning to the Stour from the Blackwater, they had been becalmed. *Trader Horn* had no power except her sails, for Bill had a great contempt for yachts with motors. Night came down. They had no navigation lights and it was not until about 11 pm that a bit of a breeze had come up. They must have been somewhere off Walton-on-the-Naze when the mainsail suddenly jibed and the boom knocked him into the water. As his brother Albert said afterwards:

"He was a round little chap, he'd got no more stability than a hen's egg." His poor wife, who had been resting below, heard a shout and came up into the cockpit to find he had gone overboard. He shouted at her to chuck him a rope. She picked up the end of the mainsheet and threw it to him. He grabbed it for a moment, but a puff of wind must have filled the sails and it slipped from his grasp.

Eventually the poor distracted woman, though she had little experience of boats, brought *Trader Horn* alongside Walton Pier. She was helped ashore and a boat put out immediately, but with no success.

Bill's body was washed ashore the day before we returned from Holland. This tragedy put our little troubles into perspective. We were devoted to Bill and it was also a terrible lesson. Stanchions and lifelines, and in bad weather a personal lifeline and harness, are absolutely essential for any offshore work.

* * * * *

The return from Holland. Griselda at the helm near the Kentish Knock, on passage from Ramsgate to Woodbridge.

The Sandettie lightvessel, which we passed on our passage from Dunkerque.

Patient Griselda spent the winter under the good care of Van Wijk en Zoon at Woubrugge. The following May Charles Hanson, Griselda and I collected the boat. Our return journey was notable only for a cloudless sky and a steady Force 4 wind on the beam which gave us the sail of a lifetime.

6

Return to Friesland

Two years later, as it had been an unsettled summer, Keith Cutmore and I took *Patient Griselda* over to Rotterdam a couple of weeks before our holiday was due to begin. It was late on a June afternoon when we sailed out of the Deben in company with an old Channel Island pilot cutter. At the Sunk lightvessel she bore away to the south-east, heading for Ostende. Soon we had the North Sea to ourselves. A faint breeze on our quarter wafted us along, but by the evening it had died away. We ploughed our way along under power over a sea as smooth as the Serpentine. Imperceptibly it grew dark, but the sky was brilliant with stars and at midnight precisely the full moon arose. It was a night of rare tranquillity.

We sat in the cockpit and talked about life. Keith was a good shipmate and he was not only a very good seaman but with his handsome bearded face, lit by the glow of the binnacle lamp, he had the reassuring quality of actually looking the part. As the eastern sky began to lighten, it turned colder. I climbed down into the cabin and started up the primus stove.

"What about a cup of coffee?" I asked.

"Good idea."

We were sipping our hot drinks as the sun came up over the horizon. There was a faint haze on the water.

"I wouldn't mind betting it's going to be a hot day," Keith said, stripping off his canvas smock as he spoke. And so it proved to be.

We passed the Goree lightvessel as breakfast was cooking and tied up in the little basin at the Hook of Holland in time for lunch. That evening, with *Patient Griselda* safely moored outside, we relaxed and dined in comfort at the Maas Yacht Club.

"It's been a nice trip, John," Keith said, leaning back in his chair. "I must say if all our crossings were as smooth as that one life would be easy . . . and maybe that much duller."

"I'll settle for the dullness," I answered.

"OK, let's drink to dullness then," and we solemnly toasted each other.

A fortnight later I was back at the Maas Yacht Club with Griselda and my cousin Paul.

"I think she's here somewhere," I said as, heavily loaded, we staggered and tripped over the slippery stagings. It was pitch dark but for one feeble light at the head of the steps.

"I told you we ought to have come over on the night boat," Griselda gasped.

"Couldn't we stay the night in the Club?" Paul suggested.

"Nonsense! We'll be perfectly all right once we are aboard." As I spoke it started to rain, cold, stinging, wet Dutch rain. Griselda and I were laden with kitbags and baskets of food and Paul was carrying a huge suitcase which must have been loaded with bricks, judging by his grunts and groans.

At last I spotted our boat. She was lying some feet out from the staging.

"Give me a hand with these stern warps, Paul," I said. "We shall have to pull her in a bit." I grabbed the line nearest to me. It was repellently slimy to the touch. Paul must have made the same discovery, for I heard him say:

"Oh God! what am I to do with it, it is covered in oil!"

"Just hang on a moment and I will make this one fast." I took a couple of turns round a bollard and joined my now dejected young cousin.

"The filthy thing is all greasy!" he remarked in a rather querulous tone.

"I know it is," I answered, "must have been an oil spillage. Here, give it to me." This was hardly the moment for instruction in belaying ropes.

We stepped on to the boat. As I opened the cabin hatch the reeking smell of diesel oil greeted us.

"It will soon blow away," I said, not really believing what I was saying. Griselda opened her mouth to say something and then thought better of it and remained silent. I lit the cabin lamps.

"Come on in Paul, I'll show you your bunk and then we can stow our gear. Mind your head!" but I had spoken too late. He had banged into the deck beam that separates the cabin from the foc's'le and collapsed stunned on to the nearest bunk.

"It's only safe sitting down on this boat," Griselda said.

"I expect I shall get used to it," Paul said in a muted voice. Bed-making in the dark, barging into each other, with rain driving in and in the choking atmosphere of diesel fumes, was not a promising beginning to our cruise. Paul had had no experience of living in confined spaces and Griselda is, at times like this, apt to take a rather acid view of the sport.

"Just my weather," she muttered as she climbed into her fleabag.

"We shall be able to go ashore quite a lot, shan't we?" Paul asked in a voice loaded with doubts. "There must be quite a lot of things worth looking at in Amsterdam."

"We are not going to Amsterdam, we are going to Friesland," I answered tersely.

"Oh, what's in Friesland?"

"Cows!" Griselda's voice was muffled by blankets. "Just lots of bloody black and white cows. Oh, for God's sake listen to that!" A carillon was clanging out the hour.

"I don't expect it will go on all night," I said hopefully.

"I bet it does," Griselda replied. And it did; I awoke every time it started up. Once I heard Griselda muttering about a leak dripping on to her pillow. Paul made no sound, but I had a feeling that he was lying awake wondering why he had come.

At seven o'clock I finally got up and looked out of the hatchway. The storm had blown itself out but had left a grey drizzly morning. Ragged clouds were scudding across the leaden sky and the Maas looked choppy and uninviting.

Our breakfast was a dismal feast as we sat round the cabin table, hollow-eyed and uncommunicative. Everything felt damp to the touch. The primus stove showed some reluctance to get going and the boat still stank like an oil rig. While Griselda washed up Paul and I set off in search of diesel fuel and water. When we had filled our tanks, we spent nearly half an hour freeing our oil-soaked bow warps, which were made fast to a buoy under the water. At last, as grimy as a couple of greasers, we got them aboard. The Lister diesel at least started up at the first press of the button.

We threaded our way out of the jachthaven and crossed to the south side of the waterway to await the opening of the Konnings Haven Bridge. We tied up to a German barge. Our bow line was taken by a rosy-cheeked boy who said he came from Poplar. I asked him if he liked the life.

"I love it," he said, "we go just everywhere." Before I could find out where "just everywhere" was we had to cast off, for the bridge was opening.

We left the Maas and turned into the Ijssel. The clouds slowly dispersed, the sun came out, our spirits rose and *Patient Griselda*, even if she did smell a bit, went efficiently about her business. We had left Rotterdam with its huge conglomeration of modern docks and industry behind us, but the banks of the canal were still flanked with warehouses. We passed one great rambling, ramshackle, old clapboard building.

"It looks as though it would make a good setting for *Our Mutual*

Friend," Griselda remarked, "just the sort of place Rogue Rider-hood or Gaffer Hexham would have lived in." Paul, with a contempt for anything but contemporary literary allusion, said:

"I should think it is more likely to provide the *mise-en-scène* for a Simenon story." As we drew level with this ancient structure we could see a brightly-painted notice with the prosaic words "Jachtwerf, Plastic Booten en Water-Skij".

By evening we had reached the Kaag. We tied up to the staging of a café we had visited previously.

"Let's get out of this dieselly smell," Griselda said. Then, turning to my cousin, "ever eaten pannekooken, Paul?"

"Not to my knowledge."

"Well, they are something particularly Dutch. They are pancakes, each about the size of a manhole cover, with fillings made from bacon, smoked sausage, fried apples and Lord knows what else."

"I'll try one," Paul said nervously.

An hour later, after we had consumed a mountainous pile of pancakes, Paul leaned back in his chair, beamed at us and said:

"I feel as stuffed as a Perigord goose."

The next morning the smell of diesel oil was getting worse, so we pulled in to the boatyard at Lisse where two years before in our hurried flight from Friesland they had cleared an airlock in our fuel line. A nice old man came aboard, sniffed, muttered something and then attacked the engine. After some heaving and grunting, he turned to me and said: "Ja, it is de filter," and showed me the offending object. It was choked with dirt and water, and we had no spare, nor had the yard.

"I will clean it for you, and the yard man, he will order some new ones for you."

The cause of the smell was cured. Later on, when we arrived at Hoorn, we collected six filters from the Poste Restante. I still have two of those original filters, and since that day *Patient Griselda* has never offended our sense of smell.

By the time the engineer had finished cleaning up our fuel system the sun was beating down on us. We continued on towards Haarlem, tying up for lunch at a place called Cruquius. Paul, who has a nose for museums, informed us that we were quite near to the Cruquius Pumping Station Museum. Somewhat reluctantly Griselda and I allowed ourselves to be piloted into a large building, there to be faced with a huge relief map of Holland. At intervals, with a clattering din, this map was submerged in turbulent floodwater and then rescued and dried off by the ingenuity of the

Dutch water engineers. Weak from hunger but much inspired by this demonstration of Dutch courage in the face of adversity, we returned to the boat and our belated lunch.

That evening we moored in a small mere, the Mooienal, a few miles north of Haarlem. It was a pleasant anchorage, quiet after the busy Spaarne, though even this quiet may soon be threatened by the spread of Haarlem's industry. On this lovely evening it was just a rather wild lake dotted with islands and reedbeds. A few camping cruisers were moored with their bows pushed firmly into their reedy resting places. As we came up to our mooring one of these craft roared past us, propelled by an outboard and driven by a pretty plump blonde who seemed immodestly anxious to reach her bedding-down place. Her young man, with an air of resignation, was draped over the boom.

"He looks like a lamb being led to the slaughter," Griselda said.

"What a glorious death!" Paul answered. "I didn't expect the Dutch girls to be so appealing. She was pretty dishy."

The sun went down, and still the outboards and motorpeds buzzed away in the distance. Overhead giant KLM jets from Schiphol headed off for New York or over the North Pole to Vancouver, and nearby a redshank called. Our little boat looked disgustingly dirty after her stay on the Maas.

The next day we crossed the North Sea Ship Canal and squeezed into the big lock at Zaandam, in company with a fleet of huge tanker-barges. In spite of the turbulence from their propellers we suffered no hurt, and at last we reached the peace of the North Holland canal. We travelled slowly past reedy banks and grazing cattle. Our companions on this lovely waterway were ducks of every variety and permutation. We were passed by only one boat, a barge bound for Rotterdam.

At the market town of Purmerend we tied up in the basin. There were four bridges to be opened, so Paul and I went in search of the Brugwachter.

"Do you think we might buy some cakes?" Paul asked, peering into a shop window filled with mouthwatering pastries. Inside the shop his attention was diverted from the cakes to the girl behind the counter, whose staggering beauty galvanised my cousin into fervent attempts at chatting her up. The fact that the maiden had no English and Paul no Dutch finally limited the progress of his courtship to ordering twice as many cakes as we needed. Reluctantly we came out of the shop. Paul said, rather unnecessarily, I thought: "Gosh! Did you notice that girl? If there are any more like that I'm going to enjoy this holiday. I must go and buy a phrase book. Do you think we might stay here for a bit?"

"No," I answered firmly, "we are going to Friesland, and to get to Friesland we have got to find the bloke who opens these bridges. We'd better ask someone." As I spoke, a man leaning on a bicycle looked up, so tentatively I said: "Dag, Mijnheer! Waar ist der brugwachter?"

"Certainly Sir, Mr Bridge opener, he lives just over there, in the little green home on the left," pointing to an octagonal toll house.

"Dank u wel," I answered.

"Alstublieft. Not at all, Sir, a pleasure." I walked up to the little green toll house and rang the doorbell. The door was opened a few inches and a woman peered out. She had a face to shatter the nerves of a strong man. It was the Brueghel troll, poor old dear, who had opened the bridges for us on our previous visit in *Dowsabel*. She spoke most kindly and in excellent English:

"In a moment the bridge keeper would come." He came, true to her word; and in as short a time as he and his grim-faced wife (if indeed she was his wife) could make it, he on a bicycle, she on foot, the three bridges were opened (the fourth had been demolished), and we were on our way to Edam. The evening was quiet and the reed-lined canal was quite deserted except for ourselves and the coots and ducks.

Our entry to Edam lacked dignity. A new bridge was being built at the end of the once delightfully quiet stretch of canal where we had moored on our first visit. A lighter was blocking most of the channel, and in avoiding this obstruction *Patient Griselda's* mast and forestay cut a way through the overhanging greenery of a large sycamore tree. Leaves, seeds and branches showered down on us and in a moment we were piled high with foliage. We would have done credit to anyone's production of *Macbeth*. We tied up in the same place and to the same tree as two years before. The beautifully mown greensward was now unkempt and cars were parked all the way along the canal. Things change, even in Holland.

Paul, reading from his guidebook, informed us how Edam cheese was made and that the Grote Kerk, notable for its stained glass, was worth visiting. "To enter the church", he read, "one has to obtain the key from the sacristan who lives at 39 Kerkstraat. That, as no doubt you know, means Church Street," he helpfully explained.

Next morning, after calling on the sacristan, who said that the church was open because of the bouwmeester, we visited the Grote Kerk of St Nicholas. The reference to the bouwmeester was

Patient Griselda moored alongside the Juliana Park at Hoorn.

explained by a vast screen of tongue-and-groove pine planking
which divided the church in half. One half was in use, the other
half was under repair. As we admired the stained glass we could
hear, from somewhere up in the roof where the builders were
working, the unmelodious sounds of the current top-of-the-charts.

We locked out into the Ijsselmeer and under the gentlest of
south-west winds we drifted up towards Hoorn. We launched the
Avon dinghy and Paul bathed. Except for the distant company of a
solitary hoogaarts, we had the sea to ourselves. As the afternoon
drew on the wind died, so we finally dropped our sails and
motored into the inner harbour. There were only a dozen yachts
moored under the trees alongside the greensward, and none of
them was English. Of all the harbours in Holland, this is the most
beautiful. Hoorn was once one of the important ports of Holland
in the days when the Dutch were the great ocean carriers of
commerce. The harbour still is a combination of a mercantile
quayside and a tree-shaded greensward which divides it into two.
Griselda voiced our thoughts when she said: "Being moored
alongside this parklike place gives one the impression of being
anchored in the middle of the Bois de Boulogne." Not to be
outdone, Paul said:

The Hoofdtoren from the Binnenhaven at Hoorn.

"It looks just like Seurat's 'Sunday on the Grand Jatte'."

That evening we dined in the restaurant on the first floor of the famous *Oude Waag* in the middle of the town. The ground floor of this old "Weigh House" building is a museum. The room in which we ate was lofty and oak panelled and we were served by two pretty girls in sixteenth-century costume, dressed like little Puritans in attractive mossy green with white aprons and caps.

As we wandered back to the harbour, Paul said:

"I think there is something rather seductive in those Puritanical costumes." I could not but agree with him.

"Boo – boop, boo – boop!" I was dimly conscious of this noise, but it was not until I had opened my eyes and looked out of the companionway that I realised it was a fog signal. It was something I had not expected in the Ijsselmeer. Visibility was down to about thirty yards. The sails were covered in droplets of water.

The fog lasted until mid-morning, but we were in no hurry. We spent the day in harbour cleaning up our very dirty little ship. It

Patient Griselda coming into Lemmer. Griselda and my cousin Paul.

was thirsty work and we bought from an itinerant grocer on a tricycle all the Amstel pils that he carried.

The next day we had an easy sail over to Lemmer, across what seemed like tropical seas. Looking back, the Dromedaris Tower at Enkhuizen in a flickering mirage seemed to be dancing in the sky. At Lemmer we tied up to the breakwater where the tar was bubbling in the heat. We waited for three large barges to pass out of the lock. One of them was registered at Regensburg, some five hundred miles away on the Danube. Visions of travelling across Europe opened up before our eyes, but for the moment Friesland was our objective and we had arrived. We left the locks behind us and were soon turning up the narrow Langesloot on our way to Sloten. The warm evening light, the winding reed-banked canal and the inevitable black and white Frisian cattle provided a Constable-like scene.

"There are your cows, Griselda," Paul said.

"They wear overcoats in the winter," was her only comment. When we at last reached the jachthaven at Sloten our idyllic scene

225

was quickly dispelled. It was packed with boats. We squeezed in between two half-deckers and tied up. Once again I wondered about the wisdom of returning to a well-loved place. After dinner I walked along to a café called the *Zeven Wouden* to telephone to Matthew, Paul's brother and the fourth member of our crew, to tell him where to meet us. Heavy clouds were rolling up and I could hear the distant sound of thunder.

It took me over two hours to get through to London, so I sat and drank a great many bottles of pils. The locals came in for their Saturday evening drink and to play bar billiards or cards. It must have been raining hard, for the newcomers as they came into the bar were shaking themselves like wet dogs. Sitting there alone, I felt like a character from a Simenon novel. I began to wonder which of these respectable Frieslanders had murdered his mistress or was about to run away with his neighbour's wife. I was weaving quite a fantasy about a poor mousy little man whose luck at cards seemed to be no greater than his success in life when at last my call came through and I gave some rather hazy directions to Matthew to meet us at Sneek.

As I came back into the bar, I felt a hand on my shoulder. I turned to see old Captain Tjalma.

"I still regret that you did not allow me to pilot you across the Noord Zee, when you had that illness to your face," he said. "It is a good little ship, yours." I made a deprecatory movement. "Oh, yes, she's a bit little, but I think she could take more rough weather than *you* would enjoy. When I was working with the Royal Navy in the war, there was a saying I learned about seaworthiness. 'Boats is all right, it's the men in them'. Have you heard that?" I admitted I had.

"So, it is still a good saying. No?"

"Yes," I answered. As it was still pouring with rain I postponed my return to the boat. We talked at length about ships and the sea and the long, cold Frisian winters, and of heroic feats by skaters on the tour of the eleven Frisian towns—and I still don't know which they are. It was nearing midnight when Captain Tjalma said:

"I am afraid I must leave you now. I will come to pay my respects to your wife in the morning. You are coming?"

"I think I will wait a little longer to see if the rain stops."

"Good," then turning to a waiter, "Ober, another Bokma for my friend." I was just finishing my drink when the door of the café burst open and Paul and Griselda, wild-eyed and in streaming oilskins, came bursting in.

"While you have been sitting here boozing, we have had a fearful time," Griselda said, wiping the rain off her face. "It has been blowing a blinking hurricane."

"It was more like a tornado! All the boats were jumping about," Paul said. "We had to shorten our warps. Climbing over one of the camping cruisers I trod on top of a loving couple. You should have heard their language—not that I could understand it."

"I should have thought the rain would have cooled their ardour," I said.

"Not a bit of it—the steam was positively rising off them."

"Aren't you going to buy us a drink?" Griselda asked rather plaintively. "I'm wet and I'm frozen."

"What would you like?"

"Bokma, and plenty of it," she answered.

"Same for me," from Paul before I had time to ask him. I mollified them with Frisian gin and told them of my meeting with Captain Tjalma.

It was still blowing hard and still pouring with rain as we walked back to the boat. Griselda had had the forethought to bring my oilskins. By one o'clock the storm had passed. The haven, presided over by a ghostly windmill, was being intermittently illuminated by flashes of lightning. There was a sound of muttering in a nearby camping cruiser. They probably had something to mutter about, I thought, for by that time their boat must have been practically awash.

We left Sloten early next morning, with old Captain Tjalma waving us farewell. It was a bright morning with mountains of cumulus sailing over the immense Frisian skies. We had the Slotermeer to ourselves. As we travelled northwards the same pattern of farm and barn, all in one, kept repeating. As well as the innumerable Frisian cows we saw an occasional Frisian black horse. Our wake set the reeds along the canal banks rustling. A heron flew slowly across our path and a black tern dived almost into our cockpit.

We arrived at Sneek in time for lunch; we wandered round the town, bought food and a Frisian flag to fly while in their waters.

Our visits to Friesland had originally been inspired by reading H. M. Doughty's *Friesland Meres*. This charming description of a family cruise in a Norfolk wherry gives a slightly misleading impression, for it was published in 1889. On Doughty's recommendation we were now heading for Grouw. On a summer's day in the eighteen-eighties when Doughty visited it there were, apart from his wherry, only two tjalks from Groningen loading peat. When we arrived at Grouw at about five o'clock on that particular

227

afternoon there must have been several thousand yachts milling around. Cowes during Regatta Week would have seemed like a watery desert compared to this. We tied up to an overcrowded jetty; consulted the chart and decided to make for a place called Wartena. We cast off and threaded our way out of the meer. Paul opened Doughty and read:

"Wartena is an attractive village; there is a bridge, a church with a tall spire, a snug house for the pastor . . ."

"And probably a Butlin's Holiday Camp too!" Griselda interjected. Quite unmoved, Paul continued: "Above it the stream expands into a pretty pool, surrounded and paved round the sides with lily leaves; it is called 'de Wyde'. . ." Griselda interrupted any further nostalgic excursions by appearing from the cabin with the familiar square bottle of Bokma and glasses. As she poured the gin, she said:

"Better fortify ourselves and be prepared for the worst." For once she proved to be wrong, for the further we sailed from Grouw, the quieter the canal became. When we reached Wartena it was very much as Doughty had described it, and though there was a little jachthaven we tied up in 'de Wyde' to a telegraph post. It was a pleasant, quiet anchorage.

"Good old Doughty," Griselda remarked, as we sat on deck warming ourselves in the evening sun. "He would not have been so shocked at this." All Paul had to say was;

"I don't think Friesland rates very high in the cultural stakes— not that it isn't very pleasant," he hurriedly added. "I hope we shall be able to get to Amsterdam. It would be a pity to come to Holland and not to visit the Rijksmuseum."

We assured him that his cultural thirst should be slaked when we reached the southern end of the Ijsselmeer.

The next day we returned to Sneek and met Matthew, carrying a briefcase and a neatly-rolled umbrella. He arrived sitting on the back of some stranger's bicycle. He greeted us with:

"Never walk if you can ride!"

Over supper we discussed our plans. Paul said:

"When we get near Amsterdam, John says we can take a day off to visit the museums and churches in Amsterdam."

"Sod culture!" replied his more earthy brother, "I'd like to chat up a few birds. The thing we ought to see is that street where all the tarts sit in the windows, showing off what they've got to offer!"

"Where on earth did you hear about that?" asked his elder brother with an unexpected gleam in his eye.

"Chap at Guy's told me. Said that no-one with any self-respect could visit Amsterdam without seeing the red light district."

"Let us see where it is," Paul said, prosaically unfolding the guidebook's map.

The next morning was grey and dank. We left the Sneek haven and pottered off towards Makkum, the most north-easterly port in the Ijsselmeer. The waterways past Ijlst and Bolsward were almost deserted. The Frisian countryside was peaceful and pleasant and faintly reminiscent of Suffolk. We arrived at Makkum in the early afternoon and went ashore to buy some pots, for Makkum is famous for its pottery.

In the late afternoon, well reefed down, we sailed out of Makkum into the Ijsselmeer. To clear the off-lying banks we sailed almost up to the dyke that encloses the Ijsselmeer and then turned south for Hindeloopen. It was blowing hard, and we had one of the few exhilarating sails of our almost windless holiday. The tower of Hindeloopen church was a splendid landmark, but as we came up towards the harbour we could not for the life of us see the two buoys that mark the channel. We were surrounded by broken water, so finally Matthew, who was at the tiller, put *Patient Griselda* about and we made for the open sea, lowered sail and then very gingerly once again approached the shore under power. As a penalty for dropping our sails, we had a fearful tumble in the broken water. At last, when we were very near in, Matthew spotted one of the buoys. They seemed to be almost on the beach, but they clearly marked the channel, so we rolled our way into the harbour and tied up to a steel tjalk. All night long our fenders squeaked, for in this rather exposed harbour when there is an onshore wind there is always something of a swell. Outside quite a sea was running. The following morning it was blowing even harder, so we delayed our departure and spent the time exploring Hindeloopen, which is an intriguing old town with unexpected little alleyways and canals. To satisfy Paul's wish to improve our minds we visited the museum, which was full of the painted furniture for which Hindeloopen is justly famous.

"It looks rather like the painting on the English canal narrow boats," Matthew remarked. We were taken in tow by a guide. He showed us a handsome painted wall bed, a pretty little sledge hanging from the ceiling with its underside painted to represent the sky, and a few ship models.

"Is that a pastry-cook's delivery cart?" Paul asked, pointing to a kind of pushcart that was decorated with paintings of buns and cakes and loaves of bread.

"Not at all," answered the guide. "It is for a sacred purpose. It

Hindeloopen. Top left: Street scene. Top right: The Museum. Bottom left: Canals and sluices. Bottom right: Harbour. *Patient Griselda* is flying the Friesland courtesy flag.

belonged to the Bakers' Guild and was for carrying their dead lijken."

"Their dead what?" Matthew asked, rather bluntly.

"Lijken, koarpsen in der doodskist—koarpsen in vooden boxes."

"Oh! coffins."

"Ja, that is right—coffins. It is a very beautiful conveyance for coffins." We agreed.

"Seeing all those loaves of bread must have made them go hungry to their graves," Matthew remarked as we trooped after the guide into the exhibition of old Hindeloopen costumes, which were displayed on some ungainly models that seemed to have been frozen into their gawky poses. Griselda said:

"Looks as if rigor mortis got them before they were properly posed."

That same afternoon we set off with our mainsail still reefed and cleared the harbour entrance. There was a tumble of sea off Stavoren, then we had a fast and lively sail to Enkhuizen.

From Enkhuizen to Hoorn is barely ten miles, but now we were beating into a head sea. It was a bright clear day but there was a lot of cumulus about. Enkhuizen was suddenly illuminated by the sunlight.

The clouds thickened. A cold front was approaching and the Ijsselmeer became a grey, heaving waste of water. We tacked back and forth and slowly rounded Oosterlijk. The only craft we saw was a large harbour launch carrying men who had been working on the new polder dyke. As she careered past us her wake practically rolled our cabin sides under.

No sooner had we tied up in the inner harbour at Hoorn than the wind dropped and the skies cleared. The little depression had passed to the north of us and that night it felt as warm as the south of France.

The next day Matthew and Paul went off to Amsterdam to do homage to Dutch art and anything else they had a mind for. Griselda and I cleaned the ship and fitted a new filter to the diesel. The warm night had given way to an even warmer day. We scrubbed the cabin out and cleaned the boat from end to end. Then we each had a bath in a small basin of hot water. It is remarkable how far one can make a small amount of water go.

Feeling clean in mind and body, we set off on a shopping expedition. An hour later, returning laden with food and drink, I felt someone tugging at my basket. It was Eddie Kahn, the young son of *Zeekaag's* owner, whom we had first met on a previous cruise.

"We have come up from Muiden looking for you," he said, as he relieved me of a basket of Amstel beer that I had been carrying. "My parents are on the boat waiting for you." We were soon sitting in *Zeekaag's* cockpit drinking the Kahns' gin, and then, in an alcoholic state of euphoria and without any apparent action on our part, we were doing the same thing aboard *Patient Griselda*.

Reunions aboard small boats seem to have some special quality. Casual acquaintances become friends and friends become more than friends. They become part of the pattern of one's life.

During the evening our crew returned from Amsterdam and were soon absorbed in this innocent orgy. At one stage one of them was doing hand springs, another cartwheels along the quay. Towards midnight Eddie and his young sister Lucie started climbing our masts. Eddie performed the Indian Rope Trick, finally disappearing into the darkness overhead. He was not seen again that night.

Next morning we were a somewhat chastened party; we could barely face each other, let alone cope with a cooked breakfast. The most we could take was a little black coffee. The day promised to be a scorcher. At about a quarter past ten we chugged across the harbour to collect water. There was no sign of life aboard *Zeekaag*, so we sailed out of the harbour into the Ijsselmeer. It was a perfect day with just a little wind. We sailed quietly eastwards for an hour, then came about and fetched back to Hoorn. There was quite a number of sailing boats out, including several botters and tjalks. Before we reached the harbour mouth *Zeekaag* appeared and for the next few hours we sailed in company. The day grew hotter and the wind dropped and the crews of both boats were soon in the water swimming around. The horizon was dotted with stationary craft. As the sun sank into the west it seemed as if we were sailing into the isles of the Hesperides. In fact we were making for Vollendam, which is a tourist attraction, with all that that implies.

From Vollendam our journey southwards as far as Dordrecht was uneventful, and we arrived there after a very long day. We were a little tired and the jachthaven has an awkward entrance. As a result of this and the fact that there was quite a swell running from passing tugs, we lost a bit of paint by banging against the piles. They were honourable scars.

Once inside we found a sheltered little haven lying under the shadow of the Grote Kerk. This church was founded, so Paul informed us, through the good offices of a thrifty virgin called Sura. In spite of being murdered by three workmen she came back from the dead and, for some reason best known to herself, saved her murderers from the hangman. She lived to a ripe old age and finished the building of the church. For her efforts she was canonised.

"Probably set up house with her assassins," Griselda said, as she passed out drinks and cast a dismembered chicken into the frying pan, "Poulet à l'estragon, or at least the boat version of it." We drank our geneva accompanied by the delicious smell of tarragon from the galley.

The meal, and it was a memorable one, was Griselda's swan song, for that night she was to return to England. After dinner we pottered round the old town, which had a markedly Dickensian atmosphere. In the fading light the river looked like a Whistler *Nocturne*. There was a constant flow of shipping; some we saw as dim silhouettes, others we could see only by their navigation lights. At ten o'clock Griselda left us for the Hook of Holland and we returned to the jachthaven. We sat for a while on deck, drinking a final nightcap. Though we were in the middle of a large town, it was remarkably quiet; the only noise was an occasional hoot from a passing tug.

I was awakened by the sound of woodpigeons; I thought for a moment I was back in Suffolk. Soon after breakfast we were away from this pleasant haven to catch the opening of the railway bridge. We circled slowly round, dodging barges and tankers, until it opened, followed somewhat reluctantly by the road bridge which lies beyond it. As we cleared the second bridge we saw an old six-metre flying a blue ensign approaching; some way behind her was a huge Swiss tanker barge.

"That yacht is in a bit of trouble," Matthew shouted from the fore deck. "Her engine must have conked out." The yacht drifted to port and the tide swept her alongside a moored lighter.

"Hang on Alistair!" a very English voice cried out. It came from a yachting-capped, reefer-jacketed figure at the helm. On the foredeck a lanky figure in sun hat and long Bermudan shorts was impotently scrabbling at the edge of the lighter. His only answer was a despairing cry of:

"There's nothing to hold on to!"

"Don't be feeble, Alistair, there must be a ringbolt or something."

"I think I've got her! There's a little cleat I can just hold."

"Well done! There's nothing to worry about." The scene that followed is etched in our minds. Caught by the tide, the stern of the yacht slowly swung away from the lighter. The man called Alistair was still frantically holding her bow in. Meanwhile, the Swiss barge, which must have been every bit of a thousand tons, was fast coming up on her. The barge's lookout man was sitting on the foredeck smoking his pipe and gazing in a ruminative manner in the opposite direction to where this little drama was being played out.

"Pass me the boathook, Alistair!" the yacht's skipper shouted.

"How can I pass you the boathook and still hold on, you dolt!" yelled the now-frantic Alistair.

"No need to panic, I'll give you a hand." So saying, the skipper climbed out of the cockpit, and then—as if a carpet had been pulled from under him—with a pitiful cry he fell flat on his face. It was not a carpet but his boat that had been pulled from under him, for at that very moment some projection on the barge had neatly hooked one of the yacht's backstays and was towing her backwards towards the bridge. The unfortunate Alistair had the presence of mind to let go his hold of the lighter and was clutching the forestay in despair. His skipper, knocked cold, lay supine on the deck.

Matthew cut into our spellbound silence by saying:

"There is not going to be room for both barge and yacht to get through the bridge together."

Alistair clearly recognised this predicament at the same moment.

"What shall we DO!" we heard him scream. His skipper came to, sat up, then in a somewhat bemused voice said:

"DO, why luff, you silly fool! Always luff if you are in trouble!" His brain seemed to be clearing, for in an alarmed voice he shouted:

"I say, where are we going!"

His further words were drowned by a loud crash as mast, rigging and all came tumbling down around his ears. The crew of the barge were still quite unaware of anything untoward having happened.

Tragedy was averted by the bridgemaster's coming to his senses just in time. He switched the traffic lights from green to red and slammed the bridge shut in the face of the oncoming craft. With a great roaring of its diesel and a churning up of water the barge came to rest a dozen feet or so from the bridge. Only then did the crew realise what had happened. There was a silence for a moment, and then a familiar voice rang out:

"I say! You in the barge, don't you know the rule of the road? That power has to give way to sail! I shall have to report. . ." He was silenced by a flood of gutteral and no doubt uncomplimentary Schweizer-Deutsch as the barge's crew disentangled their rigging and cast them off.

"Phew! that was a pretty near thing," Matthew said as we came about to see if any help was needed. "They're all right, a boat has got them in tow already."

Of the barge there was no sign; it was no doubt half way to Switzerland by this time.

"I wonder what would have happened if the bridge had not closed at that moment?" Paul said.

"Their boat would have been smashed to matchwood."

"And the crew?"

"Dead—drowndead," I answered in the immortal words of Mr Peggotty.

The morning mist was dispersing, and as we left the Oude Maas to starboard the sun came out. What little wind there was was right on our nose. By noon we were on the wide waters of the Hollandsche Diep. We had the whole of the ebb tide in our favour, so for the next few hours we had a pleasant beat to windward against a light south-westerly wind.

For the next two days, though, we had an increasingly strong south-west wind against us. In the East Scheldt there was a fearful tumble of sea, but this was not enough to stop a number of large yachts from racing. They were all well reefed down, and most of them were leaning over at most unholy angles, except for one fine boeier that went charging past us leaning only a little from the vertical. These large yachts racing in the grand style over the heaving wastes of the Scheldt made a scene of Victorian splendour. A black tern flew with us for a while, not diving but swooping low over the water scooping up beakfuls of some kind of marine life. Apart from this solitary creature, there were no birds to be seen over these almost limitless estuaries.

We had a short wait at the Zandkreek lock, then we were in tideless but far from tranquil waters, for the wind had if anything

The skyline at Veere.

strengthened. The sombre greyness of the day was giving way to a
broken sky. The intermittent sun, the scudding clouds, the waving
yellow grasses and the green water made a scene of infinite variety.
This was the Zandkreek at its best, still the loveliest thing in the
watery wastes of Holland, with its lagoons and islands, seabirds and
waders and the distant view of Veere, with its idiosyncratic skyline
made distinctive by the bulk of the old church and the spindly
onion-spiked tower of the Raadhuis.

With the closing of the Veersegat, Veere had changed. Its fishing
fleet had departed and it had now become a museum town for
tourists. Hendrik Willem van Loon's ghost must be saddened, for
this once popular Dutch-American historical writer loved this place
above all others.

The Campveerse Toren's excellent restaurant was full, so we
went aloft to the bar and drank a succession of Bokmas as the light
faded over the estuary. At last a table was free and we could eat.
Mellowed by good food and good wine we became less critical. As
we walked back to the boat, Veere seemed in the dark to have

recaptured something of her former charm. We were moored just under the Raadhuis, which was now floodlit; against a purple velvet sky it looked as if it had come out of the *Arabian Nights*.

A couple of days later, after a delectable sail under burning skies over a windblown sea, we arrived at Ostende. Keith rejoined us that same evening. Fifteen hours after leaving Ostende we hove to for the Customs in Woodbridge Haven. After the first four or five hours, we had had yet another utterly windless passage.

It had been an enjoyable little cruise. The memories of our previous shingles-ridden flight from Friesland were forgotten.

On our return from Holland we fitted *Patient Griselda* with a bowsprit so that she could carry a Yankee. The effect was remarkable, for in light airs she had been under canvassed. Also with a jib set outside the staysail, the change to a cutter rig made her modest performance to windward somewhat more purposeful.

Patient Griselda's new rig with bowsprit.

Patient Griselda up against Everson's scrubbing posts.

A few weeks later I put the boat up against the scrubbing posts by Everson's boatshed and spent a long, hot Saturday scrubbing her bottom. She had collected a pretty thick coat of barnacles. Late in the evening the tide at last floated her. I cast off, put the diesel in gear and she leaped through the water like a porpoise. She was clearly grateful for the scrub. The river was bathed in the evening sun as we sailed down to a sheltered anchorage under Shottisham woods. As I tidied up on deck, I could hear the primus stove roaring. Griselda's head appeared through the hatch.

"Dinner will be ready in a few minutes, what about a drink?"

Before going below, I stood for a moment looking about me. There were a couple of boats moored a hundred yards or so from us, and a converted lifeboat was slowly dragging a trawl up Shottisham Reach. A little old open boat, with much-patched, very dingy sails drifted past us on the tide. There was a boy at the tiller and a girl sitting astride a thwart. They looked blissfully intent on what they were doing. It reminded me of our old sailing punt and pre-war days at Oare Creek. And it brought home to me the fact that the real pleasures of sailing are probably to be found in an inverse proportion to the size and cost of the boat.

Epilogue

On the night of 16th October, 1987, the south-east corner of England was hit by an appalling gale. The forests just north of us at Rendlesham and Butley were decimated, leaving a scene reminiscent of Flanders after the battles of the Somme or Ypres.

We were awoken at about 3 am by brilliant flashes of light coming from broken electricity cables outside our bedroom window. Tiles were flying off roofs and trees were crashing down. It was not until about ten o'clock in the morning that we dared to venture outside. We picked our way over fallen trees and broken branches down to the waterside. It was a sight of utter devastation. The harbour was chock-a-block with wrecked boats piled up one on another.

We found *Patient Griselda* underneath a large and very damaged fibreglass motor cruiser. She had dragged her two heavy mooring anchors and had been driven half a mile upstream and right into the harbour, as if she wanted to come home. She was hard up against the quay by Frank Knights' workshop, with her bowsprit pointing skywards and her rear pulpit badly adrift.

On inspection, the damage to the old boat, if considerable, was only superficial. Apart from her displaced bowsprit and stern pulpit, half of one rubbing strake had been ripped off, she had been badly scuffed round the stern and had lost some rail capping. Lastly, her samson post had been driven inboard by the bowsprit. As I looked at her, I thought of the Lloyd's surveyor's remarks when she was being built. Looking at her massive stem post, he had said "Going to the Polar Ice, I suppose."

Patient Griselda was no longer my boat. After twenty years of unalloyed pleasure, with several cruises to the West Coast of Scotland and to the Outer Hebrides and a final trip to Holland in 1981, I had sold her to John Healey, a retired Civil Servant. He not only looked after her well but spent the winter after the great gale repairing her damage with dedication and skill. When she was afloat again she looked as good as she had on the day she was built.

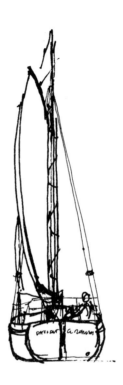